Different and Wonderful

RAISING BLACK CHILDREN IN A RACE-CONSCIOUS SOCIETY

Darlene Powell Hopson, Ph.D.
and
Derek S. Hopson, Ph.D.

Foreword by Alvin F. Poussaint, M.D.

A Fireside Book
Published by Simon & Schuster
NEW YORK LONDON TORONTO SYDNEY TOKYO SINGAPORE

FIRESIDE
Simon & Schuster Building
Rockefeller Center
1230 Avenue of the Americas
New York, New York 10020

First Fireside Edition 1992

FIRESIDE and colophon are registered trademarks
of Simon & Schuster Inc.

Designed by Irving Perkins Associates
Manufactured in the United States of America

1 3 5 7 9 10 8 6 4 2

Library of Congress Cataloging-in-Publication Data is available.

ISBN: 0-671-75518-8

To the Hopson and Powell families, especially our parents, whose love, support, Black pride, and strong kinship bonds greatly influence our lives. This commonality attracted us to each other when we first met. Both families taught us to never forget who we are and to strive to be the best that we can be. Our most precious times are those we spend with all of the children and families together.

And to the beautiful Black African-American princess that God blessed us with: DOTTEANNA KARYN HOPSON.

ACKNOWLEDGMENTS

The research which was the impetus for this book was conducted through Hofstra University. The late Dr. Julia R. Vane, Chairperson of the Psychology Department, was a White woman who was dedicated to Black issues and supported the research to fruition. Thanks to all of our colleagues who shared their experiences related to the research and the book and who continue Dr. Vane's efforts at Hofstra University. We are indebted to the Association of Black Psychologists and the American Psychological Association for granting us the opportunity to present our research and receive critical feedback and suggestions from our colleagues.

For technical assistance and support at various stages of the manuscript, we are especially thankful to Selbourne Brown for his ability to point out psychological jargon and help translate it into meaningful language for the general public; Barbara Lowenstein, our agent, for her initiative in encouraging this book and working through the different stages; Malaika Adero, for her ethnic and cultural style during the development of the initial proposal; Suzanne Lipsett, for her stylistic and creative suggestions in the proposal; Marilyn J. Abraham, editor-in-chief at Prentice Hall Press, for her sensitivity and insightful input; Robert and Leanna Powell, for their wisdom and meaningful analysis; Attorney William Grant Bumpus, for the time and attention dedicated to giving invaluable comments and for showing his commitment to Black youth; William and Bernice Sampson, for their faith and reassurance; Karyn Berkley, for her keen perceptions and insights; Attorney Marvin T. Braker, for his generous personal and professional advice; and many other friends and family, too numerous to mention, that we would like to thank for their enthusiasm and belief in this book.

Most of all, thank you to the children and families who shared experiences with us; to the children who are different and wonderful in this race-conscious society.

CONTENTS

FOREWORD

Black people have made great strides since the civil rights movement of the 1960s. Discrimination and segregation are illegal nationwide, affirmative action has forced open some doors of opportunity, and in America there are Black role models at high levels of achievement.

Yet black children in America are still born into a society with strong racist undercurrents that continue to damage their sense of self-esteem and diminish their sense of control over the environment. In addition, the high rate of poverty (estimated at about 50 percent for Black children) combines with lower-caste "minority" status to create additional self-doubt and feelings of powerlessness in both Black parents and children. A home atmosphere that breeds low self-confidence can foster a negative self-concept from infancy.

Racism for a Black child starts with this society's working definition of a Black person in America as an individual with any known Black ancestry. Because this concept of race is bizarre and without scientific merit, it was manipulated as a sociopolitical weapon designed to instill in so-called Black people feelings of inferiority and "impurity"—"Black blood," genetically speaking, is depicted as a pollutant. Such racist illogic suggests that Black children are born with a taint, that they are suspect, inferior persons until they have proved themselves worthy and "exceptions" to well-embedded negative racial stereotypes.

From an early age Black children are made to feel tarnished and unwelcome in the United States, a country that, despite being multiethnic, is dominated culturally by those of White European heritage.

Black parents who read traditional fairy tales and folklore to their children send them messages very early on that kings, queens, princes, and princesses are White and that the world is controlled and run by White people. In addition, important cultural symbols and the fantasy heroes who exercise dominant power over children are White, among them Superman, Batman, He-Man, Master of the Universe, and even Captain Midnight. Religious symbols in Black churches display a White God, a White Jesus, a White Mother Mary. Is it any wonder that Black children often feel a general sense of societal rejection? Race relations have been changing for the better, but we still have a distance to go before America establishes solid social and psychologic equity for citizens from all ethnic backgrounds.

Predictably, many Black children still do not perceive themselves as "different and wonderful." The Hopsons report that when they reenacted Drs. Kenneth and Mamie Clark's famous doll studies, Black children, despite all the progress that has been made, still preferred the White dolls and saw them as "better." However, the Hopsons also demonstrated the impact that modeling a positive interaction with the black dolls had on the subjects. Their research points out not only how far we have yet to go, but also suggests the corrective action that must be taken to enable Black children to grow up with self-respect and dignity.

Now that we have laws to support equality, and the example of many active Black middle-class participants in American life, it is even more important that our children have expectations of success. The opportunities exist, but because of racist legacies many Black youngsters do not believe it is worth struggling for long-term goals because they feel trapped, without hope and vision, in inner cities as members of the so-called underclass. Self-hatred under such circumstances leads to antisocial and self-destructive behavior that shows a lack of regard for their own community. The obvious byproducts are crime, drug abuse, high rates of homicide, and further disintegration of the Black family.

Civil rights leaders have recognized these problems for a long time. For decades the powerful message that the Reverend Jesse Jackson delivers to young Black people—"I am somebody!"—has been greeted with rousing cheers. It saddens me that our youngsters still have to be told that they are "somebody." I have spent twenty-five years speaking about the need to build a strong self-image in Black children.

I have seen the great hunger for advice of Black parents anxious to instill pride and self-esteem in their children. This sense of urgency is expressed as well by interracial couples, White adoptive parents of Black children, teachers, and social service workers from many ethnic backgrounds. In this highly readable book for parents and other caretakers, the Hopsons have been very specific about what it takes to accomplish this mission. They give examples of incidents that occur at home and at school, and—of utmost importance—suggestions for effective responses.

They emphasize the necessity of being positive, not simply silent, about our children's Blackness. In a society that views white as better, cleaner, purer, and holier than black, our children need to have their self-image actively bolstered in the home. The style of positive parenting the Hopsons describe is the ideal for all parents. The authors provide examples of the need to focus more on a child's efforts and less on outcomes, to encourage a child to value her or his own ability. They seek to empower parents to model an assertive style of dealing with racial incidents and realities. *Different and Wonderful* seeks to aid in the process of developing a free-flowing style of communication in the family around issues of race. The Hopsons also explore more general issues of peer influence and adolescent vulnerabilities.

A helpful aspect of this book is the series of self-evaluation tools interspersed throughout the text to help parents examine their own attitudes and feelings about being Black. Self-knowledge is the important first ingredient in the ability to present a positive and assertive model to Black children.

If our children are to succeed in an increasingly technological and white-collar society, they must believe in themselves and their talents. They must be encouraged and supported in their efforts to achieve in school and in their adult lives. Black children are often told that they are "natural athletes" and "natural entertainers." The reality is that they see many Black role models in sports and entertainment but very few in the professions or other more academically oriented fields. Children who receive such messages may exert maximum effort to succeed in entertainment and sports. On the other hand, Black children may internalize both from society and from themselves that they are unable to attain high levels in reading, writing, science, and math. Low teacher and parental expectations can cause them to withdraw and fail at these basic subjects. Their own racial self-doubt is turned on its head when such youngsters encounter academically serious Black students, whom they accuse of "trying to be White."

We will lose a generation of children if they feel that "being Black" is synonymous with failure and a lack of hope for accomplishment in a wide range of areas. The decrease in college enrollment for Black males and the fact that about 25 percent of young Black males are under the supervision of the criminal justice system in jail, on parole, or on probation are particular causes for concern. Parents, teachers, and social service agencies must show a greater interest in the gender differences among Black children in order to respond effectively to their varying needs, behaviors, and expectations. This is the challenge for the future.

In the final analysis, Black parents and others must be eternally vigilant in fighting racism in the society in which their children must grow and develop. Being a parent of a Black child requires supporting your child at home, helping him or her develop a strong sense of self-worth, and working outside the home on behalf of your child for social change to ensure that fairness and equal opportunity exist in every aspect of life. I believe that this helpful book, *Different and Wonderful,* will make a significant contribution to these efforts.

—Alvin F. Poussaint, M.D.,
Harvard Medical School

INTRODUCTION

As Black clinical psychologists who specialize in children and families, we've had a long-standing professional interest in the positive racial identity development and self-esteem of Black children. It was a series of personal experiences, however, that finally led us to begin formal research into the subject.

As Christmas 1984 approached, we like many others were caught scrambling to do our last-minute shopping. With the shelves emptying fast, we were afraid we might not be able to find everything on our list. Our biggest worry, however, was a shortage of the season's biggest hit—the prized Cabbage Patch dolls. Between our two families there were six adorable children whom we knew would love the popular funny-faced dolls.

As we reached the top of the escalator in one store, we saw a group of people huddled by a table under a sign marked "Cabbage Patch U.S.A."

"Too bad, they're all sold out," someone said as we approached. The crowd looked disappointed. Our hearts sank. We'd been *this* close, but too late. The crowd was reluctant to leave. We all seemed to be hoping that by some miracle someone would discover a shipment that had been overlooked.

"When will you get a new supply in?" a woman asked the harried clerk. "Will they be in before Christmas? Are you keeping a waiting list?" We pressed closer into the crowd to hear what the clerk had to say. Just then Derek said, "Hey, look at this."

By now we both could see that the table was covered with packages of the precious dolls—about twenty in all. Their faces peered at us through the cellophane window on the boxes. We looked around at the crowd. Their faces still showed their disappointment. We looked back at the dolls. They were all different, as Cabbage Patch Kids are guaranteed to be, but there was one characteristic that they all shared: All were Black. To the all-White crowd they might as well not have been there at all.

We bought our dolls, the very ones we were afraid we might not be able to find, and made our nephews and nieces very happy. But this incident stayed with us. It served as a turning point in our years of thinking about self-esteem and racial identity. We had been focusing on the inner reality of the children we saw—their self-concept and their self-esteem—but perhaps it was time to look outward again at the messages that society was sending them. Perhaps it was time to pay attention to how these signals were affecting Black children's sense of who they are.

Not long afterward we watched a television documentary about an inner-city New Jersey neighborhood near the one in which Derek grew up. The filmmaker carefully presented the full range of inner-city "types": drug dealers, addicts, high school dropouts, and the unemployed of all ages. Angry renters, welfare recipients, and single mothers were interviewed. Poverty abounded. The scene was all the more numbing for its familiarity. Everyone interviewed was Black.

Another "serious" news program had portrayed Black America with no mention of the Black middle and professional class now firmly established alongside the still struggling inner-city and poor rural Blacks. Derek had grown up within the radius the program covered. His "gang" of friends who grew up in the area had gone on to become a physician, an attorney, a journalist, and, in Derek's case, a clinical psychologist. But most viewers of the documentary would have been surprised to learn that, and would probably have assumed, incorrectly, that Derek and his friends were exceptions. We were galvanized into action. This book is the result.

* * *

While electronic media have taken steps to correct much of the racial imbalances in situation comedies and dramatic presentations, when it comes to serious news reporting, the Black community is still portrayed as an inner-city entity with "disadvantaged" stamped across it. But the problem doesn't end there. It's not only White America that has failed to keep pace with the changing demographics of the Black community: The hard-won advancement of Blacks in the professional and white-collar work force, the movement of many Blacks from cities to suburbs, and the new successful demands of a stable Black middle class for top-grade educational resources remain unsung. As Blacks, we, too, have been slow to revise our view of ourselves.

As practicing psychologists interacting with new clients every day, we can attest to a disturbing prevalence of self-devaluation throughout the Black community. Too often, in a reflection of a crippling psychological pattern that has its roots in slavery, Black people think of *themselves* as lacking in self-worth. And nowhere is this problem of low self-esteem more widespread or more critical than among children.

Based on cases in treatment, our impressions were that low self-esteem, as it relates to racial identity, was rampant among Black children. In 1985, to examine those impressions, we undertook to replicate a famous study conducted in the late 1930s and early 1940s. In this classic study, designed to document the impact of negative racial images on children, Black social scientists Drs. Kenneth and Mamie Clark reported that 67 percent of Black children who were given a choice between White and Black dolls chose White dolls. In effect the children were rejecting the Black dolls with which they might have been expected to identify.

When we repeated the doll tests in 1985, *65 percent* of the Black children in our sample chose White dolls. Further, 76 percent said that the Black dolls "looked bad" to them. In forty years, despite the civil rights movement, landmark legal decisions, and acts of Congress, the numbers had barely changed. And the meaning behind the numbers remained clear: Black children, in great numbers, were identifying with White images

—even when they had the opportunity to choose Black images. Our empirical results confirmed the messages Black children were sending us every day in our practice: "We're not as good, as pretty, or as nice as Whites. . . . We don't *like* being Black. We wish we could be like *them.*"

Psychologist Arthur Dozier touched on the root of the problem when he addressed a conference sponsored by the American Psychological Association (APA) in 1987. Dr. Dozier said:

> Authority, beauty, goodness and power most often have a white face. Most of the heroes, from He-man to Rambo, are white. In the '60's we were naive, too, in thinking that saying "Black is Beautiful" was enough. The change has to permeate society.

Our results were greeted with shock and despair around the world. Our presentation to the APA was reported in the *New York Times* on page one of its science section. At least 150 other newspapers and magazines gave prominent attention to the study as well, including the *Chicago Tribune, Chicago Sun Times, Los Angeles Times, USA Today,* and *Time, Newsweek, Parenting, Jet,* and *Essence* magazines. Publications worldwide echoed their interest. What did it all mean?

For Christina, an eight-year-old girl we saw in therapy, it meant confusion and self-consciousness. She told us she used to think her hair was very pretty, but when she went to an all-White Catholic school, a little White girl came up to feel her hair and told the other children it "felt funny." In an attempt to make this a learning experience, the nun told all the children to feel Christina's hair. Before bringing Christina to see us, her parents could elicit only a hysterical outburst from the little girl about how "I hate my hair."

For Elyse, a fair-skinned young Black woman engaged to a dark-skinned man, our results reflected an inner threat to her future happiness. She loved Carl, but her family disapproved of him because he was dark. Though she herself was light-skinned she was the darkest of her siblings, and as a child she frequently felt her parents loved her the least because of it. She married Carl, but when they discussed starting a family, Elyse began to have serious reservations. Her mother told her she should never have married a dark man. According to her mother, Elyse would have only dark children, and they'd never have a chance. When Carl insisted he wanted to have a child, Elyse panicked. She divorced Carl and then struggled with her guilt and unhappiness in therapy.

For Jonathan, whom we saw in a crisis situation following a difficult sophomore year in high school, our report underscored the stubbornness of negative racial stereotypes that he had personally experienced. "This White girl I took out stopped me in the hall," he told us. "She had a black eye and was crying real hard. She said, 'I know you'll understand. My dad, he treats me as bad as Black guys treat their kids.' I looked at her thinking maybe she knew something I didn't. My dad is the gentlest guy in the world."

For us, our findings and the tremendous interest our study evoked meant that the time for action had arrived. Obviously making racial discrimination illegal twenty-one years ago at the time of our initial study hadn't banished race consciousness or racism from American life—it had merely made it less overt. Black children's self-esteem continued to be at risk. But the overwhelming response to our study indicated that people across the nation were prepared to do something about it.

We have received hundreds of calls from people requesting written material on our research. Many asked for suggestions as to how they can counteract the effects of negative racial images. There were so many requests that we prepared a pamphlet summarizing the information for private distribution.

Requests continue to come in from parents, teachers, psychologists, and people in many other fields. They want to know how they can root out the subconscious taboos they were raised with, and how to begin discussing race-related issues with their children. They ask us what to do when their children express self-contempt and how to deal with race consciousness and outright racism when it surfaces in schools. Some ask us how they can instill ethnic identity and racial pride in their children who live in White environments and attend predominantly White schools. Others come in despair, seeking ways to help their youngsters develop the inner resources to avoid self-destruction and embrace the goals that only healthy, self-accepting young people can pursue.

Different and Wonderful is designed to provide answers and guidance to these parents—and to the hundreds of thousands of others who may not know where to turn. Psychology has much to contribute toward the healthy development of Black children in a race-conscious society. Our objective is to make that contribution available to those who need it so acutely.

Our replication of the Clarks' doll experiment differed from the original in one crucial way. We designed an intervention to encourage the children to take a positive view of Blackness and to select Black dolls. After giving them choices of Black or White dolls, we made *our own* doll choices. In carefully developed ways, we spoke enthusiastically to the children who chose the Black dolls, applied positive adjectives to the Black dolls, read a story depicting Black children in positive ways, and, of course, made certain to choose Black dolls in the children's presence. We then tested them again.

Those few minutes had an enormous impact. Now 68 percent, not 35 percent, chose *Black* dolls. And only 27 percent, not our original 76 percent, pointed to the Black doll as the one that "looked bad." With concentrated time and attention we had turned the results around!

The secret weapon against low self-esteem and poor racial identity in Black children is *talk*—open acknowledgment of racial issues, positive modeling, and reinforcement of Blackness.

As borne out both in our research and in our practice, it is through communication and careful attention to detail that we will succeed in counteracting the negative racial images all around us. In a simple, accessible style, marked by a wealth of anecdotes and case studies drawn from our practice, *Different and Wonderful* will guide its readers in fostering confidence and strong ethnic identity in Black children from infancy through adolescence, and into young adulthood.

NOTE: Throughout this book we have made a conscious decision to use the term "Black" instead of "African-American" because it covers all groups of Blacks, including Caribbean Blacks.

"African-American" is a progressive term and connects us

with a land; however, we believe that the desire and interest in this connection vary among Blacks. Our ancestry needs to be understood and appreciated, those who do not take conscious steps to develop contemporary connections need not be criticized. Changing our racial name from Colored to Negro to Afro-American to Black to African-American was intended to foster positive racial identification and self-esteem. The external means, such as our name, are not the most important factors, however. Internal appreciation, unity, support, and positive leadership are.

PART I

The Growing Garden:

RACIAL IDENTITY AND THE SEASONS OF CHILDHOOD

Chapter One

LOOKING INTO THE MIRROR: OURSELVES AS BLACK PARENTS

As Black parents we face a unique and formidable challenge: preparing our children for the race consciousness and outright racism that still pervade American society while helping them remain positive, productive, and self-respecting. Juan Williams, a *Washington Post* reporter, accurately describes the dilemma:

> For me, as a Black parent, the principal tension is between raising a child who feels good about himself (as an individual and a Black person) and also raising a child who can function in a race-conscious—if not always racist—society. A Black child has to be aware that mainstream White society often judges Black people as less intelligent, less attractive, and less trustworthy. A Black child has to live with that generalization without letting it destroy him or his dreams.

Different and Wonderful gives you the tools to protect your children's right to dream. We have tried to make it as practical and as easy to use as possible. We have designed it to apply to all phases of child rearing, for in each phase of a child's life distinct issues related to race, self-image, and self-esteem arise. In the next two chapters we lay the groundwork for the important job of parenting by defining the basic psychological concepts and tools upon which the book rests. The concepts are *self-image* and *self-esteem,* especially as they are affected by racism. The tools are *modeling, reinforcement,* and *free-flowing communication.* Armed with these basic concepts and tools we can attack and counteract the destructiveness of racism.

The effectiveness of these approaches depends, however, entirely on our preparedness and our willingness to use them. We therefore begin not by looking at our children but by closely examining *ourselves* as Black parents to see how well we understand the task before us.

A LOOK AT ME

Thinking about yourself as a Black parent can be something like looking into a mirror. All the features will be familiar to you. Some will please you; others will not. For example, when we talk about parents who take the time to communicate with their children, you will rightly feel good about yourself if that's your style. On the other hand, you will be saddened to realize that even seemingly innocent racial comments you might have made could have damaged your child's image of himself.

Don't despair if you feel you have been less than the perfect parent. You are not alone in this. In reality, there is no such thing as a perfect parent. We can all use a hand in some aspect of child rearing. The thing for you to remember is that there are things you can do about whatever problems you find. In fact, you can feel good about yourself for having taken the time and effort to begin reading this book. That action in itself expresses your concern and intention to act.

YOU AS A BLACK PARENT

Few of us actually sat down and decided what kind of parents we wanted to be, or even if we wanted to be parents at all. In most cases, circumstances or other people made these decisions for us. Most of us had children simply because that seemed to be what was supposed to happen after we got married. And once our children entered the picture, we became so busy trying to keep up with them that there was barely any time to think about *how* to prepare them to live in society. For the most part all we could do was "go with the flow."

In this section we encourage you to catch your breath and then take some time to think seriously about the job of raising your children. What does it mean to be a Black parent? Is it really different from being a White parent? How do you feel about being a Black parent? This is an important step in preparing to work with your child.

To help you with your self-evaluation we have adapted for your use a tool that we often use in our practice, a questionnaire that helps parents gauge the way they feel about being parents of Black children. There are no right or wrong responses to any of the statements below. The purpose of this section is not to test you, but to help you think about how you feel about these important issues. The way you feel about them influences the way you relate to your children, and that in turn has a big impact on their lives.

Read each of the italicized statements and note whether you agree, disagree, or feel somewhere in between about them. Then read the comments that follow each statement to help you evaluate your feelings about the subject.

Black parents have to sacrifice more than other parents when raising young children. Many Black parents feel that they have to sacrifice more because of the added burden of racism. They believe that advantages that are readily available to Whites—for example, good basic education for their children—are not available to them.

"You have to be twice as smart to go half as far as White people" is a "fact" that most Blacks come to realize early in life. Yet being *that* smart in itself can create a whole different set of problems. For example, the daughter of one of our family friends was having serious behavior problems in school. The parents asked us to talk to their child, Anna.

All the behavior reports that Anna had brought home from school alluded to the fact that she was capable of doing her schoolwork, but that she spent a lot of her time misbehaving. Her verbal and reading skills suggested that she was exceptionally intelligent. We immediately suspected that Anna was simply bored in school. Tests showed that we were correct. We were able to advise her parents on how to get help for their child.

We have found that school authorities seldom consider that a Black child's poor behavior might be due to boredom because of his or her exceptional intelligence and giftedness, although this situation is as common as it is among Whites. Such a possibility does not fit the way they see Black children or what they expect of them. They see poor behavior as normal for Black children. This is only one example of the many hurdles that Black parents have to routinely clear on behalf of their children.

Blacks should help their children feel that they are the same in all ways as other children. This has long been a point of debate among some Blacks and some liberal Whites. It is sometimes assumed that unless Blacks are seen as the same as Whites in every way, then they are seen as inferior to Whites.

Cultural variations make people different from one another, but no one race or culture is superior or inferior to another. Our art, music, poetry, dance, literature, and oral history tradition all contribute to our uniqueness as a people. We believe that every culture is different and wonderful in its own way.

It is important to look at this fact positively but realistically, and not fool ourselves. White America has never seen African peoples as the equals of any other race. It has always seen us as inferior to Whites in particular. And we have always had to prove our humanity to the world.

One of our clients, a nine-year-old boy named Jeremy, took part in his school's science fair. He was the only Black child at the event. Somewhere in the course of the evening one of the organizers pointedly asked him where he lived. The question sounded innocent enough, but the boy was confused because it didn't seem to make sense at the time. Although he lived in the same community as the other students, he felt he was being singled out.

After the fair Jeremy asked his father, "Why didn't he ask the other children where they lived?" His father told him that the man had reacted to the fact that Jeremy was different and stood out. He told his son that the man's question wasn't necessarily right or wrong, but that it was at least inconsiderate of him to ask Jeremy the question in front of the other children, and not ask it of *all* of them.

The question sent the boy a message. He felt that as the only Black child in the fair, he had to prove his right to be there by proving that he lived in the town. He was different. That was the reality. White people sometimes treat Black people differently simply because they *are* different. Telling our children that they are the same will not change the way others treat them. It will only set them up to be disappointed or confused when they are mistreated, or treated differently.

Black parents should help their children feel that they are unique, yet equal to all other children. Throughout history many Black Americans and well-meaning Whites have eschewed the idea that Black people are in any way different from other peoples. It is perhaps a natural reaction to the common notion that Black people, by being Black, are somehow inferior to other races.

But the things that make Black people different from others are nothing for you or your children to be ashamed of. The most obvious difference is, of course, skin color. Along with color comes the full range of our cultural expression: music, dancing, socializing, communicating, literature, art, and the way we dress. Even the foods we eat reflect our distinct cultural heritage. Your children, as the products of Black culture, share these distinctions.

Yes, in many ways Black children are different from other children—not superior, not inferior, just different—and wonderful!

I feel that Black parents are faced with more problems than other parents. As long as there is racism in America Black parents will continue to be faced with more problems. We have to deal with that. If your child is having difficulties, although the problem might have nothing to do with racism, you have to consider it as a possible factor.

The same would be true if the child were gifted, retarded, handicapped, or even significantly shorter or taller than his classmates, for example. If your child is different from others in any readily apparent way, it would be unreasonable not to take that difference into account, particularly when it comes to relating to others.

We know of one particularly gifted child who frequently got into fights. In fact, every marking period he came home bruised and battered. It turned out that his classmates were beating him because he kept getting *A*'s and making the honor roll. They called him a "nerd."

Children have a way of focusing on and emphasizing characteristics that they believe make others different from them or less important than they are. The difference might be in height, weight, speech—or skin color. As long as Whites continue to see Blacks as inferior, the role of Black parents will be more difficult than that of other parents.

It is hard to know what to do when a child is afraid of White people. Sometimes children become fearful as a result of negative experiences. They might not cry or cling to parents, although they sometimes do, but Black children might be quieter and more bashful with Whites than they are with Blacks. This could mean that they are holding back because of discomfort, fear, or anxiety. Perhaps the best solution to this problem is for you to have your child associate with White people with whom you yourself feel comfortable.

Two-year-old Carol shows no consciousness about race. She is very comfortable with her Black "aunties" as well as her White "aunties," who are in reality family friends. Latasha, who is the same age, has a completely different reaction to Whites. She pulls away and stares suspiciously. She has had no contact or routine interaction with Whites. The difference between these two toddlers is striking to see. Clearly, unless something changes for Latasha she will have difficulty relating to Whites when she grows up. If you want your child to be comfortable around people of different cultures it helps to give them such exposure as early as possible.

It is difficult to know whether to be lighthearted or serious about racial or color differences. We can't let racism devastate us. And one way to alleviate the pain is to acknowledge that some situations lend themselves to humor. While in-group humor is acceptable, however, we must not condone ethnic humor across racial lines. It is usually offensive and tends to perpetuate stereotyped views of Blacks.

As Blacks we certainly don't want to take racism so lightly that we never discuss it seriously with our children. We know from our own lives that these experiences can hurt for life.

Children's own lightheartedness sometimes hides their deepest feelings. Aaron, a mixed-race fourth-grader, has a reputation for being a real "cutup" among his friends. He has a sharp wit spiced with liberal doses of ethnic humor. His jokes are usually aimed at his Black friends, however: "You are so Black," he might say, "I wouldn't let you into my house. You might scare somebody." He told one of his friends, "You're so Black even ghosts are afraid to come to your house."

Unfortunately, when Aaron is angry at his Black friends he also expresses his negative feelings in ethnic terms. He has been sent to the principal many times for calling his classmates "nigger." A private conference in the principal's office reveals that Aaron's unmarried parents are separated, and that his mother, who is White, has custody of him, and has nothing good to say about the boy's father, who is Black.

Aaron is using humor to express some negative feelings about himself and about his home life. This is a case where someone needs to take the child seriously and address his concerns. If we take something lightly that our child takes seriously it could be very damaging to him or her.

It is a rare parent who can be even-tempered all the time when discussing racial issues with children. While we would all like to be calm and cool all the time, when our children have been hurt or offended, it is difficult to remain even-tempered. It's fine to let them see us get upset over some things. But after the upset, it's imperative to calm down and let them see you handle the situation constructively for your benefit and theirs.

Some Black children are naturally more aggressive than others. This has long been a controversial topic, with some researchers attempting to prove that Black people are naturally more aggressive than other racial groups. Such studies have proved largely inconclusive. People are born with differing propensities for aggressiveness. Each individual's circumstances are then further compounded by environmental factors affecting his or her life.

For example, a child raised in a quiet Detroit suburb might begin to show a higher level of aggressiveness after living in a city such as Belfast, Northern Ireland, for a few years. If the child were to then move back to the same Detroit suburb, his level of aggressiveness would probably be seen as inappropriate.

There is no conclusive evidence that race is a factor in aggressiveness. So, the fact is some Black children *are* more aggressive than others, just as some White children are more aggressive than others. It is an individual trait—it has nothing to do with race.

It is hard to know when to let Black boys and White girls play together when they are preteens. Some parents, especially liberal Whites, find this to be their most challenging problem. Interracial dating remains the last and greatest taboo in the uneasy relationship between Blacks and Whites in America. And the fear of this possibility haunts many parents even before their children are old enough to date.

Some people object to interracial dating because of the problems they know might await such couples. Rejection by family members and friends, disapproval by total strangers, and public discourtesy are only a few of the complaints. Others object because of what they perceive as their own racial superiority. Some racial extremists or hate groups have been known to target interracial couples for violence and even death. Many Blacks, thinking back to years of forced sexual contact with White slave owners, object on pride and principle.

Often people who support interracial dating do so because they see it as consistent with their ideal of racial equality. It is possible to believe in racial equality, however, and *not* support interracial dating. This is a very personal issue, one you have to think about and decide for yourself.

Whether you support or object to interracial dating is up to you. In any event, open communication, both within the family and between the families, is the best way to arrive at a solution that causes minimum harm to the children. Talking freely is the only way to find out how the other parties really feel about the issue. As parents you might be pleasantly surprised to find out that you agree with the other parents and are actually able to influence your children in their decision.

With all that children hear at school and from friends about race, there is little parents can do to influence them. The earlier you start to plant the seeds in your children's minds of positive feelings about themselves, the better will be your chance of influencing them. But it is never too late to start helping them prepare for the society in which they must live. At every age children present us with opportunities to provide them with guidance, although what you will be able to do depends on your child's age.

Your toddler, for instance, learning about the world through her parents, can be taught to appreciate Black people as a source of love, strength, and protection. Your school-aged child is better prepared to learn about the historical contribution of Black people to world culture, and to develop a greater sense of pride in who he is. Your adolescent child can be taught that she is at an age where she can begin to make significant contributions to her community and culture. There is something that can be done for your children at every age.

A child may learn racial prejudice from playing games such as "Cowboys and Indians." It's true. Usually children get the idea from television that the Indians were the bad guys and the cowboys were the good guys. We know that in fact the reverse was usually true. But we don't necessarily need to stop them from playing such games. We can use the opportunity to talk to them about the facts. We might find that they choose to change the games on their own.

We want to teach them the real story of Native Americans because the history of both Native and Black Americans has been distorted.

Talking to children about racism most often makes it more of a problem. Some parents feel this way, but we have found that talking about racism helps children deal with it more effectively. And research has shown that whether or not we bring it up, children can become aware of racism as early as three years of age.

Many Black girls in integrated or predominantly White schools discover racism in the seemingly innocent class play. That is where their usually White, but often Black, teacher somehow makes it clear that they are not suitable to play the part of the fairy princess or some such character.

One of our clients, Lisa, ran into this problem. She and a White girl tried out for the leading role in a class play. At first the teacher told her that the other girl got the part because she had taken dancing lessons. When informed that Lisa had also taken dancing lessons, the teacher said that she still felt that the other girl better fit the part. In a meeting with the parents, the teacher, pressed to explain how she had made her decision between the two girls, stated, "Well, the princess was White in the story."

Faced with two girls, one Black and one White, the teacher could not conceive of the Black girl in the lead role as the fairy princess. Such heroines are almost always White with blue eyes and long blonde hair. With most children's literature biased toward such images, it takes sensitive and imaginative teachers to see that their Black students are treated fairly in situations such as Lisa's.

If our children are put at a disadvantage at such young ages because of their race, it would be unfair not to be straightforward with them about it.

It is a parent's obligation to learn a child's innermost thoughts about race. As with any other thought or feeling, children sometimes guard the way they feel about racism. The way to get them to open up to us is to help them feel comfortable about sharing their thoughts with us. We can do that by listening to them and showing them that we respect their feelings without being judgmental.

A lifetime of conditioning teaches us that "parents always know best." As a result we always have an answer to our children's problems, often before we even know what the problems are. Responding in this manner is a sure way to turn them away from us. It will take self-discipline to force ourselves to listen to them. But the reward of their confidence in us will be worth it.

A child should always accept the parent's view of race. Children will develop their own views and attitudes about race just as they do about anything else. Many families we see include siblings who think very differently when it comes to race. For example, Lewis is heavily involved with soccer and has almost all White friends while his sister, May, is involved in Black youth organizations and has little contact with Whites.

Their parents were concerned at first because their children seemed to be moving toward extremes. We assured them that their children were developing their own independent views and that it was a natural step in their maturing process. Your children might eventually choose to look at things the way you do, but ultimately the choice is theirs.

It might be helpful to remember that whatever we *force* our children to do will usually be only temporary. As soon as they take control of their own lives they will do as they choose anyway. Force is definitely not the way.

Children should be taught about race at the earliest possible time. We believe this is very important. It is not necessary to lecture them and force them into direct racial experiences. Instead it might be helpful to distinguish between the subjects of *race* and *racism.*

Teaching your children about their race and who they are as a Black people *before* they are exposed to racism can be a positive and rewarding experience for you and for them. Choose books by Black authors that treat Black people and Blackness with dignity and pride (see Resource Guide on page 209). This kind of exposure is a great way for you to help your children begin to build positive views about themselves and their race. And it helps you, as a parent, to reinforce your own beliefs.

When you sense that your children understand and appreciate themselves as Black people, you can begin to talk to them about racism. Explain that there are people who might feel differently about Black people and will treat them differently. At this stage they will be better prepared to deal with the subject than if they encountered racism cold.

CAN YOU TALK TO YOUR CHILD ABOUT RACISM?

There is one more thing we need to do as a part of our self-examination before we go on to working with the children. We want to take a look not only at what you believe but how you feel today when you discuss racism with your children. It is important to do this because our feelings at these times are mirrored back to our children. Our attitudes and actions as well as our words have meaning to them, so we want to be sure we are sending a consistent message at these critical times.

Think about each of the italicized words below. Does it describe the way you feel when you discuss racism with your child? Circle the number that comes closest to the way you feel about the word (1 = Never true, 2 = Rarely true, 3 = Sometimes true, 4 = Frequently true, 5 = Always true). Read the remarks that follow each word to get an idea of how to gauge your reactions. There is no right or wrong answer; just respond as honestly as you can.

A. Exhausted (1 2 3 4 5). As parents we sometimes *do* feel exhausted dealing with racism. We cope with it all our lives. Then, just at a point where we feel we know how to deal with the problem, along come the children and the battle begins anew. We have to teach *them* how to combat racism.

The exhaustion you feel at these times is no different from any other and the remedy is the same. Take a break. Play your favorite sport or go jogging. Do anything you can to work off the frustration. Talk to a friend about the problem. Talk to your children. Communication is the key. (We'll discuss communication in depth in chapter 4.) All of these steps can help you regain your perspective on things and make it easier for you to help your children deal with racism.

B. Nervous (1 2 3 4 5). Many parents are understandably nervous when they discuss racial issues with their children. Talking about racism is a lot like talking about sex, religion, or politics—it creates anxiety. It's okay to let your children know that you are nervous about the subject. They will probably sense it anyway. But it's also important to find ways to reduce your anxiety so that you can concentrate on the problem.

In most cases the familiar tactics that we use to fight nervousness about speaking on any subject can be just as effective when race is the issue. Take a walk. Count to ten. Take a few deep breaths. More important, plan and mentally rehearse what you are going to do and say. If possible, practice discussing the problem with someone who is not involved. If that's not possible, practice by yourself in front of a mirror. Different things work for different people. Use whatever technique works best for you.

C. Frustrated (*1 2 3 4 5*). Many parents are frustrated because they feel powerless to help their children deal with racism. The frustration usually comes from the feeling that nothing will change no matter what they do. It may not always be easy, but we assure you that there is plenty you can do. In our practice we frequently see parents turn around bad relationships with their children when they discover that they can do things differently. There is no reason for you to give up on your child.

D. Irritated (*1 2 3 4 5*). Irritation can come when parents understand their child's feelings in a given racial situation, yet find it difficult to begin to deal with them. It is a normal reaction. It can even help your child to know that you understand how he or she feels, but that you alone cannot help him or her cope with the problem. What's more important is what you *do* about it. So, at some point you have to put aside the irritation and come up with a plan of action. You and your child can explore your possible reactions to the problem, and choose one he or she is comfortable with.

The more you understand that there are things that you can do to help, the less time you will spend being irritated.

E. Disappointed (*1 2 3 4 5*). Disappointment is particularly common among parents who have raised their children to feel that they are the same as all other children. Our philosophy is "different but equal." As long as our children understand that being different does not mean "better than" or "worse than," they won't be disappointed. If we acknowledge the extent of racism in America and the fact that our children cannot avoid it, we won't be as disappointed. But if we raise them to think that people will treat them by their character and not by the color of their skin, we are setting them and ourselves up for disappointment.

If you find yourself in this situation a good approach might be to "network" with support organizations such as the Urban League or the National Association for the Advancement of Colored People (NAACP). The first thing you will probably discover is that you are not alone. You can then learn how people in your situation have successfully coped with the problem.

F. Regretful (*1 2 3 4 5*). In therapy, people who have not openly discussed race with their children usually express regret. When racism surfaces the child is often devastated. ("Why didn't you tell me?" is a sad but frequent refrain.) Such events often lead children into therapy and leave parents burdened with regret.

The best antidote to regret is to realize, and to tell yourself as often as you need to hear it, that there is *nothing* you can do about what has already happened. On the positive side there is *a lot* you can do from now on that can make a difference.

G. Depressed (*1 2 3 4 5*). Depression is often tied in with a sense of hopelessness, a feeling that there is nothing you can do to change the situation. Occasionally we may run into a type of racial discrimination that we thought had disappeared from society. It is enough to make us doubt that anything will ever change for the better.

At those times it might be helpful for you to connect with someone, White or Black, whose attitude, philosophy, or behavior can reassure you that there is reason to hope. Remind yourself, or let others remind you, that there are many positive interracial experiences every day. Making a conscious effort to focus on such experiences will help you feel more optimistic.

H. Angry (*1 2 3 4 5*). Racism naturally breeds anger. And it is important to find ways to express such anger before it becomes rage. Expressing anger is fine as long as it is done in a controlled manner. We don't want our anger to take us to the point where we do things that are self-defeating. Any parent whose child has been called a "nigger" feels violent. That anger must be expressed somehow. We should always keep the goal in mind, however, to help the child find effective ways to deal with racism. That fact must dictate how we react.

I. Embarrassed (*1 2 3 4 5*). Parents express embarrassment at having to explain to their children that they are being judged by their race. They don't want their children to know that they themselves are sometimes judged that way. Obviously, such embarrassment serves no positive purpose; however, it does provide a clue to the parents that they too need to reassess the way they feel about themselves as Black people before they begin to work with their children.

J. Guilty (*1 2 3 4 5*). Parents sometimes feel guilty that they have not been able to better protect their children from racism. We would all like to have been better parents. But feeling guilty about where we have fallen short cannot make the past better. Such guilt only wastes time and saps creative energy that parents could use to improve things in the present. Guilt, like regret, belongs in the past and is best left there. Besides, by feeling guilty about race-related problems parents can end up blaming themselves for racism. Racism is not the parents' fault; it is a problem with the society around them. We all have a part in working to change it, however.

If guilt is preventing you from helping your child deal effectively with racism, talk to your child about it. Let him or her know why you feel the way you do and how difficult the problem is for you. Talking out your guilt is the best way to get rid of it.

K. Desperate (*1 2 3 4 5*). Some parents get to a point where they feel desperate about dealing with racism. Perhaps, for one reason or another, they have had to put up with a lot of racial discrimination with no end in sight. If you truly feel desperate, you probably need outside help. You might just need to talk to someone who can give you a different perspective on things. You might need a social service agency to help you deal with your child's school problems. Or you might need to talk to a mental health professional. Again, if you feel that things are out of your control, don't hesitate to seek outside help.

L. Calm (*1 2 3 4 5*). Calmness is an asset well worth cultivating by parents. It is important to be able to show feelings of anger with appropriate expressions. Letting our anger get out of control, however, could hurt more than help a situation. No matter how angry you get, never forget your ultimate goal—to give your child a positive way to deal with conflict. Always come back to that.

M. Confident (*1 2 3 4 5*). The more confident you are about your own worth, the more confidence your child will place in your advice on coping with racism.

N. Patient (*1 2 3 4 5*). We have seen parents who are instinctively very patient in discussing race with their children. This is another valuable asset for a parent to have. Children need to see that you are willing to put in the time to listen to them express their feelings and experiences, and to try to help them solve their problems.

O. Helpful (*1 2 3 4 5*). Feeling confident that you can help your child deal with racial issues or outright racism will come with practice in using the tools we give you in this book.

P. Enthusiastic (*1 2 3 4 5*). Our children need to see us as enthusiastic about Black concerns. Discussions about historical figures, Black history events, and present-day progress such as Jesse Jackson's 1988 presidential campaign are opportunities for us to show the excitement we feel. Even two-year-olds will show signs of recognition and enthusiasm for such things if they see their parents do the same.

It doesn't do us any good to tell our children that we are pleased with ourselves and proud of our accomplishments if we show little pleasure in our own lives. Participation in cultural events such as theater, dance concerts, and art exhibitions can serve to show them that we do enjoy expressions of Black culture.

Q. Friendly (*1 2 3 4 5*). Our children need to see us interacting with people from different backgrounds and ethnic groups in a friendly manner. It is a way to show them that we can be friends and connected to different kinds of people while still loving and appreciating our own ethnicity.

R. Happy (1 2 3 4 5). This relates to what we said earlier about enthusiasm. It is good for our children to see us being happy about who we are and about being with other Black people. When you are with a White friend in public and you greet someone Black, your White friend might ask, "Do you know her?" She might be surprised if you say no.

Black people share a strong historical and cultural kinship bond that Whites largely do not understand or appreciate. In the many situations where there are few other Blacks, it can be very reassuring to feel connected to someone you don't even know. It's an excellent quality to pass on to your children.

S. Concerned (1 2 3 4 5). Our children need to know that we are concerned about Black issues—apartheid, for example. Throughout adolescence our children need to know that we are willing to do something, however minor, to change racist policies and practices.

Appraising the Reflection

Now let's take a look at your results. Note that the words in A through K suggest negative feelings, while those in L through S represent positive feelings. It's not important for you to get a particular overall score, or one for negatives and one for positives. What's important is that you look at each word and decide whether you need to change that particular feeling when you work with your child.

For items A through K, if 1 or 2 best describes your feelings, you've probably developed your own healthy reactions to those aspects of racism. Well done, and keep up the good work! For those items where you circled 4 or 5, it will be helpful for you to pay particular attention to the times you feel this way. Ask yourself why you feel the way you do. Use the discussion that follows each word to help you find alternative ways to respond.

Items L through S represent positive feelings. For those items where you circled 4 or 5, you should be very proud of yourself. It isn't easy to think positively where racism is concerned. But it is essential to be able to do so when it comes to communicating with your children. If you scored low (1 or 2) on any of the positive items, don't be discouraged. Again, use the discussions to help you come up with alternatives to the way you feel now.

Wherever you circled a 3, whether on a positive or negative feeling, it means that you, like all parents, have your good days and your bad.

If we were perfect parents we would circle 1 on all the negative feelings and 5 on all the positive ones. But since we are less than perfect we have to work on those feelings we need to improve. By becoming aware of how you feel when you discuss race with your children you will find yourself responding more positively to your children.

GETTING IN TOUCH WITH YOUR FEELINGS

To be able to control or change your feelings when you discuss race with your children, you need to first learn how to identify those feelings and their sources. "Getting in touch with your feelings" is one of those expressions that we all hear a lot but are probably unsure of its real meaning.

To give you an idea, let's imagine that your daughter is turning her room upside-down looking for a textbook that she needs for tomorrow's test. Her room, which is usually messy anyway, looks particularly disastrous when you walk in. She tells you what the problem is and immediately you start in on her.

"Is it any wonder you can't find anything in this room? How many times do I have to tell you to clean up your room? What are you going to do if you don't find that book? How can anyone keep the room they live in this messy? . . ." And so you play the old familiar refrain.

But instead, stop. *Take a break.* Force yourself to calm down. Do whatever it takes. Sit in the backyard, take a walk in the park, take a hot bath. Anything. Then, *label the feeling.* What are you feeling? Anger? Frustration? Disappointment? Find a name for the feeling and acknowledge it to yourself. Say, "I am angry," or "I feel frustrated."

Once you have labeled it you can then *process the feeling.* Processing takes two steps. First, you identify the obvious source of the feeling. In this case, the immediate source is the fact that your daughter's room is such a mess that she can't find her textbook in it. Next, you try to see if there are any other causes for the feeling. For example, why might you become so angry or frustrated at the fact that your daughter's room is such a mess? You've never really felt *that* strongly about her room before. Perhaps there is something else that is causing the feeling of frustration.

If you think harder you might discover you are frustrated because your daughter is doing poorly in school, and failing this test will just put her further in the hole. You might think back to your own school days when you refused to listen to anybody's advice about studying. As a result, you got poor grades and you have never been able to get the kind of work you know you are capable of doing. You are concerned and frustrated because your daughter seems to be making the same mistake.

By getting in touch with your feelings you've put your finger on the fact that your daughter's poor school performance is a source of frustration for you. Processing has helped you to make that connection to the way you feel. You are now prepared to deal with the problem.

We would like to mention here that although many people are sensitive enough about their own feelings to go through the process by themselves, others need help. A spouse, a relative, a friend, even an older child can sometimes help in getting in touch with one's feelings.

To recap, the steps for getting in touch with your feelings are:

1. Take a break.
2. Label the feeling.
3. Process the feeling.
   a. Identify the obvious source of the feeling.
   b. Identify other, less obvious sources, if any.

As an extension of getting in touch with your own feelings it is also helpful for you to try to get your child to see things the way you do. In this way you help your child to build *empathy* for your point of view. This can be very helpful in problem solving. If you can get your child to understand how *you* feel about a problem it might be easier to arrive at a solution even though you and your child might still disagree.

HOPSONS' RACIAL ATTITUDE ASSESSMENT PROCEDURE

We develop much of our thoughts and feelings about race and what racial differences mean within our families. In our daily routine we seldom have the time to analyze these feelings. Yet, they influence the way we interact with the people around us. So, let's take a few minutes to ask ourselves how we *really* feel about race.

The following sentence-completion exercise that we call Hopsons' Racial Attitude Assessment Procedure (Hopsons' RAP) is a tool we use in assessing children's and adolescents' racial attitudes. We suggest that you take it to become familiar with the process and experience of expressing your attitudes. We also suggest that you have your child complete the sentences and discuss the responses openly together. Still, Hopsons' RAP is designed to encourage you and other family members to begin to examine the feelings and thoughts that form the basis of your attitudes about race. As you complete each sentence you'll begin to notice, perhaps for the first time, that some of these thoughts make you feel more or less comfortable than others.

No scoring is necessary. Putting such thoughts down in writing is just a way to help us become more aware of ourselves and what we may want to change, improve, or develop further.

1. Black people are
2. White people are
3. I like Black people who
4. I don't like Black people who
5. Black and White people should
6. Black people should
7. White people should
8. I like White people who
9. I don't like White people who
10. Black people in my neighborhood
11. White people in my neighborhood
12. In school Black people
13. In school White people
14. My greatest fear of Black people

15. My greatest fear of White people
16. Black people are best at
17. White people are best at
18. My parents think that Blacks are
19. My parents think that Whites are
20. If I had one wish concerning race relations it would be
21. Black is positive because
22. Being Black in America is
23. Being White in America is
24. White is positive because
25. Black people like me because
26. White people like me because
27. The thing I have most in common with White people is
28. The thing I have most in common with Black people is
29. I sometimes call Whites
30. I sometimes call Blacks
31. I like my race because

At the beginning of this chapter we hinted at the importance of fostering a positive self-image and healthy self-esteem in our children. Now that we have a better understanding of ourselves as parents and what we bring to the child-rearing process, we can turn our attention to the task of building self-esteem in our children.

Chapter Two

BUILDING SELF-IMAGE AND SELF-ESTEEM

Now we turn to the subject at hand, the raising of healthy, self-confident Black children in a racially conscious and sometimes explicitly racist society. To do this, let's return for a moment to the very important concepts of self-image and self-esteem presented earlier in chapter 1.

SELF-IMAGE

Everybody talks about self-image, but what is it, anyway? Self-image describes how we imagine ourselves to be. It begins to develop when an infant first becomes aware of his or her own body, and continues to be refined as the baby starts to recognize body parts. The game in which Mommy says to the baby, "Where are Tommy's eyes?" and responds with a reassuring "Right!" when the child points to his own eyes, helps the baby practice building a self-image.

In learning about themselves as part of a social world, children start comparing themselves to other children. Carrie might show great interest in other people's eyes after she first becomes aware that hers are brown. Gerald might become fascinated with skin color, constantly comparing his own with that of everyone he meets. This sort of interest provides great opportunities for parents to praise their child's own physical attributes.

Our praise helps our children feel that their eyes or skin or hair are important parts of being attractive. The same is true for height, weight, and other characteristics, whether or not they are visible. Whatever the adults around a child emphasize consistently eventually becomes important to a young child. If the emphasis is positive, the value is positive. If the emphasis is negative, the value is also negative.

For example, if you continually tell your daughter that her curly hair is attractive and makes her look good, she will develop pride in her appearance. If you complain about her "nappy" hair and how difficult it is to comb, however, she will probably come to resent her hair and think that it is inferior to other types of hair. So, by pointing out their attributes in positive ways, we can help our children to form healthy mental pictures of themselves.

How Negatives Creep In

No matter how positive and aware your family might be, you are almost certain to find some pocket of negative Black images lurking somewhere. How can you deal with it? First, don't panic. Divide the problem sources into two categories: yourself and everybody else. As with any other personal relationship, it is much easier to change yourself than it is to change someone else. With that in mind, let's see what we can do to identify those negative images that originate within ourselves. After we have had some practice at this, we can then tackle the world around us.

Let's look at some of the ways in which bias against Blackness and in favor of Whiteness can show up in even the most innocent forms without our being aware of it. Imagine, for example, that you are a young woman with two children. You are dark-skinned and your husband is light-skinned. Your son turned out to be light-skinned like his father, and your daughter's skin looks more like yours. You love them both regardless of their skin color. You know better than to show a preference for one skin color over another.

You have a girlfriend, Anita, who is also light-skinned, however. Whenever Anita comes to visit you often talk about beauty care. You always compliment her on her lovely skin. You think nothing of the fact that your daughter is listening to this. You have never told your daughter that her dark skin is anything to be ashamed of, but you have never told her that it is beautiful either. What effect do you think this experience, repeated again and again, will have on your child?

Without knowing it, you are building in her a preference for light skin. You have not actually said light skin is better than dark, but you repeatedly *reinforce* in her the perception that your friend's light skin is lovely. Your young daughter listens to this and *learns* it. She doesn't even have to be able to ask if that means that dark skin is not lovely. Just hearing repeatedly that light is beautiful is sufficient to build up a prejudice against dark skin. And when your daughter grows up, she might not only think that light skin is lovely but tell her daughter that it is better to be light than to be dark. How can you deal with such a situation?

You don't have to stop complimenting your friend on her lovely complexion. Instead, tell your children in a warm and loving way that both of them have lovely skin. Say, "Janet, I love your smooth, dark skin. It is so lovely. With your rich, dark complexion I bet you are the prettiest girl in your class." Say to them both, "I have the two loveliest children in the whole wide world." Say to your son, "I love your brown skin. It makes you as handsome as your daddy."

If your children hear such compliments repeatedly they will come to understand that they and other people can be attractive at the same time even though they look different. This way your daughter can learn to appreciate someone else's beauty without feeling that it diminishes hers.

As we've said before, the things you say, do, and take for granted influence the way your children feel about themselves as Black people. It requires a conscious effort to monitor our words and our behavior to catch and eliminate negative ideas about Black people.

If you say, "I don't use this makeup any more. It makes me look too dark," your daughter hears, "It's not good to look too dark." You are better off if you say, "I have found makeup that better *matches* my complexion."

If you ever said that Black people are always late because

they operate on C.P. (Colored people's) time, think about it again. Sure, it sounds funny and we say it good-naturedly to one another. But how many times have you deliberately gone late to a gathering on the assumption that it is a Black people's affair, and they will all be late anyway? How many times have you been surprised to find you were among the last to arrive? Black people are not always late. Exposing your children to such misperceptions works against them if they come to believe them. In a work environment, a Black person who believes this would probably have a problem with tardiness. A boss who believes it wouldn't trust a Black person with time-sensitive assignments. Such perceptions cost us in the long run.

When you look for those pockets of negativity think about the things you normally take for granted. A very common one is a distrust of Black professionals. Is your doctor White or Black? Ask yourself if you could not find a competent Black doctor that you could trust. Do the same for your dentist. How about your accountant or attorney? Did you think of finding Black ones?

Obviously, when you hire these professionals your first concern has to be whether they are good at what they do; however, it is worthwhile to remember that these seemingly unrelated choices also have an impact on your child. If all your friends and day-to-day contacts are Black but your professional "advisers" are White, your child will grow to believe that the law, medicine, finance, and so on are the domains of White people.

It is possible for you to find competent Black professionals. By choosing to do so when you can, you provide positive role models for your children. If you have deep doubts about trusting a Black doctor, for example, ask yourself a few basic questions. As an intelligent person, do you think that with proper training *you* could be a doctor? Do you think your daughter could grow up to be a good doctor? If not, why? Do you think that Black people are incapable of such skills and responsibilities?

If you are otherwise confident in yourself and other Black people, where did this doubt about Black professionals come from? Look into your background for the reasons you feel this way. In all likelihood you adopted your opinion from some influential person or people in your past and have never had occasion to question it.

Counteracting Negative Images

What can you do to counteract the negative images of Black people that come from sources outside the home? The best way to blunt their power over your children is to expose the children to appropriate positive images in the first place. The more deeply they appreciate their own worth, the less negative influence society can exert on them. However, we know that it is not possible to shield the children completely. For instance, if all of this is new to you there is probably much negative programming that you will have to overcome. But even if you have been setting positive examples for all your child's life, some negative outside influences are bound to have slipped through.

For example, imagine that your retired father, who lived most of his life in the segregated South, now lives with you in a northern city. He takes care of your son after school before you get home from work. He takes the boy fishing frequently. They love each other and your son idolizes his grandfather. After a while you notice that your son has become very shy in the presence of Whites. He seldom speaks to them, and when they address him he looks down at the floor. He is completely at ease in the company of Black people. You gently question the boy about his change in attitude.

"Is everything okay?" you ask.

He is not sure what you mean, but he answers, "Yes, Mommy!"

"You didn't seem like your old self when Mrs. Smith was here today. Is something wrong?"

"No, Mommy!"

"You seemed a little uncomfortable when she was talking to you. Were you?"

"No, Mommy."

"Why did you look down when she spoke to you? Why didn't you look at her the way I taught you while she was speaking to you?"

"Because Grandpa told me not to." Now you begin to see the picture. By gently questioning the boy further, you find that his grandfather has been teaching him a whole new way to relate to White people. At first you are furious that your father seemed to have undone all your careful work with your son. However, you soon calm down and begin to think rationally. You have to do something right away. What should you do?

We know it's tough to do, but first take a moment to appreciate what is happening. Your father is giving your son what he considers to be basic tools for survival in a White-dominated society. He grew up in a time and place when deferring to White people was a way of life for Blacks, particularly for Black males. He knows well the penalty of stepping out of bounds. It would be good to at least show your appreciation for the ways in which our culture passes valuable information from one generation to the next. We suggest thanking him for his concern. You do not want to patronize him. You want to show sincere appreciation for what he is trying to do.

Of course, you will then want to let your father know that you are teaching your son to behave differently and ask for his cooperation. If he is willing to support your approach, fine. If he is not, as a first step you will have to ask him not to discuss such things with your child. If that is not sufficient, you might have to reduce the amount of contact he has with the boy. Finding a new baby-sitter could be one solution.

At the same time, you will want to explain the situation to your son. Make sure he understands that your father had good intentions. But then tell him to follow only the instructions that you give him on the subject.

These may seem like harsh conditions to impose on your own flesh and blood. But your child will suffer the consequences if you do not intervene. By being as careful and considerate as you can when you approach your father you can minimize any negative side effect of the experience.

Obviously, this would be an extreme case. We are confident that most of us will have to face nothing so dramatic; however, the basic approach should be the same in similar situations.

WHEN FRIENDS AND NEIGHBORS ARE THE SOURCE

When it comes to friends and neighbors influencing your children, you will have to gauge your response based on the nature of your relationship to the person. If an old family friend tells your daughter that nursing is a high enough career goal for Black girls, you might respond differently than you would if the advice came from your new next-door neighbor. But in both cases you will want to firmly set them straight: "Thank you for your concern, but I'm raising my daughter to believe that she can do whatever she decides and believes she can do."

The images of Black people that your child will get from society as a whole are perhaps the most difficult to monitor or control. You can't be there when your son is hanging out with his playmates to nip self-defeating attitudes in the bud. You can't be at school to sift out the prejudice from teachers, classmates, and textbooks. And you can't always be there to point out the lies, half-truths, and omissions in their favorite television shows. Still, you are not powerless.

Peer pressure is one of the most powerful influences on your child. You could spend your last dollar to buy your son a shirt you think he will love, only to discover he would not be caught dead in it—until he finds out that all his friends are wearing the same shirt. And if one of them decides that it looks better with one sleeve torn off—watch out, that sleeve is coming off. That is peer pressure. What can you do about it?

Early in your child's life, show an interest in who his friends are. Encourage him to invite them home for lunch. Sit down and talk with them. You can find out much about parents' views by talking to their children. Of course, your intent is not to interview the child but to see how the children might be influencing each other. You can perhaps find out if their views contradict views you consider important.

Imagine, for example, that you find that Carey, your son's best friend, is from a home where there is much fighting and cursing. Carey is respectful enough to avoid cursing in front of you. You suspect that he curses when he is with other children, however, including your son.

An extreme reaction might be to tell your son to stay away from Carey. But he might resent this if he really likes the other boy. A better approach would be to remind your child that you object to cursing and to explain your reasons for objecting. Tell him to be careful not to slip into the habit himself. You might also be able to have a positive influence as a role model for your child's friend.

A word about explaining your reasons to your children: It's easy to fall into the trap of feeling that you are the adult and therefore do not have to explain yourself to children. We all do it sometimes, but try to avoid it. When you do that, you are playing a dictator's role and inviting rebellion. When you explain your reasons, you show the children that you think enough of them to be straightforward with them. You are far more likely to get their cooperation with that approach.

TELEVISION'S NEGATIVE PICTURES

What can you do about the many negative images of Black people that our children see on television? A first step is to sit with your child and watch the shows he usually chooses to watch. If your child is like most, he probably spends all of Saturday morning in front of the television. Join him one Saturday. Look at the roles that any Black characters play. Think about the level of aggression the characters display. Note the many fighting scenes. If you do not want to encourage excessive aggressiveness, you might want to restrict them from watching programs that teach them that fighting is an acceptable way to settle a conflict.

There is another disturbing reality for your Black child when he sits down in front of the television. Note how many of his favorite shows are about Black people or even include Black characters. Chances are you will find few Black characters and fewer Black shows. In fact, someone watching Saturday morning television for the first time might guess that America was peopled entirely by statuesque White people with blond hair and blue eyes. Of course, there is nothing wrong with showing those images on television. But why should Black children be denied Black shows with Black heroes? Black children eat the same cereals that sponsor the shows. They go to the toy stores and buy the same action figures from those shows, so why are there so few Black characters? The people who program these shows simply cannot conceive of credible Black heroes and heroines.

We cannot wait for this bias toward White heroes and the continued portrayal of negative images of Blacks to end. We must take action to protect our children. We recommend sharply limiting your child's television time. An hour a day, two at the most, is sufficient. We also suggest that you and your child go through your television program guide at the beginning of each week. Mark the shows you wish to watch with him so that you can help him understand them. These might be the news or programs about racial violence. Identify those shows he can watch by himself, for example, shows like "Sesame Street" for children that present a balanced view of different ethnic groups and have no violence. Note those programs you do not want him to see and explain why. Many of the police shows, in addition to their violence, are highly biased against Blacks. Tell your child, "That program shows people being mean to each other. They also treat Black people like us unfairly. When you are older we can watch it together and talk some more about it."

We should warn you that breaking children of the television habit is not an easy job. If you find it necessary to do this, prepare yourself for a long struggle. It would be helpful if you could find alternative things for the child to do. For young children, it might be sufficient to distract them by reading to them. Older children are more of a challenge, and you will probably have to give them a say in choosing an alternative. Don't overlook reading as a choice for them as well. At whatever age they discover the adventure in reading it will pay dividends for the rest of their lives.

Some people have been known to bribe their children with money to get them to give up television. Paying the cost of a hobby such as collecting baseball cards might be a less expensive alternative that could do the trick and send a better message as well. On the positive side, children who are persuaded to give up television for even a couple of months usually find that they don't miss it as much as they thought they would. It's worth the effort.

When you have done everything you can to combat the negative images that confront your children, your best defense will still be the positive images that you have laid down as a part of the children's upbringing. If your child knows and loves the person he is, appreciating his physical appearance as well as his personal character and his culture, there is little that can undermine him. Biased films and television programs, indifferent teachers, and a hostile society will only sharpen his determination to assert himself as a complete and worthwhile person. It stands to reason that this aspect of your child rearing should receive the greatest amount of your attention. No matter where you are in the process of raising your child, work to replace those negative, demeaning images of Black people that your child sees with positive, affirming images.

SELF-ESTEEM

Like self-image, self-esteem is a much-overused term. What does it refer to? Self-esteem is the feeling children (and, of course, adults) have about their self-images. Children who feel good about themselves are said to have high self-esteem; those who feel bad about themselves have low self-esteem. Since we all have negative feelings about ourselves sometimes, we use the term self-esteem here to refer to the self-view that a person has most of the time.

How do young children come to feel good about themselves? They find ways to please the adults who are important to them. They try to do well in order to receive praise for completing a task. In general, they do things to promote our love and approval of them. As these positive rewards ebb and flow, so does the children's self-esteem. If a child feels there is no chance for love and approval, he or she will stop trying to please and begin to behave in undesirable ways.

Fifteen-year-old Cheryl is the daughter of a biracial divorced couple. She admired and identified with her Black father. Her mother, who is alcoholic, let her know she took after "that nigger father of yours," and never misses a chance to insult his memory even though he is no longer involved in their lives. Cheryl grew up confused about being Black. She considered herself worthless and stupid, with no chance of earning a living. By the time she reached her teens she knew she was going to have a life on the streets. With the encouragement of her boyfriend she began to abuse drugs and finally dropped out of school.

Cheryl had nowhere to turn for the encouragement, affection, and self-respect that she needed to nourish her self-esteem.

Without those things she was all but doomed to resignation and despair. Perhaps without realizing how it would affect her daughter, Cheryl's mother had sent powerful negative racial messages about the father. Clearly, that enormous amount of negativity contributed to Cheryl's poor self-esteem and low expectations.

SIGNS OF LOW SELF-ESTEEM

How can we tell whether our children's experiences so far are building up or breaking down their self-esteem? There are several clues that point to low self-esteem in a child. Frequent self-deprecating remarks are a common sign. Eva might say, "I'm not important. Nobody wants to play with me." Black children with poor self-esteem often say, "I wish I had blond hair." Some come right out and state, "I wish I were White." Others, such as eight-year-old Marlon, will openly question characteristics of Black people as a whole: "How come Black people never invent anything?"

Here are some signs of low self-esteem:

Disrespect. In a family setting, children who have doubts about their own worth behave inappropriately toward other family members. They might be disrespectful to adults, or make negative remarks about brothers' and sisters' Blackness.

Jamie's case is a good example. She was the lightest-skinned child in her family. She had a different father from that of her two brothers. When the family entered therapy, her mother reported that they were always fighting. After several sessions, the older brother admitted that Jamie was calling them "blackie" and saying that their father was a bum. In reality, their father was involved with them and frequently took them out on weekends. Jamie's father, on the other hand, was uninvolved. Jamie was using skin-color differences as a way to hurt her brothers because their relationship with their father was so much better than her relationship with her father.

Self-defeating behavior. Children with low self-esteem might deliberately do things that are self-defeating. Daniel's case described in chapter 4 shows this kind of behavior. Although he was highly intelligent he did poorly in school and had behavior problems. He was struggling with racist treatment from his classmates.

Feelings of inadequacy. Some children find ways to hide their feelings of inadequacy. Harold might behave in a grandiose manner, bragging about toys he does not have or events that never took place. In relationships with other children he might be aggressive and tend to bully others. Youngsters like Harold are often quick to reject other people. They fear that they themselves would otherwise be rejected. They also tend to express anger indirectly. For example, Harold might deliberately break John's toy instead of standing up to John in a conflict.

Other children accept their feelings of inadequacy as fact and live up to them, creating a self-fulfilling prophecy. In therapy a single mother expressed her negative feelings about her son's father in front of the child, calling the father a "no-good nigger." She then said of the boy, "He is just like his father, always getting in trouble. He never listens to me." With sufficient reinforcement, the child would undoubtedly come to believe this description of himself and behave that way. Fortunately, after feedback in therapy the mother was able to see how such comments could be self-defeating in the relationship with her son.

We also pointed out that it was important that she pay attention to the effect that her words might possibly have on her son. We explained that regardless of how she perceived his father, how the boy turned out depended very much on her. In other words, even if the father was a saint, those words from his mother would have a negative impact on the boy. And even if they were not true, by setting up such negative expectations of the boy she was almost guaranteeing that he would turn out that way.

Even mothers who love their children and wouldn't say negative things about them will degrade an absent father in front of their child. Disappointment and frustration are often high in such situations, but it's important to refrain from the negativity in the child's presence. Children often pick up on such feelings and blame themselves for their parents' unhappiness. It could haunt them all their lives.

Withdrawal. In some cases, children with low self-esteem withdraw altogether into a fantasy world, attempting to block out the rejections they feel from other people. Lynn, for example, frequently complained to her mother that she didn't like her short, kinky hair. Other children teased her about it. She preferred to play alone in her room. There she would put a pair of her mother's stockings on her head and pretend that they were two long braids. When encouraged to play with other children, Lynn would say that her stuffed animals were her friends. This type of fantasy is very common. Actress Whoopi Goldberg portrayed such a little girl in one of her television specials. The girl puts a shirt over her head and twirls it around, fantasizing that it's her long hair.

A good indication of a child's self-esteem level is the way he or she relates to others. A child who is confident with herself will socialize easily with whomever happens to be around, whether Blacks or Whites. Black children experiencing race-related self-esteem problems will often behave inappropriately when they deal with Whites. They might become unduly aggressive or they might withdraw and refuse to participate. Sometimes children in these situations say things like "I don't want to be with those White kids." Children who behave this way are usually telling us that they are uncomfortable relating to Whites.

Another clue as to how our children feel about themselves is the way they react when they face racial conflict. If your child had a toy and a White child took it from him, how would he try to get it back? Would he cry, fight, throw a tantrum, forcibly take it back, do without it, get someone else to ask for it, bargain for it, yell, buy it back, or simply pout? Would he behave differently if he had been dealing with a Black child? The response indicates how he or she relates to others. Your child might say, "Give me back my ball and I will lend you my Transformers," or "I am going to tell the teacher if you don't return my ball." If your child would normally behave in one of the other ways, it might be helpful for you to show him a more effective way to respond. (Modeling is discussed in depth in chapter 3.)

Self-esteem in the classroom. Evidence of low self-esteem sometimes appears in the classroom. If your child is in a predominantly White school, you might have received complaints that he or she is disruptive, acting out, hostile, or belligerent. Obviously, such behavior is not unique to race-related problems. In our practice, however, we often see such terms used when schools refer Black students to us for evaluation or counseling. It is possible that the child might be reacting to racial conflicts that leave him feeling that he is not as good as Whites. Frequently, the child is accused of creating a problem. To the contrary, we find that he or she is often reacting to racial prejudice or discrimination in the school environment.

Such discrimination is often unintended, but the effect is still negative. Thirteen-year-old Tanya attended a largely White school. She complained that she was never invited to birthday parties or afterschool activities at her classmates' homes. The other students might not have intentionally excluded her, but they did not see her as someone with whom they would normally socialize outside of school. Her reaction to the situation was to behave negatively toward her classmates. She began to call them names and start rumors about them.

A teacher in a predominantly White junior high school described this incident to us: She had arranged a special program in honor of Martin Luther King, Jr. There were two Black students in the class. One of them said loudly enough for the other children to hear him, "Boy, did he have a big nose and lips!" Later, when the teacher talked to the student after class, he became teary-eyed and got very defensive. He said he was just having fun. He admitted he was just trying to make everybody laugh.

The pressure to be accepted by his peers was too great for the boy to resist. He felt uncomfortable because through King his own Blackness became a focus in that nearly all-White environment. To deal with his anxiety he used humor at his own expense. The teacher was surprised that he would try to make fun of something she thought would be very serious to him.

A complicated process was taking place in that classroom. The Black student thought that the White students were feeling as uncomfortable as he was. His reasoning might have gone something like this: The White students probably think Dr. King is funny-looking. Maybe I'll feel more comfortable if I say what I think they are thinking and feeling. That way I'll fit in with them. The boy who made the remark was actually putting *himself* down.

Self-esteem is fragile. It can just as easily be damaged by neglect as by direct assault. If Grandma always hugs and kisses the grandson with the light curly hair, thin nose, or light complexion and says, "What a sweet boy you are," she will do wonders for his self-esteem. At the same time Jerome, with the tightly curled hair and flat nose, will begin to wonder why Grandma never says such nice things to him. Before long he will come to believe that his features are less attractive than his brother's. The effect will be almost the same as if Grandma had said, "Don't you wish you had good hair like your brother's?"

These are some of the behavior patterns that can help you assess your child's self-esteem level. The important word here is *pattern.* All children at one time or another will behave in one or more of these ways. It is usually not cause for alarm. However, if your child shows a prolonged pattern of such behavior, or perhaps has come to believe that it is okay to act in that manner, he or she might need you to intervene and help.

In addition to observing your children, there are some practical things you can do to find out how they feel about themselves. Make a list of the things you believe influence or reflect your child's self-esteem and racial identity. Does your child often compare himself to White children? Does he use derogatory names for Black people? Many children who are uncomfortable with their Blackness express this discomfort by attacking other children's Blackness. We have to watch out for these instances when our children put themselves and one another down for being Black.

Next, ask yourself, "How do I deal with these things? Do I get angry about them? Do I ignore them? Do I talk about them?" Again, the way you deal with those experiences helps shape the way your child thinks of himself. Take a look at this example and picture yourself as the parent involved.

Several children were playing together at a birthday party. They were all Black, but two of them had very light skin. The parents were sitting together in a separate room. One of the girls came in and said to her mother, "I don't want to play with that White girl anymore." She was referring to one of the light-skinned Black children. Her mother, and all of the other mothers, thought it was amusing. The mother of the girl who made the remark chose not to say anything to the child about it. She felt it was better to let the children work it out among themselves.

We are not saying the parent was right or wrong. Where and when you react to such things should depend on the child and the circumstances. But as an alternative the mother might have said, "She's not White, she's Black," and say something about the different skin tones among Black people. The advantage to correcting the child on the spot is that it allows the parent to discuss the issue while it is on the child's mind.

Another practical exercise that can reveal your children's self-image is to ask them to draw pictures of themselves. Lay out an assortment of crayons, the more colors the better, and allow them to draw at their leisure. What color do they make their skin? What color is the hair? What expressions do they draw? Are the figures smiling and cheerful or are they sad? How big did they draw themselves? Unfortunately, many Black children draw themselves with White skin and long blond hair. Some draw themselves small and insignificant among others. Such drawings can reveal a great deal about a child's self-image, but they require professional interpretation. Just look for obvious things such as hair color and skin color, and whether the child in the picture appears happy or sad.

To summarize, here is a list of some of the signs that will clue you in to the possibility that your child's self-esteem needs work:

- Frequent self-deprecating remarks
- Consistently disrespectful to family members
- Self-defeating behavior
- Grandiose manner
- Overly aggressive or bullying manner
- Lives up to negative expectations
- Withdrawal into fantasy world
- Difficulty socializing with other children
- Passive in the face of racial conflict
- Hostile, disruptive, or belligerent in class
- Draws himself or herself as White or with blond hair

SPOTTING POSITIVE SIGNS

It is just as important to identify signs of budding self-esteem and to offer support. When your son says, "I know I can do it if I try" or "I know I am good at this," he might be working to convince himself that what he is saying is true. Your support will reassure him that he is good at the task, or that he can do whatever he puts his mind to. Self-affirming statements such as "I like my beautiful brown skin" or "I have lots of people who like me" are also opportunities for parents to boost their children's self-esteem.

As a parent, you can further the development of your child's self-esteem by listening and eagerly responding when he or she expresses interest in hobbies, jobs, or careers. Although these interests are likely to vacillate or change many times over, it's your child's efforts to discover what he or she wants to be that you applaud. Whatever you do in the way of active support and encouragement can send the important message to your child, "you are a very special and important person," and thereby enhance self-esteem.

SELF-IMAGE, SELF-ESTEEM, AND RACISM

Negative racial attitudes and racism are communicated to children in both overt and subtle ways. In our era, when racial discrimination is illegal, it is the subtlest forms of race consciousness and racism that are the most dangerous. If someone calls you a "nigger," there is no question as to how he feels about you. If a store has a sign that says "We do not serve Blacks," we know that there are legal remedies that we can seek. When your rental application is mysteriously turned down, or when people who enter a restaurant after you are seated before you, however, it is more difficult to prove racism.

Antonia, a nine-year-old girl, was brought to us for counseling because she was having difficulty relating to her teacher. In the initial session she was tearful, sullen, and uncommunicative. Later, she told us she was upset about something she had seen happen to her mother while they were shopping. A White woman in front of them in line cashed a check at the register. But when Antonia's mother wrote a check and presented the same forms of identification the clerk refused to cash the check. Visibly upset, Antonia's mother rushed out of the store without her intended purchase and hushed Antonia abruptly when the child asked her to explain.

Understandably, the mother was too frustrated and angry—and perhaps too embarrassed—to use the opportunity to discuss racial discrimination and teach Antonia by example how to handle it (never a simple matter). Antonia came away knowing that the two women were treated differently but not *why.*

In therapy it became clear that she thought that perhaps Blacks weren't allowed to cash checks and that there might be a good reason why. Maybe, in some way that was beyond Antonia's understanding, the White woman was better than her mommy, as the clerk had seemed to suggest. Antonia needed guidance in understanding that racism exists, that those who practice it are wrong, and that despite its existence the value of Blacks *and the value of Antonia* are unchanged. After explaining racism and discriminatory treatment to Antonia, we assured her that she and her mother were different from Whites *and wonderful,* and she repaid us with a smile of great relief.

As this story suggests, negative stereotypes can slip into a child's world all too easily. Comings and goings in the marketplace provide many examples.

Journalist Juan Williams tells the story of a mother's experience in an ice cream parlor where the waitress simply ignored her. "I had a difficult choice to make," the woman said, "whether to walk out and face the kids' howling or sit there and sizzle." The same thing happened to another Black parent in a restaurant: "You keep sitting there," she said, "wondering when you're going to get waited on, watching everybody else being waited on, and it just makes you feel bad. And then it makes you want to be violent; you're wondering if you should get up and do something."

RACISM ASSAULTS SELF-ESTEEM

For adults and children alike, racism is a direct assault upon their self-esteem. In each of the above examples, the victims received the message through a simple act that by being Black they were less respectable, less deserving, and somehow less worthwhile. Without help from a concerned adult, the danger is that Black children will *identify* with, or see themselves in, the negative images of Blacks mirrored back to them by society: "If all Black boys are bad and I'm a Black boy, that must mean I'm bad." In fact, the idea that all Black boys of a certain age are bad is common in American society, and it haunts Black neighborhoods as well as White ones. Imagine, then, how many little Black boys are in danger of becoming adolescents with a negative view of themselves. As Jesse Jackson pointed out to the whole nation during the 1988 Democratic campaign, the inevitable results of low expectations are hopelessness and despair.

YOU CAN HELP YOUR CHILDREN FIGHT BACK

Children need adults' help in identifying and separating themselves from negative racial images. Even adolescents are too young to do so for themselves. Whether we like it or not, as Black parents we have an extra responsibility: to point out negative racial images, explain their inaccuracy, and teach our children how to separate themselves from them and protect their self-esteem. Elena's example below and her mother's actions illustrate an effective response to these situations.

Elena, a dark-skinned Hispanic girl, has been taking dance lessons most of her life. She tried out for the lead part in a high school production, but the dance teacher told her not to get her hopes up because "people of her background" have not done well in "serious" dancing. When pressed as to what she meant, the teacher, flustered, responded, "Your thighs are a bit heavy."

Crushed by the remarks from a teacher she had respected, Elena ran from the dance class. Her mother, Luz, was furious when she heard what had happened. She forced herself to calm down, however, and deal with the most important issue—her daughter's feelings. Luz explained to Elena that the teacher was expressing her own prejudices and that she was wrong. She cited examples of successful Black and Hispanic dancers, and helped her daughter to see that with her talent there was no reason why she could not be a successful dancer.

When Luz subsequently met with the teacher and the school's principal about the incident, the teacher admitted that she was wrong. She explained that she simply did not want to see Elena disappointed.

By helping her daughter to interpret the situation and by bringing the matter to school officials, Elena's mother was taking steps to solve the problem. But she was also showing her daughter an effective way to deal with such situations.

Chapter Three

MODELING AND REINFORCEMENT

In *modeling* we have the first of the basic tools that you can use to help build your child's self-esteem. Modeling means demonstrating a particular behavior or action and encouraging the child to imitate it.

For example, in our research, described in the introduction, we modeled choosing Black dolls and playing with them as a way to encourage the children to do the same. A more dramatic example of how modeling works involves an instance of *negative* modeling—demonstrating undesirable behavior. A young Black man in therapy had many memories of being taught that Black men should be passive because asserting themselves could be dangerous. On a bus trip, when he and his brother got off at a rest stop, a White man yelled at them for drinking at a "Whites only" fountain. Upset and angry, the boy ran back to the bus to tell his grandfather. "Why didn't you just stay on the bus like me?" the old man asked him. "Now, you just stay on the bus for the rest of the trip so you don't get into any more trouble."

This and other such incidents in his family could have taught the boy never to assert himself to a White man. But there's a happy ending to this man's story that demonstrates a tradition of *positive* modeling. Growing up in the rural South, the young man witnessed many occasions in which his father had to choose whether to challenge White people. One experience had such a powerful effect upon the boy that it directly influenced the course of his life.

Pigs belonging to a White neighbor often wandered onto the boy's family's farm and ate the crops. After repeated complaints the boy's father told the neighbor that if the pigs ate the crops again he would have to destroy the animals. The neighbor ignored the warning. Furthermore, he seemed to be deliberately allowing the pigs onto the farm. The next time the pigs ate the crops the boy's father shot one.

The owners threatened the boy's family, forcing them to hide. The family attempted to pursue the matter in court, but that brought them no guarantee of safety. It soon became clear that they could no longer stay on their land, so they decided to move to the North.

From this, the boy learned that it was indeed risky for a Black person to stand up for his rights in this country. He respected his father for choosing to assert his rights in the conflict. His father fled only when the safety of his family was at risk. As a result of this experience, the young man decided to commit his life to serving as a corrections officer. He strongly believes that some Black men who are in prisons are there simply because at some time in their lives they asserted their rights as human beings. He takes it as his responsibility, wherever possible, to prevent less sensitive corrections officers from dehumanizing Black prisoners.

Today the man proudly observes that each generation of men in his family grew up to be stronger and more assertive as a result of the tradition his father cultivated. His own son owns a private preschool; most of the students who attend are White. The son feels he has an opportunity to educate some of these children about what it is like to grow up Black in America, and to help promote racial harmony.

YOU ARE ALWAYS MODELING

An important fact about modeling is that we do it whether we know it or not. When you walk away in tears because of a racial slur, you are saying to your child, "This is the way to behave in this situation." Cursing at a store clerk who ignores you in favor of White customers gives your child the same message. Whatever you do in your child's presence, you are modeling. The reactions you model in response to racism will *inevitably* affect the way your child thinks of himself or herself as a Black person. In other words, modeling has a direct influence on the child's self-esteem. That's why it is important to model appropriate behavior.

STYLES OF BEHAVIOR

The first step in modeling appropriate responses to racism is to understand that there are many ways to react to this type of conflict. The reason that many Black children have such difficulty with racist practices is that they simply have no idea how to react to them.

People tend to engage in one of four basic styles of behavior: *passive, aggressive, passive-aggressive, or assertive.* The style we usually choose to respond by reflects the way we generally approach life's challenges. We all have a little of each style in us, but most people tend to favor one above the rest, particularly in times of crisis or conflict, such as when we have to deal with racism.

Passive. A Black person who is passive accepts racism and does nothing about it. George works in the headquarters of a bank. He is the only Black person at his level in the organization, so he usually has lunch with his White colleagues. Just about every day one of the other guys has a new ethnic joke to tell.

George hates ethnic jokes, but he doesn't know how to react when his White friends use them. Although he never contributes any, he smiles when the others tell such jokes. They have become very comfortable using even derogatory terms such as "darkie" around him. They think he likes "a good one" as well as any of them. But in fact it eats him up inside every time he has to listen to these jokes. Nevertheless, he does nothing about it.

On the day George was promoted to head of his section, one of his friends came up to him and said, "Congratulations. I see they made you top nigger around here. What do we Anglos have to do to get noticed?" George was angry. He couldn't tell for certain if his "friend" was serious, but he knew he did not like the remark. Nevertheless, he just smiled and walked away.

When it comes to racism, George is passive. Deep inside he knew he should not have let the remark pass without saying or doing something. But he could not bring himself to react. He has trouble stating his feelings and standing up for his rights.

Aggressive. At the other extreme we have the aggressive person. Helen, for example, resorts to name-calling at the first sign of racial conflict. She takes no time to think of an appropriate response, and will not hesitate to throw the first punch when she feels wronged. She may even go looking for situations where she can release her anger at an offending person.

Aggressive people like Helen are easy to spot. They seem to take pleasure in tormenting and intimidating others. Although few people like them, they get their way because people would rather give in to them than deal with them. They have few friends and are usually very unhappy people.

Passive-aggressive. On the surface, Nelson resembles George somewhat. Nothing, it appears, gets him angry. He does get angry, however; he just doesn't show it. Although he will smile at the cruelest ethnic joke, the joke teller is likely to find his tires slashed later. Nelson is passive-aggressive. He expresses his anger in sneaky ways. He doesn't know how to deal with anger directly and openly.

Assertive. Karren always says what's on her mind. She expresses her feelings honestly but is considerate of other people's feelings. "I find those jokes offensive," she might say. "I would appreciate it if you would not tell them when I'm present." Karren is an assertive person. Her friends and colleagues respect her honesty.

Janet is another example of someone who is assertive. She is the only Black student in her prep school class. She uses a styling solution to make her hair easier to manage. It leaves her hair damp. One of the boys in her class touched her hair and asked, "How come your hair is always so greasy?" Her classmates chuckled. Janet stood quietly until the snickering stopped; then she turned to the boy. "What I do with my hair is my business," she said. "You have no business touching my hair. Please don't do that again." Janet was offended, but she was not embarrassed. Rather than crying or remaining silent, she told the offender firmly what she expected of him. No one criticized her hair after that.

When we act assertively we defend our rights without violating the rights of others. Children who learn to be assertive grow up to be confident in themselves and well equipped to deal with racism. We feel that is appropriate behavior worth modeling for Black children.

Take a hard look at the above behavior styles and ask yourself which one is most like yours. Whichever one it is, you can be sure that you have been modeling it for your child. In chapter 5 we'll take a closer look at individual styles of interacting when we talk about family influences. We adopt much of our particular styles from influential members of our families. For now, let's look at some ideas for modeling appropriate behavior for your children.

IDEAS FOR MODELING

One of your best sources of modeling help is your fellow parents. Start paying attention to those you know. How do they behave in front of their children? Do any of them demonstrate assertive behavior? Discuss the question with them. Let them know that you are trying to develop the same style with your child. There is no need for you to postpone your work for want of a teacher, however. You can begin modeling on your own by following some of the examples given below.

Because children of different ages respond to different approaches, you will want to take a different tack in approaching your five-year-old than you would with your ten-year-old. Here are some examples.

MODELING FOR YOUNG CHILDREN

Denise, one of our White coworkers, has a daughter, Jill, who is the same age as our daughter. Denise asked us if we could help her find ways to expose Jill to some positive experiences with Black children. Our first reaction, even though we didn't say so, was, Why is this necessary? Every day Black people go about their business as positively as does anyone else. Why is there a need to set up special circumstances? Upon reflection, we realized that the request was not unreasonable. Denise lived in a predominantly White community, and although she interacts with Black Americans in her work, her daughter's exposure to Blacks was quite limited. We decided to help. We also figured that the best way to teach Jill about positive interaction between Blacks and Whites was to demonstrate (model) it for her.

We invited mother and daughter to our home for coffee and dessert. We set the kitchen table and, at the same time, we set our daughter's toy tea set on a play table next to the kitchen table. When we sat down to dessert, we had the girls sit down with the toy tea set at the play table. Denise and I made a point of speaking clearly so that the girls could hear us and see our reactions to each other. "This tea is very good, where did you buy it?" "I love your dress, I have one just like it." "How are things at the office." And so it went.

At first the girls merely eyed each other warily, but then they started to pay attention to us. After a short time the girls started to imitate our actions. In less than fifteen minutes they were laughing and playing like the best of friends, which they are today. In this simple exercise of modeling we showed the girls that Blacks and Whites can interact comfortably with one another.

MODELING FOR AGES SIX THROUGH TEN

Look for modeling opportunities that lend themselves to your child's interests in this age range. For instance, Doreen takes her six-year-old son Eric to play in the park. Normally he runs to the monkey bars as soon as they get there. On one occasion, however, he stood hesitantly a few feet away. A group of white children were climbing the bars. Doreen could tell that he wanted to play, but he was unsure of the situation. She took him by the hand and said, "Let's go meet those kids. Maybe we can make friends with them."

She began by admiring what the other children were doing on the bars: "That's a great flip! How'd you learn to do that?" As she talked to them, Eric became more and more comfortable with the situation. Before long he was clambering over the bars with the other children. Doreen's example showed Eric how to help ease the tension in new social situations.

Modeling for Adolescents

Of course, the way you model for your teenage children will reflect their particular needs. We've dedicated chapter 8 to the difficulties that adolescents face. So for now, let's just look briefly at some examples of modeling for adolescents. One of the facts of life is that what you say to adolescents will often have the opposite effect of what you intend. It seems that teenagers instinctively reject verbal advice. Therefore, teaching by doing—modeling—becomes even more important.

Marcia, the teenage daughter of a friend, gets annoyed because her White friends ask her questions about Blackness: "How come your hair is like that?" "What kinds of foods do you eat at home?" "What's it like in your church?" She feels that those questions point out the differences between her and her friends, and that she has to suppress her Black culture if she wants to be friendly with them.

One day when Marcia was visiting us, we unexpectedly found an opportunity to model an appropriate response for her. Our family is always on the lookout for Black cultural activities in our area. Alice, a White friend of ours who lives in a "university" town, keeps urging us to move to her town because there are lots of cultural events there. Whenever she visits us, she brings flyers and notices of upcoming events.

As we went over the brochures, Alice pointed out Black theater productions, a lecture at the university, a gospel concert, and a Black fashion show. Marcia sat wide-eyed at the spectacle of a White person who had taken the time to find out what was happening in the Black community. Furthermore, Alice talked about these events comfortably, calmly, and confidently.

When Alice left, Marcia asked, "How come she knows so much about Black stuff?" We were able to help Marcia understand that Alice was comfortable discussing Black culture with us because we had shown her that *we* were comfortable with it.

At the time of the Bernhard Goetz shooting in the New York City subway, seventeen-year-old Larry felt that Goetz had a right to shoot his assailants. His parents felt differently, and after one heated discussion Larry refused to talk to them about it again. Shortly after that, Larry's aunt and uncle came to visit, and the subject of the shooting came up. The aunt and uncle shared Larry's opinion, and the four adults had a very calm discussion instead of a "fight." They stated their points of view and found areas where they agreed and others where they agreed to disagree. Larry learned that it was okay for Black people to have differing opinions on critical issues that concerned Blacks.

In your search for help in modeling for your children, check with your church or your child's school. You might find that a group concerned with such issues exists. If there isn't one, you could try to start one. It doesn't have to be formal; it could even be just a sharing of ideas over the phone.

If you feel that a particular problem is more than you can manage, it would be helpful for you to seek counseling. You can get help from social service agencies such as the Urban League, the NAACP, or other groups that are sensitive to racial problems. For even more serious problems, you might want to consider seeing a mental health professional.

PROFESSIONAL HELP WITH MODELING

The first step when you choose a mental health professional is to find someone who is licensed or certified in the state where you live. Check with professional associations such as the Association of Black Psychologists, the Association of Black Social Workers, or the Black Psychiatrists of America to see if they have a list of professionals in your area. An equally important consideration is that the person you choose be caring and sensitive to your particular racial problem. For that qualification, word of mouth is often your best guide. If possible, find someone who can recommend a therapist with whom he or she has had a good experience.

You might find it difficult to admit to "strangers" or even to your close friends that you are concerned with the perception of Blackness your child has been receiving from you and others. It is easy to feel that you have failed and to try to hide it. That would be your biggest mistake, and a disservice to your child. It will take time to get the results you are looking for, but you will be rewarded with the knowledge that you have equipped your child to function in society.

PEER MODELING

Another form of modeling is to draw your child's attention to another child who clearly displays assertive behavior. We call this *peer modeling*. It's quite simple. Let's say your eight-year-old daughter is new to a suburban school. Her teacher is the first White person she has had to deal with. She is very shy and cannot bring herself to speak to him. While it would be a good idea for you to talk to the teacher about your child's reticence, at the same time it would be helpful to introduce your child to another Black child who has successfully dealt with the problem. Tell your daughter to watch the other child and do as he or she does.

Peer modeling can be quite effective. It's just a positive form of peer pressure, and we all know how powerful that can be. When we work with groups of children in our practice, we always try to include at least one child who is skilled in the behavior we are modeling. It makes the work much easier.

AUTHORITY FIGURES

Black authority figures can be good models of assertiveness for Black children. Doctors, dentists, policemen, and other professionals come to mind. Take your child to see a Black doctor. Call the child's attention to professional symbols such as diplomas or instruments in the office. Explain to him or her about the doctor's responsibilities, and allow your child to speak directly to the doctor as much as possible.

Of course, you will want to model assertiveness in your communications with the doctor. Look the doctor in the eye. Listen attentively to his or her questions. Answer them clearly in words; don't just nod. If assertive behavior is new to you, you will want to plan, as best you can, how you are going to behave. You might find it helpful to write down any questions you plan to ask the doctor. You can even plan the whole thing out with the doctor in advance. Both you and your child will feel very good about yourselves after an encounter like this.

HISTORIC FIGURES

Historic figures can also be good models of assertive behavior. Martin Luther King, Jr., devoted his life to asserting the rights of all people. His speeches and writings can help Black children understand how to stand up for one's beliefs. Harriet Tubman, Sojourner Truth, Malcolm X, and Marcus Garvey are all figures from whom we can learn much through books and films about asserting ourselves.

Some libraries have special collections of Black literature dating back to slavery. Learning about the courage of some of the slaves can be very enlightening for your child. If your local library does not have such works perhaps they can suggest places near you where you can find them.

Contemporary history is also full of fascinating and inspiring examples of the courage and assertiveness it takes for our people to succeed. Reading just the newspapers can give you plenty of material to work with. For example, think of the Black mayors elected in recent years in cities around the country. Many of them came to power after bitter fights with political organizations that simply did not think Black people were capable of handling the responsibilities of the mayoralty. The late Mayor Harold Washington of Chicago and Mayor Wilson Goode of Philadelphia are excellent examples. They fought incredible odds to achieve the results they did.

Recently on the state level, the first Black governor in U.S. history was elected, in Virginia, the Honorable Lawrence Douglas Wilder. His immediate family background includes being a direct descendant of slaves, a grandson. He clearly serves as a powerful role model and inspiration for Black people.

On the national level we have figures such as Jesse Jackson; Ron Brown, the head of the Democratic National Committee; Justice Thurgood Marshall of the Supreme Court; and former Texas Congresswoman Barbara Jordan. These people have had to overcome enormous obstacles to reach their goals. Their stories are as close as your daily newspapers. Read them to your children so they can have an idea of the cost and the possible rewards of asserting themselves.

MODELING FOR CHILDREN IN NON-BLACK SETTINGS

If your children are enrolled in a predominantly White school, their exposure to Black role models might be severely limited. Many of those school systems have little concern for information about Africans' contribution to American history. They celebrate Black History Month and Martin Luther King Day with posters in the hallways and classrooms; however, these all but disappear at the end of February (Black History Month), and it's back to business as usual. Sadly, this is sometimes true even in predominantly Black school systems.

We visited one classroom at the end of February and watched as the student teacher walked around the room and removed every picture of a Black person, replacing them with symbols of the upcoming spring. All of the pictures that remained on the walls were of White historic figures. This incident happened in a school that was 80 percent Black. It was not the teacher's intention to deliberately strip the room of Black images. As far as she was concerned, she was just providing new material to stimulate the children's interest. But in doing so she had treated Black history with no more significance than the changing of the seasons.

Enrolling your children in White suburban schools is good in one sense. It will give them a chance to get the basic education that too often is lacking in the schools that many Blacks attend. But to make sure your child is not cut off from positive Black authority figures, you will have to seek out the community programs, books, and role models they need to develop a respect for Black people and culture.

To do this you have to take the initiative in areas that might be completely new to you. For example, if you belong to a church, you might discuss the problem with the minister. Perhaps you can suggest that Sunday school classes profile at least one Black figure each week and encourage the students to research and report on him or her the next week.

ROLE PLAYING

Role playing, which is closely related to modeling, is another technique you can use to teach your children appropriate behavior. Whereas in modeling you *demonstrate* the desirable behavior for the child, in role playing you have the child *act out* the desirable behavior in a hypothetical situation.

For instance, one of our clients, a boy named Carl, came home with an unusual complaint: "There is a boy in my class who, every day when I am getting ready to have lunch, comes over and takes my white milk and tells me I should be drinking chocolate milk." Carl's mother consulted us after deciding that she did not know how to handle the situation. We used role playing to help the child find an appropriate response.

We obtained a carton of white milk and sat down with Carl and a third person who played the part of the bully. Together we practiced several reactions Carl should consider. We practiced being passive, moving to different seats. Of course, each time the "bully" found Carl and continued teasing him. We were able to point out that passive responses usually do not work.

We asked Carl what *he* wanted to do about the bully. "I just want to tell him, 'Get away from me, honky,'" he replied. He was having difficulty getting past his anger. We explained that that would have been inappropriate because it was too aggressive and would probably make the situation worse.

One of the responses we suggested was that he tell the bully, "What you are doing is racist and I don't like it." Carl objected to that because he felt uncomfortable with it. "Can you say it in a way that is more comfortable to you?" we asked. He thought for a while, then suggested, "*Look.* What you are doing is racist and I don't like it." He thought that would better show the bully that he was angry. Still he wasn't satisfied.

We tried different kinds of assertive responses to show him that assertiveness can escalate. In other words, he could start off by telling the bully, "I drink what I like. It's no business of yours." If that did not work, Carl could go a step further by reporting it to the cafeteria staff. He could say, "John Smith is bothering me. He keeps telling me I can't drink white milk. He takes away my milk and tells me I have to drink chocolate milk because I'm Black." If that were not effective, he could say to the bully, "I really don't like this, and if you don't stop I'm going to tell the principal."

In the end, Carl chose to ask the other boy, "If being Black is so bad, why do you go outside to try to get a tan?" He wanted the bully to know he was comfortable being Black. He just did not want to be bothered with the teasing. That was the end of his problem.

One important lesson from this experience is that the reactions you role play with your child should offer him or her an assertive but *comfortable* way to deal with the conflict. The last thing you want is for your children to try to assert themselves and have someone laugh in their faces. Make sure your child shows that he or she is comfortable with the reaction. A good way to do that is to imagine how someone might react to the assertions and practice how to deal with that.

For example, if the bully were to respond, "I never try to get a tan," Carl could simply say, with all the confidence in the world, "You will." He could use that as his routine response whenever the bully came around.

It might seem as though Carl would be merely taunting the other boy with this response. However, because the boys are not yet mature enough to "talk out" their conflict at this age, a response such as this would be aimed at getting the bully to experience and hopefully later on to understand the discomfort caused by offensive racial teasing.

Still, another alternative is to enroll your child in martial arts classes. He or she will learn not only to physically defend against bullies but also valuable lessons of self-discipline when threatened.

ROLE PLAYING CAN BE ANTICIPATORY

Role playing is good for helping children deal with problems after they occur. However, it is also helpful in preparing them for the difficult situations we know they will encounter sooner or later. Think of a racial situation that was especially difficult for you to handle as a child. For example, how did you feel the first time you heard the word "nigger" and you looked around and found you were the only Black person present? Wouldn't it be great if you could help your child prepare for that experience?

How did you feel the first time you were the only Black child in a group of children? How will your son feel in that situation? If this all seems silly, consider this: Most of the neighborhoods in this country are segregated. Your children could reach the age of ten before having to deal with White children. How would they feel at an overnight scout camp? Role-play such experiences with your children to help remove some of the anxiety they might otherwise experience.

Imagine that your daughter is the only Black child in her unit at a sleep-away camp. Most of the girls know each other from previous years, but this is your daughter's first time. Imagine that there is a White girl your daughter's age who has never had anything to do with a Black person before. She tells your daughter, "I'm not sleeping in the same tent as you. I don't want you stealing my stuff." How would your child react?

For situations such as this, you could play the role of the other girl and encourage your daughter to practice responses such as these: She might ask the other girl, "How do I know that *you* won't steal *my* things?" That should get the girl to say why she thinks your daughter might steal. "Do you think Black people steal?" your daughter might also ask. She could also say, "I don't believe all White people steal, and you have no reason to believe all Black people do."

Here is a situation that put one girl to the test. Diana lives in an affluent White suburb of an eastern city. She is a freshman in her town's only high school, and one of only four Black girls attending. Her school is in the same athletic league as the nearby city, so their football teams play at each other's fields. The city's Jefferson High School is 100 percent Black. For the first game of the season, Diana's school was to host Jefferson High. The Friday before the game, as she was leaving school, she heard someone remark, "We're playing Jefferson tomorrow—lock your car."

As she left school that day, she heard the same remark repeated several times in the hallway. Even her friends were saying it. It was a tradition. Diana felt embarrassed, insulted, and confused. She did not know how to react to the open display of racism. When she told her father, he shrugged and said, "There's a lot of that out there. You'd better get used to it."

A better response would have been for Diana's father to say, "There's a lot of that out there, so don't be shocked when you hear it. Here's what you can do. You pretend to be your friend, and I'll pretend to be you. Now, what did she say?"

"We're playing Jefferson tomorrow. Lock your car."

"Why do you say that?"

"Because they will rob you blind if you don't."

"Do you think I'll rob you, too?"

"No!"

"Why not?"

"Well . . . you're different."

"If you get to know those kids from Jefferson, you might find that most of them are 'different,' too." This is only one of many scenarios that could give the girl an idea of how to deal with such remarks.

Role playing might feel uncomfortable to you at first, but you don't need to set up complicated situations in order to practice. A less threatening and less complicated way to get your child interested in role playing is to simply ask the child "what if" questions, and help him or her work through the solutions. Such questions are useful because they can start your child thinking about these types of issues before they become a problem. With your help, by the time the child has to deal with these situations he or she will be very confident in handling them. Here are some useful "what if" questions and some suggested responses. We're sure you can come up with some of your own:

What if someone calls you "nigger"? People who have to call other people names like that to feel good must really feel bad about themselves. I feel sorry for you. You should get help.

What if Whites make fun of your hair? My hair is naturally different from yours. I don't know how you feel about yours, but *I'm* perfectly happy with mine. I don't care how *you* feel about it.

What if someone asks you why your skin is Black? People come in different colors. One color doesn't make a person better or worse than another. I don't think any less of you because you aren't Black. Treat me the same way.

What if you feel that someone is being unfair to you, but you're not sure if it's because of your race? If you're doing this because I am Black, I want you to know that's unfair and I object to it. I will report what you're doing to [the appropriate authority].

What if you heard a White person you considered a friend make a racist remark? Do you really feel that way about Black people? I'm sorry, but if you do I can't be your friend.

What if someone accuses your White friend of being racist? I know [Janet] and I'd be surprised to find she feels this way. I'll have to talk to her about it.

Of course, no list can cover every possible situation. Most of these situations tend to generate the same kinds of feelings, however. And those feelings are what tend to dictate our responses. By learning how to control these feelings and developing controlled responses such as those above, your child will be better prepared to handle most racial conflicts that develop.

A word of caution: It takes time to learn any new skill. We don't recommend that you read this chapter, put away the book, and start role playing on the spot. Please take the time to assess your own attitude and behavior by using the statements in chapter 1 (included in "You as a Black Parent" and "Can You Talk to Your Child about Racism?"). Think carefully about what you are doing. Give yourself time to understand and feel comfortable with the ideas before you try to communicate them to your child. By the same token, don't expect your child to become assertive the very next day.

REINFORCEMENT: GOOD OLD-FASHIONED REWARD

Reinforcement is the second of the three major tools that will help you build your child's self-esteem. Reinforcement is simply a reward given after an action to encourage the person to perform the action again. An adult's smile or praise works magic on children's behavior. Any parent who has acknowledged the smallest instance of good behavior in a difficult-to-manage child knows this.

SEIZING REINFORCEMENT OPPORTUNITIES

Reinforcement is a simple concept, but knowing when to apply it is sometimes difficult, and those missed opportunities can send negative messages. For example, Naomi, an extremely bright eight-year-old who attended a predominantly White school, came home with a poor report card even though her grades had been outstanding throughout the year. In conference, the teacher agreed that Naomi had been doing very well academically but that she had the habit of overenthusiasm—she called out the right answers in class and corrected the other children when they were wrong. Naomi's parents joined the teacher in criticizing this overzealous behavior, embarrassed that their daughter was drawing attention to herself in class. In the confusion, all three adults showed little interest in Naomi's achievements. The little girl came away with this message: Good grades don't mean so much when you do something so audacious and bad as criticizing White children. Her parents were proud of Naomi's intelligence, but they took it for granted. They did not see that in focusing negatively on Naomi's behavior in class the teacher was failing to credit her real achievements. Naomi needed her parents to reward her for the good work she had performed, but they missed their chance to give her the reinforcement she deserved. In addition, Naomi was demonstrating leadership that could have been channeled.

As a first step, Naomi's parents could have congratulated her and let her know they were proud of her because she usually knew the right answer. "Not everyone is as quick to solve problems as you are," they might have said. "Most children need more time to solve the problems than you do. It would be very helpful if you would wait a little before you answer to give the others time to figure it out."

"But she never calls on me!" Naomi might reply. Her parents would then have to work out a solution with the teacher to make sure that their child got recognition for knowing the answers. It might be as simple as having Naomi write the answers on the board as other children call them out and write the solution as the teacher explains it.

Kim's case illustrates another missed opportunity to reinforce positive behavior. She is a very bright child with an IQ above 130. Like Naomi, she attends a predominantly White, upper-middle-class school. During our observation, she sat with a group of children in her class. There was a six-pointed star on the chalkboard. The teacher asked how many triangles made up the star. Most of the children shouted out that there were two: one right side up, the other upside-down. Kim counted all of the smaller triangles and said there were eight. The teacher ignored her. Kim kept raising her hand. She answered all the questions that the teacher asked, trying to get the children to look more carefully. But the teacher, attempting to make the other children feel good about themselves, kept ignoring Kim because she usually knew the answer. Kim became disruptive. She began poking some of the kids next to her and making fun of their answers. She was not getting attention and reinforcement for her positive actions, so she began to taunt the children around her, knowing that the teacher would pay attention to her then. In her concern about boosting the other children's self-esteem, the teacher had failed to attend to Kim's needs.

Kim's teacher could have said, "Thank you, Kim, but wait just a moment and you'll have your turn." Since Kim was first with the right answer, the teacher could have rewarded her by having her demonstrate the answer at the board.

Black children who are exceptionally bright need special reinforcement. More than others, they do not fit the image that many teachers have of Black children. As a result, teachers do not always know how to treat them. These children might not need as *much* attention as other children, but it is important to make sure they do not have to use negative tactics, as Kim did, to get the attention they deserve.

Parents should let teachers know they would like to hear from them when their children are doing well, not just when they are misbehaving. One teacher remarked, "We see the parents we *don't* want to see, and never see those we *need* to see." He was implying that he doesn't need to see the parents of children who are doing well. That may be reasonable from his point of view, but as a Black parent you should find that approach unacceptable. Take the time to go to the school and say, "I haven't heard from you. I hope my child is doing well. If so, I'd like to know some of the things she is doing well." That would be an assertive way to let the school know that you are actively involved in your child's education. Imagine how surprised and pleased your daughter would be if you said to her, "I spoke to your teacher today, and he said you are doing very well in school."

Focus on the Positive

In our day-to-day contact with our children, we tend to focus on the negative things they do, and this is only natural. When a child does something wrong it catches our attention because it disturbs us. It breaks our concentration, and we can't resist reacting to it. Let's say your daughter comes through the front door and shouts, "I got a *B* on my math test." "That's nice," you say from the kitchen, not quite sure what she said. But just imagine she said *F* instead of *B*. "What!?" you say. She's got your attention now. "Get in here this second!"

The greater part of our conversations with our children is spent telling them what they shouldn't do. As a result they don't get the rewards they need and deserve for the things they do appropriately.

Reinforce Promptly

For reinforcement to work, the child must be able to relate the reward to something he or she has done. Try to reward desirable behavior as quickly as possible. When you hug your daughter to encourage her assertiveness, she shouldn't have to ask you, "What was *that* for?" If your son questions the way Blacks are portrayed in a book or a television program, reinforce his action. You could say right then and there, "I'm very pleased you noticed that. It's important for you to be aware of those things." Your son hears, "I care about these things, and I'm glad to see that you do too."

ANYTHING CAN BE A REWARD

We said reinforcement means reward, but you do not have to be rich to reinforce your child's positive actions. A hand on the shoulder or a pat on the back can be more meaningful than any amount of money. Likewise, a hug or a smile is a way of saying to your child, "You've done well" or "I know you can do it." Money and other material rewards have their place, but it's important that children do not come to expect them in exchange for appropriate behavior.

By now you are probably saying to yourself, "Where am I going to find time to do all these things? I barely have enough time to *breathe* at the end of the day. Besides, I don't know 'modeling' from ironing." We understand that. But before you put all of this aside and forget about it, there is an important point for you to consider.

It is reassuring to know that in modeling, reinforcement, and open communication we have the tools to shape our children's future. But we must keep in mind the peculiar nature of those tools: They are always at work whether or not we have control of them. Modeling takes place whether we intend it or not. For better or for worse, we somehow communicate with our children. And whatever we reward, consciously or unconsciously, gets repeated by them. The result is that your children have been influenced by what you have said and done long before you read this book.

Fortunately there is plenty you can do if you feel the situation needs improvement. The techniques presented here are the tools that you need to begin using. Don't feel badly if you think you are poorly prepared. Most parents are in the same boat as you. Start practicing with little things like complimenting your children on their appearance or things they do well. You can't go wrong with this, and the results you get will give you the confidence to address the more complex issues involving race.

We've talked about some sophisticated concepts and techniques in this chapter. Our goal is to help you understand how critical good self-image and high self-esteem are to your children's future. Modeling and reinforcing appropriate behavior are the main tools you will use to build up their self-esteem.

The techniques we discussed are easy enough to follow, but they need time and patience to work. Don't let that discourage you from starting. You don't need to do *everything* we suggest, and you don't have to tackle everything you choose to do at once. As you read, pick out the minor activities that catch your attention and start with those. The success you have with them will give you the confidence to try the more complex exercises.

Chapter Four

FREE-FLOWING COMMUNICATION: THE ESSENTIAL INGREDIENT

Racism, always tangled with emotions, is difficult to discuss rationally or constructively. Yet frank, open expression in the family is essential to combating the negative racial messages that bombard Black children every day. Some basic steps are necessary if an honest sharing of feelings is to take place. We must be willing to admit to our children that they *are* different from Whites. They need to know that although the most obvious difference is in the color of their skin, there are also valid cultural differences of which they can be proud. (This knowledge could spark in them a necessary curiosity about Black culture and provide further opportunities to enhance their images of themselves as Black people.) They need to know that even though there is no inherent goodness or badness in these differences, there are people who believe otherwise and will treat them badly. It is only fair that they know this. Until they learn how to respond to such treatment we, their parents, will be their first line of defense. It is important, therefore, that we make them feel that they can discuss such experiences with us in an atmosphere free of anxiety, criticism, or punishment.

Daniel came from an interracial home and attended a predominantly White school. He constantly misbehaved in school and had trouble with his work although he was very intelligent.

His teacher routinely punished him by keeping him inside during recess. Nothing changed. In therapy he disclosed he didn't want to go out at recess anyway, but at first he didn't say why. Later he disclosed that he didn't want to go out because the children called him racial names during recess. Daniel was smart enough to figure out that if he misbehaved he would be kept in at recess and not have to face his tormentors. For his own reasons he did not feel he could tell his parents about the problem.

WHY SOME CHILDREN SUFFER IN SILENCE

Why would our children endure such discomfort, or even misery, without telling us? There are many reasons, but one appears with sad regularity. Some Black parents deny that racial prejudice exists, perhaps because they so desperately want this to be the case, especially for their children. They believe that if they teach them to deny the existence of racism they will somehow escape its effect. That approach does not work. Often when such a child encounters racism he cannot discuss it with his parents. How can he discuss something that does not exist? If the child raises the issue the parent will probably try to explain away an experience the child knows to be real. Imagine how confusing this must be for a child who has seen the face of racism.

We suspect that the majority of those who deny racism do so in the hopes of escaping its effects. Since we feel that this is an unrealistic reaction, we are concerned for the children of such parents. We can only urge the parents to consider how much they are putting their children at risk if their perception is wrong.

Parents of mixed-race Black children often tell their children they are neither Black nor White, but Brown. They attempt to raise them with a balanced exposure to both cultures. The goal is admirable, and it's true that somewhere between Black and White is a range we can safely call Brown. The language of skin coloring in America still admits to only Black and White, however. If an individual has any discernible measure of Black blood, he or she is considered Black. It doesn't matter that he or she might be lighter than others who are considered White.

It might indeed be more accurate, or even desirable, to tell mixed-race children that they are Brown, as a way of acknowledging their dual heritage. However, open, honest communication requires that they be told how the world around them will see them—as Black—and that their Blackness is beautiful.

Even positive interracial experiences sometimes require careful communication to deal with potentially negative undertones. For example, inner-city Black students enrolled in an enrichment program in a White suburban school described difficulties they were having as "academic problems." But in group therapy they admitted that White children in their classes treated them differently. Their adviser, who was White, kept telling them that no one was treating them differently. "You are a part of the community," he told them. The reality, of course, was that they *were* different. Although they were welcomed and treated with good intentions, they were not seen as regular members of the community.

Some of the children admitted that they were reluctant to talk to their parents about the problems, fearing that their parents would be disappointed to hear that they were having problems. After all, the parents had told them this would be a better chance for them. If these parents had openly cautioned their children as to what they could expect, they might have been better prepared to deal with the subtle rejection.

If we are to teach our children how to fight racism, we must first create an atmosphere suitable to the open communication of honest feelings—nothing can be off-limits in our communication with them. We must tell them what we want them to know and be willing to listen calmly to what *they* want us to know. That means turning off the radio or the television to show them that they have our attention. It also means questioning them to make sure we understand what they are saying. Only then can we begin to develop appropriate responses to their concerns and help them face a race-conscious society with pride in who they are.

BEHAVIOR COMMUNICATES FEELINGS

We communicate mainly with words, but the things we do also reveal much about the way we feel inside. For example, if a child constantly provokes other children, she is saying something about how she feels. If David, a Black child, says, "I only like to play with Billy," he is obviously saying something about how he feels about Billy. He is also revealing something of the way he feels about himself. If Billy is the only White child in David's class, David might be saying, "I prefer White playmates." On the other hand, if Billy is the only other Black child in David's class, David might be showing that he feels comfortable with someone who is also Black. If a child goes into a room full of Blacks and Whites and joins the other Blacks in the room, he is "saying" a feeling. It may be "I feel comfortable with other Blacks" or "I feel good about being with other Blacks." He might also be saying, "I don't feel comfortable with Whites."

Facial expressions, gestures, and even tone of voice all reveal feelings. Hugging, smiling, appearing angry, or throwing a tantrum provide other clues as to what a child might be feeling. Parents also communicate through their behavior. Spanking, hugging, smiling, even ignoring are some of the ways parents communicate their feelings to their children.

A Black woman who had just moved into a largely White neighborhood was concerned about how her son would fit in. Every day when she came home she cornered the boy: "How did you do today? Did you get into any trouble?" After a while the boy began to be very annoyed with his mother. He could tell she was expecting the worst from him. The feeling that the boy was "hearing" from his mother was "I can't trust you to behave properly when I'm away."

The first step in understanding what someone is trying to communicate is to observe the person's behavior and understand the feelings behind it. You can improve the communication in your family by finding out what different members are feeling. You can then take steps to help meet their needs.

Sally, a six-year-old child, never plays with other children and is noticeably unhappy about not having friends. She would rather watch television after school then get together with other children. Her behavior is expressing a feeling. Maybe she doesn't feel comfortable being with other children. For reasons that even she might not know, she might be frustrated, confused, or anxious in her relationships with other children. Perhaps they do not pay attention to her. Maybe she always says the "wrong thing." Maybe she is always the last one chosen to play games. It could be that her reaction to her playmates has nothing to do with them, but instead is related to something that's happening at home. She might be bored or depressed.

Sally's parents could help their daughter by inviting small groups of children over to play. During the play activities, the parents could offer guidance and support, as well as observe any difficulties in their daughter's interaction with the other children. They could talk to Sally's teacher and find out which children she relates to in school and if she interacts differently there than at home. She could attend a play group or organization like Jack & Jill. Finally, if appropriate, enrolling Sally in a therapeutic play group, which teaches social skills could be helpful. If serious concerns still remain, Sally's parents could locate a psychologist to conduct a psychological evaluation to determine if there are other underlying causes of her difficulties. Individual treatment might be warranted to help her build confidence and self-esteem.

Obviously, people can express a wide range of feelings in their behavior. Also, people can express more than one feeling at the same time. In fact, we usually show a combination of feelings at any given time.

If your son comes home feeling angry because a group of bullies taunted him on the way home, what else might he be feeling? He might be recalling the fear he felt at the time. He might also be feeling anxiety over what might happen the next day at school.

CHILDREN'S CONFLICTING SIGNALS

Children often show conflicting feelings. They cannot or do not express themselves in words as well as most adults do. Instead they tend to "act out" the way they feel. How many times have your children insisted that "nothing is wrong" as they slammed the door to their room? We have to take into account both what they say and what they do when we try to understand their feelings. If we are going to communicate with them effectively, we have to learn what their actions mean.

All communication skills are learned. We learn our ways of

talking and listening to one another and continue to refine them throughout our lives. We are taught by our families, our friends, our teachers, and by our culture at large. And we teach our children rules for communication. These rules may be as simple as "Speak up" or "Look at me when I'm talking to you." But as our children grow, communication becomes more complicated and demands greater effort.

For Black children, the pressures of living in a race-conscious society exert powerful additional influences that we have to consider when we teach them to communicate with ourselves and with others. For instance, your child would probably find it much easier to tell you she failed an important test than to tell you she overheard her favorite teacher talking about the "dumb spics" in his class. She would *feel* far more foolish for trusting someone who felt that way than for failing a test. When racism enters the picture, communication becomes far more complicated.

ACTIVE LISTENING

One way to improve communication with our children is to take an active role when we listen to them. Consider this example: Stephanie's seven-year-old daughter, Melanie, came home and said, "I hate going to school." How should Stephanie react to this?

The first step is for her to listen. What *feelings* is she hearing? The words offer clues, but there might be even more information that the child cannot or will not put into words. What does her appearance show? Does she seem agitated? Is her expression worried? Angry? Calm? Pleasant? Friendly? Is she speaking loudly, perhaps shouting? Is she nervous and jumpy, or relaxed and comfortable? If the mother looks for these *nonverbal clues* that are present in all communication, she will stand a better chance of understanding more fully what her child is feeling.

To further understand the child, Stephanie could employ some simple techniques of active listening. She probably already uses some of them without knowing it. For example, she might simply repeat Melanie's statement as a question: "You hate school?" Now Melanie knows her mother is listening. Usually the child will volunteer more information.

"Janice is stupid. She follows me everywhere." Now Stephanie knows that Janice, Melanie's best friend, has had something to do with her state of mind.

"Sounds to me like you had a problem with Janice today," the mother says.

"She doesn't even dress right," Melanie continues.

"What makes you say that?" her mother asks. Through gentle questioning she learns that Janice wore an ill-fitting dress to school and the other children made fun of her. She tried to stick close to Melanie for support, but Melanie was embarrassed and tried to get away from her.

After repeating the child's words—"you hate school?"—to make her aware she was listening, Stephanie, in practicing active listening, asked her daughter open-ended questions. These questions, such as "What makes you say that?" cannot be answered with either yes or no. Open-ended questions encourage the child to respond with more information about the way she feels.

Next, the mother states how *she* understands the child's remarks: "Sounds to me like you had a problem with Janice." This kind of comment can be used in almost any situation and still be appropriate. It lets the child know if you are on the right track, and she is encouraged to give you more information. One good thing about questions that begin with "Sounds to me like . . ." is that if you are wrong the child will often tell you.

In analyzing Stephanie's responses to Melanie we can detect another technique of active listening in something that she *doesn't* do. She does not pass judgment on anything her daughter says. "Janice follows you around because she likes you. Don't be so sensitive" would be a judgmental remark. Not making judgments is critical for active listening. When you are listening, you are simply collecting information. Only after you are satisfied that you understand what your child is feeling should you attempt even to offer a suggestion.

In this example, Stephanie discovers through active listening that her daughter's words do not express her true feelings. By probing gently, she discovers the real feelings and gains an opportunity to talk to Melanie about friendship and loyalty.

Active listening is an aspect of open communication that cannot be overlooked. It is simple to do, produces immediate results, and is usually quite revealing to both parent and child. Again, the steps in active listening are:

- Restate the child's remarks to make sure you are hearing them correctly and to let him or her know that you are listening.
- Ask open-ended questions to further clarify the situation.
- State how *you* understand the problem.
- Withhold judgment until you have all the facts.

OPEN RESPONSE, CLOSED RESPONSE

The way you respond to your children also determines how much information you get from them. We speak of two basic types of responses: closed and open. Closed responses tend to cut off communication, whereas open responses encourage it. Imagine that your son, Oscar, asks you, "Have you ever tried pot, Dad?" Caught off guard, you might react instantly, saying, "Drugs are bad news, son. A lot of people have been messed up by drugs. I don't want you to even *think* about it." That's a closed response. Although the information might be factual and valuable, it serves to inhibit further discussion.

An open response might be "That's an interesting question. Why do you ask?" This reply leaves the lines of communications open so that you can find out exactly what he is thinking about drugs. Keep injecting such responses into the conversation until you feel you understand what's on his mind. For instance, if he were to say, "Oh, nothing, just curious . . . I guess," you might ask him, "In what way are you curious? Let's talk about it. When I was your age, I was curious too." This way you are demonstrating empathy and an understanding of his curiosity. At the end of the discussion you might still want to say how bad you think drugs are, but by then you will have found out more about how *he* feels about them.

Open responses are an integral part of active listening. They are particularly effective in keeping communication flowing. It might be helpful for you to jot down some open-response examples. Of course, you can't anticipate every problem your child might bring to you. But that's not necessary. All you need are some general responses that will encourage your child to continue to express his or her feelings.

If Bobby says, "I hate White people" or "I hate being Black," what might you say? First of all, resist the temptation to jump in and lecture him about the brotherhood of man. As an active listener who has been practicing your open responses, you could say, "It sounds like you are really angry at someone White," "It sounds as if being Black is hard on you at times," or "It seems as though things aren't going well."

When you do this for the first time, expect your child to be pretty surprised. But it will be a pleasant surprise, because the way you communicate with him or her will be changing for the better.

I-MESSAGES, YOU-MESSAGES

A child who is involved in a conflict might be wrestling with feelings of anger, frustration, regret, fear, or anxiety. Obviously, no one feels good with these emotions churning inside him. It is normal for anyone who has these feelings to try to assign responsibility for them—to himself or to someone else.

People who see others as responsible for their feelings tend to describe their conflicts in terms of "you-messages." For example, your son Donald comes home from school and says, "Marvin made me *real* mad today. He called me a 'dumb nigger' in front of all my friends." Donald is using a "you-message" to blame Marvin for making him mad.

But Donald might have said, "I got real mad today." When you asked why, he could have said, "Marvin called me a 'dumb nigger' in front of all my friends." In this instance, Donald would have been using an "I-message."

In the first example, by saying *Marvin* made him angry, Donald implied that he had no choice in the matter. As long as Marvin said those words, the only choice Donald felt he had was to get angry. Donald is making Marvin responsible for his anger. Compare this with the second example, where Donald says, "*I* got angry today." In this case he is acknowledging that getting angry is something *he* chose to do. He is accepting responsibility for his own anger.

People tend to react to conflict in automatic ways because they forget, or do not know, that they have choices in the way they respond. Encouraging our children to use I-messages is a way to teach them that they are responsible for the way they feel in different situations, and that by controlling their feelings they can choose the way they react to situations.

Getting children to use I-messages might be a bit difficult at first. It is much easier to blame someone else for what disturbs us. One suggestion is that you encourage them, especially small children, to begin all complaints with "I"—for example, "I feel upset," "I feel angry," or "I was very angry today." With older children a subtler approach might be necessary. Imagine your teenage son Bobby slams the door and says, "Coach really *ticked* me off today, Mom. He kept me on the bench the whole second half." You might ask, "Do you mean to say he got inside you and *made* you mad, Bobby?" "What?!" he might ask, surprised. "You said *Coach* ticked you off, but *you* are the one who decided to get angry at something Coach did. There were other ways you could feel, but you chose to feel angry. It's okay to feel angry, but remember the way you feel in situations like this is always your choice."

NEVER FORCE A CHILD TO EXPRESS HIS OR HER FEELINGS

There is another important point to remember when we communicate with our children, especially when we practice open responses. When our children face crises, we are naturally anxious to see them resolve them. At times we press them for explanations that they are not prepared to give. It is always a mistake to *force* our children to express their feelings. A better approach is to listen to whatever information they can give at the time and *gradually* encourage them to express themselves further.

If you invade your children's privacy by forcing them to talk against their will, it could take a lot of work to undo the damage. A good rule to follow is to look for nonverbal clues and keep asking yourself, "What is my child feeling?"

Nonverbal Clues

Nonverbal clues, you might recall, are those actions that tend to reveal what a person might be feeling in spite of what he or she might be saying. For instance, the Richardsons, a Black family, have just moved to a White suburb. They suspect their son Garrett, a very popular student at his old, predominantly Black high school, is uneasy about attending the all-White high school in their new town. When his parents tried to discuss it with him, he denied any anxiety. "Do you think I'm *afraid* of White people?" he asked defiantly. "No," his mother said, "I just want you to know it's all right for you to be apprehensive under the circumstances. Being the only Black person in a totally new setting can make you feel uncomfortable." "Well, I'm not uncomfortable," Garrett snapped as he left the dinner table, his food still untouched. Although Garrett denied he was uncomfortable, his defensiveness and the fact that he was too disturbed to eat were nonverbal clues that suggested he was uncomfortable.

If you spot contradictory nonverbal clues in your child's behavior, try asking open-ended questions to test your impressions. A good question in Garrett's case might have been "How would you feel if you were going back to your old school tomorrow?" Again, this approach might be a bit uncomfortable at first, but you will be happy to see how quickly it all falls into place with a little practice.

RESPECT AND PATIENCE

In relating to our children we sometimes seem to forget that as people they deserve the same respect we want for ourselves and give to other people. If most of us treated our children the way we treat our friends, our relationships with our children would improve considerably. On the other hand, if we treated our friends the way we treat our children, our friendships would fall apart.

Think of how we behave when we are upset. What do we want at those times? Often we just want to be left alone. Isn't it fair to assume that our children feel the same way sometimes?

Many of us have been taught that feelings of anger, disappointment, or fear are wrong and should not be expressed. As a result, we do not know how to handle these feelings when our children express them. Confused, we tend to react by playing familiar, set roles. Sometimes we feel we have to be the person "in charge." At those times we seem interested only in keeping things under control, demanding that the child get rid of negative feelings immediately. "Get your act together," we might say.

At other times we play the know-it-all. We lecture and advise, showing that we are superior at solving problems. Sometimes we preach: "You should do this. You shouldn't do that." We judge, we question, we analyze, and we criticize. Many times all the child needs is a good listener and simple reassurance. "It's okay to be upset. . . . It will all look better tomorrow."

If we are understanding and sensitive to how our children feel, they will reward us with their trust. Prying information out of them and trying to solve their problems even before we understand the nature of the problems are guaranteed to alienate our children. A better approach is to allow them to experience their feelings and tell us about them when they feel they understand them or need our help.

Imagine that your child comes home and says, "I hate Sally." You might know that Sally is a White child who tends to be controlling or a bully. Don't be tempted to conclude that the problem has to do with Sally's being White. It is better to try to get more of a sense of what your child is feeling and why she is feeling it. Let's see where this situation might lead.

"You hate Sally?" you ask.

"She never picks me," your daughter continues.

"She never picks you for what?"

"Softball. She always picks her friends and she never picks me."

"Who would you pick to play softball?"

"Elaine and Cynthia and Deena . . . and Terry . . . but I never get to pick."

"Never?"

"Only Sally gets to pick. Miss Nelson never lets anybody else pick. I hate Miss Nelson."

At any point in such an exchange you might be tempted to intervene with a solution to what you see as the problem (Sally wouldn't let your daughter play). But by encouraging your child to express herself you find that the problem is not quite what you thought it was. In this case you find that her anger is at her teacher for always letting Sally choose.

Even when you are sure you understand what your child is really feeling, one important step remains. Because it is so simple and obvious, we almost always overlook it. If you had been helping a friend at work with a problem, at this point your next question would have been "What would you like me to do?" or "What can I do to help?" This common courtesy shows respect for the other person's feelings, and it works just as well for children. It is a very simple thing to ask "Is there anything I can do?" or "Would you like me to talk to your teacher about that?" Put yourself in your child's place. The chances are you would feel much better if someone asked, "Can I help?" instead of saying, "Here's what you must do . . ."

CRITICISM AND FEEDBACK

What do you do when you finally understand what is bothering your child? You are still his parent and he is expecting guidance from you. How will you handle the problem? Two possible responses are to give criticism or feedback. There is a big difference between them. Criticism is usually negative and condemning. ("You only got a *B* on that test! It would have been an *A* if you weren't so lazy.") We are usually angry when we criticize, and it comes across that way. After criticizing a child, it is the parent who feels satisfied, not the child. Furthermore, when we criticize someone, we often attack personal weaknesses that he cannot change by himself. As a result, he feels poorly about himself.

Feedback, if given properly, should be constructive and helpful to the recipient. Open responses make use of feedback. For example, you might say to your son, "You got a *B!* Great! Is that as well as you expected to do?" You might be disappointed that he didn't get an *A*, but this response would leave the issue open for more constructive discussion: "No, I could have gotten an *A*, but I just don't have enough time to study since I started my new job." Keep communications flowing by offering feedback when you are tempted to criticize your children. You might say, "I agree, when you weren't working as much your grades were higher and you made the honor roll. What options are you considering? What about cutting back the number of hours you work? How important are your grades to getting accepted in the college you like?"

ADOLESCENTS' FEELINGS

Active listening, open-ended questions, and feedback are all effective techniques you can use to maintain constructive communications with your children. But we don't want you to get the idea that they are perfect and foolproof. They are not. Raising children, as you may know, is a constantly changing process. What works today may or may not work tomorrow. As your children grow, they make different demands of you and you have to learn how to respond to them.

Perhaps no period in your child's life demands more from you than adolescence, the early teenage years during which children go from childhood to young adulthood. Children often experience wrenching emotional conflicts at this time. These conflicts can tear families apart.

For example, sixteen-year-old Norma became pregnant and had an abortion without her mother's consent. When Norma's mother Thelma, a devout Christian, found out by reading the girl's diary, she was devastated. Upon finding out that Thelma had read her diary, Norma wrecked her mother's bedroom. Feeling she could not tolerate such behavior, Thelma evicted her daughter from their home. When Norma and her mother started therapy, the girl was living in a shelter for the homeless.

But it doesn't have to get this bad. There are things you can do to help smooth your child's passage into adulthood. We deal with adolescence in chapter 8. Be aware that if you have adolescents in your home successful communication is going to take extra work, but it can be very rewarding.

Chapter Five

PREPARING THE SOIL: THE RACIAL IMAGES IN YOUR FAMILY

Black Americans reflect a great variety of skin colors, hair textures, facial structures, and overall body types. The way you and others in your family feel about these characteristics will determine how your child will feel about himself or herself. A dark-skinned child born into a home where Blackness is appreciated and celebrated will feel welcome and special. If Blackness is not respected, the child will grow to doubt his or her self-worth.

We obviously have a great deal of influence over our children's self-esteem. But the power is not ours alone. Relatives, friends, and society as a whole contribute to the way we see ourselves as Black people. Of course, we in turn pass those images on to our children. In this chapter we look at some of the racial images that have been passed down in our families. Our goal is to eliminate the negative images and strengthen the ones that build up our children's self-esteem, giving them the confidence to assert their rights as human beings who happen to be Black.

TWO-HUNDRED-YEAR-OLD IMAGES

Many of us had no formal training to be parents when we started. We knew even less about what it takes to be successful Black parents. We have had to raise our children in a dual culture with nothing to rely on but our own experiences as Black children plus whatever we learned from parents, grandparents, and other relatives. Many of the techniques that we draw from are more than 200 years old and have come to us through successive generations. Therefore, the way we feel about ourselves and the way we react to racism may reflect assumptions that are centuries old. The attitude of the grandfather in chapter 3 who told his grandson to suffer thirst rather than challenge a White man is typical of those assumptions.

Another example shows that at one time this kind of passive reaction was the only way to stay alive in a racist society. A grandmother of one of the authors was particularly attractive as a young woman. As she walked down the street with her husband in the southern town where they lived, White men would tease her and insult her husband for not reacting. She begged him not to respond because doing so could easily have cost him his life. As a solution, she began to dress in a way that made her appear less attractive so as to avoid the attention of White men. This was an acceptable reaction at that time but would be entirely inappropriate today. Imagine how a little girl might feel about dressing attractively today if such a grandmother had taught her to react in that way.

If we look back, we can all probably find experiences such as these in our families. It took a great deal of inner strength to emerge from them alive, let alone with feelings of self-worth to pass on to later generations. Not everyone made it. Some of our people did indeed come to resent, or at least regret, their Blackness. If you had an ancestor who had negative feelings about being Black, he or she might have passed them on to your mother, for instance, and she to you.

Negative feelings about Blackness can show up in many ways. It is common, for example, to find Black people who grow up believing they are inferior to Whites. They unquestioningly submit to White authority and show a fear of Whites even in the absence of any threats. Many also buy into White standards of appearance. They come to believe that Black features such as curly hair, a flat nose, and Black skin are inherently ugly.

Good Hair, Bad Hair

A clear illustration of the way Blacks sometimes feel about their racial characteristics is that many Blacks use the terms "good" and "bad" to describe their hair. "Good hair" refers to long, straight hair, typical of Caucasians. "Bad hair" refers to curly Negroid hair. Director Spike Lee underscores this continuing perception in his film *School Daze.* Negative views of Blackness are usually learned and internalized in childhood, and passed from generation to generation along with the positive images.

Several young boys, ranging in complexion from light-skinned to very dark, visited with their maternal grandmother. The boys were a mixture of cousins and brothers. One particularly light-skinned boy, Jeffery, received a great deal of attention from an aunt who visited frequently. She always complimented him on his soft, wavy hair and "beautiful" skin. His cousin Phil, one of the darker boys, felt he had to find some way to attract his aunt's affection. He chose to work hard and do well in school. Jeffery came to believe he was entitled to whatever he wanted and did not have to work for anything. At the age of fifteen he developed serious behavior problems when it became clear that the whole world was not about to treat him as well as his aunt did. Phil continued to excel in school, earning the respect of his teachers and family members. In time he grew to realize that it was his aunt and not he who had a problem.

Light Skin, Dark Skin

For many Blacks skin color, like hair texture, is seen as a symbol of value—lightness being preferable to darkness. Again, Spike Lee explores this issue in *School Daze* by portraying the relationships between so-called "Jigaboos" (dark-skinned Blacks) and "Wannabees" (light-skinned Blacks who want to be White). But there are plenty of real-life examples.

A middle-aged Black man recalled that his minister used to preach that when Christ returns to take Christians with him to heaven, the dead will rise up and the living will be taken up and they will all be given new *White* bodies before they are taken into heaven.

Another minister addressed his congregation on the need for them to pay attention to their appearance before they go out in public. "Put on some clean clothes," he said, "and fix up your hair." Then he added, "You can even do something about that Black skin of yours. You can go down to the drugstore and get yourself some skin bleach and lighten it up a little." This was in 1988!

A fair-skinned middle-aged woman from the West Indies swears that her skin has become lighter since she has been living in the States. She can recall, she says, that it began to get lighter in the plane on the way to America! After being exposed to the tropical sun all her life, it is possible that her skin would appear lighter after some time in the North American climate. However, the real issues lie deeper than the probable causes for any change in her complexion.

What is more interesting is that she seemed to feel that the change she perceived in her appearance was a real improvement. She spoke of it frequently and with great pride. It was as if the apparent lightening of her skin was a positive addition to all the other advantages she associated with moving to America. In her mind, to be seen as light-skinned was clearly preferable to being seen as dark-skinned.

Miriam, a dark-skinned seventeen-year-old woman, came to us after a period of mental illness. In therapy she said she heard voices telling her to reject her father, who had very dark skin and Negroid features. She described her mother as being "clear-skinned," and said she wanted to be like her mother. She was very intelligent and had started college at age sixteen. She was approached by a White student for a date. He later told her he couldn't date her because his parents would not approve. This rejection started the negative thoughts that led to her breakdown.

Miriam's parents had never discussed racial issues with her. They had always lived in White neighborhoods, and she was raised to believe that she was "just like everybody else." When she discovered that other people did not see her that way she lost all sense of herself as a worthwhile person. It was as if her world had been cut out from under her.

Another young lady said that her mother had always felt that if one of her (the mother's) children were to have been darker than the other, she would have preferred that her son be dark and her daughter be light. This mother was expressing an understanding of a situation that has been true throughout the history of Black people in America: American society has always held the White woman as the highest standard of beauty, goodness, and desirability. Her "pure" white skin, blond hair, blue eyes, and overall "fine features" contrast sharply with the black skin, "kinky" hair, dark eyes, thick lips, and broad nose of the Black woman. If the White woman is seen as the pinnacle of goodness and desirability, the Black woman is necessarily seen as her opposite—bad and undesirable.

WHITE PREFERENCE

With all the obvious advantages that accompany being White in this society, it is easy to see why many Blacks have expressed a preference for Whiteness, or at least light skin, even among their own. That preference has often extended to choice of mates as well. Historically, a light-skinned woman was far more able than a dark-skinned woman to attract a desirable man. So a mother who shows a preference for a light-skinned daughter is acknowledging the fact that even within Black culture there have been advantages to having light skin. Because in our society the man is usually expected to choose the mate, light skin would considerably improve a woman's chance of being chosen.

The people described above have all somehow come to believe that Black skin is undesirable. If they are in positions of authority—for example, ministers or elderly relatives—it would be difficult for them to avoid passing their feelings about Blackness on to other people.

We want to make it clear that we are in no way suggesting that churches and ministers in general are responsible for perpetuating undesirable images of Blacks. To the contrary, the church has been one of the greatest sources of strength and support for Black people in this country. We simply want to show that authority figures, such as ministers, teachers, and other civic leaders, have an obligation to be aware of the messages they send to the people who look up to them. Children are especially vulnerable to such messages.

If a Black child has never been told explicitly that he is good, worthwhile, and attractive as he is, there are plenty of confirming negative messages to make him feel that he would need a "clean" white body in order to face his God.

There is an old riddle that children still tell among themselves. It goes, "What's clean when it's black and white when it's dirty?" The answer: A blackboard. On the surface the riddle seems innocent, but it masks an awful truth: The reason the riddle works is that in this society black is synonymous with dirt, and white with cleanliness. Only by knowing this "fact of life" can one appreciate the riddle. The contradiction is clear: Isn't it amazing that something that is black can actually be clean!? Obviously there are already powerful forces at work convincing our children that by being Black they are less human than Whites.

Could what happened to Miriam happen to your daughter? Yes, it could. Much depends on you, and whether you are willing to be open and honest. A child who learns about racism early in life *and* learns the truth about herself as a worthwhile human being will be better prepared to cope with such difficulties. We cannot entirely eliminate these kinds of disappointments from our children's lives. However, by building up our children's belief in their own self-worth, we can insure that they are not destroyed by such setbacks. It is critical that we begin teaching our children at a very early age that Black people have a variety of beautiful skin tones, from ebony to ivory. Our children must not be allowed to continue the ignorance that perpetuates the false belief that lighter skin is somehow more beautiful than darker.

Since the elements that will make up the individuals our children will become are entwined with the images that already exist in our families, let's take a look at the Black family as an institution.

THE FAMILY TREE

The Black family in America has traditionally had a different structure from that of the White family. In White society the *nuclear family* has always been accepted as normal. It consists of a mother, a father, and a child or children. In contrast, most Black Americans belong to what is known as an *extended family*. In such a family not only parents but grandparents, older siblings, aunts, or uncles might become directly involved in raising a particular child. In many instances a child's guardian might not even be a blood relative, but a very close family friend.

When we work with families in therapy, we usually see the parent(s) and the child or children. After one or two sessions it sometimes becomes clear that *executive power* in the family lies outside the nuclear unit. In other words, a grandparent or other relative, rather than a parent, turns out to be a more influential person in the children's lives. That person might have complete say as to how the children are reared, including how they are disciplined.

A child might also adopt a relative as a role model and be highly influenced by that person. For example, Laura thought her aunt Dot was the nicest person in the world. She was a teacher who always dressed stylishly, and her perfect dark skin barely needed makeup. Dot sometimes took Laura to class with her. The little girl would look admiringly at her beautiful aunt and dream of growing up to be just like her.

Tragically, Dot developed breast cancer and died at age thirty-three. She had already taught Laura a great deal about Black pride and self-confidence, but before she died she had one more powerful lesson for the girl. Six months after she had undergone a mastectomy, Dot had demonstrated her courage by modeling a bathing suit in a fashion show!

Dot had taken the time to teach her niece the lessons that she herself had learned about what it takes to live a full and rewarding life as a Black person. Laura still feels her influence to this day. In fact Laura, who has light skin, has always wanted to be darker because of her aunt Dot's beauty.

Laura's case shows how powerful the extended family can be in shaping an individual's development. This kind of variation from the usual family patterns has to be anticipated when one sets out to study the Black family.

Because our families did not always follow the nuclear pattern, American society has long thought of Black family life as abnormal. Until perhaps the beginning of the 1980s, terms such as "children out of wedlock," "illegitimate children," and "female-headed family" were used almost exclusively in reference to Black families. And in most cases the user was describing a family in crisis. All that has changed. Today many Whites have chosen or have been forced to go the single-parent route and some have found that it can be done quite successfully. Unfortunately, most of them do not have the benefit of the extended family that has been partly responsible for the survival of Black people in this country.

In the February 1990 issue of *Ebony* magazine, an author was cited as saying, "It is from the father, or another male figure in the household, that a male child develops a strong sense of self-esteem." This frequently is clearly demonstrated in many of our families in therapy. This is not meant to minimize the role that numerous single Black women play when raising their sons. However, we can not ignore the fact that in many cases our Black male children are doing poorly because of a lack of access to positive Black male role models. There are many loving, dedicated, strong, and sensitive Black men and Black women need to support their efforts to be good fathers.

Family-life observers of the past failed to acknowledge an important fact: The extended family was a necessary source of emotional and material support for Black people in a society that was, at best, indifferent to our concerns. Today Whites who are facing some of the economic difficulties that have been long familiar to Blacks are discovering family alternatives, such as grandparents caring for children, traditionally used by Blacks. Ultimately, the terms that were once used to put down "broken" Black families have lost their stigma and other, more neutral expressions (i.e. "single parenting") have been adopted to depict any single parent situation, be it Black or White.

But whether or not White society accepts the extended family structure, we must continue to see it as the positive resource it is.

THE STRENGTHS OF THE BLACK FAMILY

Researcher Robert Hill in his book *The Strengths of Black Families* has identified what he considers five major strengths of the Black family:

1. Strong kinship bonds
2. Adaptability of family roles
3. Strong work orientation
4. Strong educational achievement orientation
5. Strong religious orientation

Let's look at them in turn.

Strong kinship bonds. This means that the extended family network we talked about is more than just a group of people that are merely *recognized* as family. Any relative—aunt, uncle, grandmother, or friend of a grandfather for that matter—might be called on to provide child care, for example. And that person would see it as a legitimate responsibility. A child might thus be raised entirely by someone other than the biological parents, and want for none of the love and affection necessary to succeed in life.

A *New York Times* article not long ago identified an interesting trend: In many cities ravaged by drugs, particularly among the Black population, addicts with children often turn to their parents for support. As a result, grandparents who thought they had seen the last of parenthood are being called on to care for their grandchildren.

On the one hand, this is a grim picture for those grandparents who thought they had earned their rest after years of struggle, only to face a second parenthood. On the other hand, it is an illustration of the support structure in the Black family. This concept of *informal adoption* continues to be one of the key mechanisms in Black Americans' survival in a hostile society.

Adaptability of family roles. For a long time, one of the main features of the nuclear family has been its division of roles: Simply put, Father went to work to earn money; Mother stayed home, cooked, cleaned, and nurtured; children went to school.

The Black family has had to be far more creative and flexible. Both parents have traditionally worked out of the home. Children often took on adult responsibilities: cooking, cleaning, child care, sometimes wage earning. Common male/female roles sometimes blurred as boys and girls shared household tasks. For example, one of the authors recalls that all of his uncles were expected to learn to cook, clean house, baby-sit, and when necessary, repair their own clothing.

This blurring of roles and the wage-earning activities of many Black women have contributed to the stereotype of the Black family as a *matriarchal* (female-headed) system. However, regardless of the father's income, he is likely to demand and receive recognition as the head of the household. His influence in his family is no less than that of a White father.

Strong work orientation. Young Black children quickly learn the importance that Black culture places on working. Steven's experience is typical. His family encouraged him as a young boy to obtain a shoe-shine kit and begin working in Manhattan's shopping district. Later he took his first supervised job shining shoes in a barbershop. The shop's owner was a close friend of Steven's family and also the boy's Sunday school teacher. By age ten, Steven had learned to succeed at a job that depended on his own initiative. He was expected to work not only because of economic need but also to learn the value of money—how to earn and save to buy something he wanted.

Strong educational achievement orientation. Black Americans have traditionally believed in the value of a good education. They have stressed this to their children and have made tremendous sacrifices to educate them. Perhaps every Black person who became successful through the 1960s could point to someone who scrubbed floors or performed back-breaking or even life-threatening work for years to enable them to achieve what they had.

A junior high school teacher told Steven that he was not

college material. Though furious at the remark, Steven's mother confronted the teacher in a calm but assertive manner: "I have gone through this school system," she told her. "I was told the same thing. I never had the opportunity to go to college. If my kid isn't college material—and I think he is—let him find out. If he fails, let him fail trying. I'm gonna see that my son has the chance I never had." Today Steven is a licensed clinical psychologist.

Like any other parents, Black parents are sometimes intimidated by imposing educational bureaucracies. Their strong achievement orientation, however, usually motivates them to seek educational opportunities for their children.

When, as sometimes happens, a child has to leave school to help support the family financially, it doesn't mean that education is not valued. It simply means that the demands of the kinship bonds take priority.

Strong religious orientation. The church has long been the focal point of Black family life. It meets our need for the communal experience of worship; it provides social, economic, and educational support; and the pulpit has been the cradle of our highest political expression. It is no surprise then that some of our most powerful leaders—Martin Luther King, Jr., Jesse Jackson, Andrew Young—have their roots in the church.

Steven distinctly recalls the church's role in his life. He had his first leadership experience when his minister appointed him to open Sunday worship service each week. He learned about great Black leaders in Sunday school. And the same Sunday school teacher who hired Steven to work in his barbershop shared a collection of Black history books with him.

Tapping the Family's Strengths

It is good for us just to know that we possess family strengths. This knowledge can boost our self-confidence and our self-esteem because it belies the negative stereotypes that continue to plague us. But for us to fully benefit from those strengths, we have to make sure we are connected to their sources. We have to acknowledge our extended families and be prepared to offer assistance as well as to request it when we need it.

The experience of Glen described below demonstrates two things: alternative family configurations, such as a single father and a daughter, can be responsive and supportive in nurturing a child; and extended families are resourceful.

Glen, recently separated from his wife, has custody of his nine-year-old daughter, Lorna. Lorna is a charming girl who, up to the time of the separation, had been very happy and successful in school. After the separation she became quiet and withdrawn. With some coaxing Glen discovered that other children were teasing her about her hair. She was embarrassed and thought her hair was ugly.

Glen's busy schedule had caused him to overlook Lorna's hair care. When he became aware of the problem, he asked his "aunt," who was really a friend of the family, to teach him how to make cornrow braids. Night after night he practiced on Lorna's dolls. He learned to make different styles of braids and was soon able to set Lorna's hair in a variety of styles for school. Lorna's self-confidence quickly returned with her new hairstyles. Fixing hair became an opportunity for a single father to show his daughter how much he cared for her.

Earl, a student in junior high school, caused a stir when he refused to give up his seat to a White girl. This occurred in New Jersey in the mid-1960s! There may or may not have been racial undertones, but as Earl saw it, "I was on the spot to give up my chair to a White girl." He refused. The principal called Earl's grandmother to report Earl's behavior. His grandmother was furious.

"If you don't have enough chairs in school for all the students," she told the principal, "let me know and I'll send Earl to school with a chair of his own." That was the end of the discussion.

His grandmother's reaction confirmed to Earl that he was right to assert himself when he felt he was being treated unfairly. The extended family had contributed to the child's development.

Pam not only draws sustenance from her religious roots but happily shares it with her friends. Every year she celebrates Kwanzaa, an African cultural-religious festival. She particularly cherishes the sharing, cooperation, and family togetherness that the festival encourages. She often brings her friend

Delores with her. Impressed with the experience, Delores now incorporates many Kwanzaa elements into her Christmas celebration. This in turn has enriched her family's Christmas observance.

As Black parents we have to tell our children that the strengths in the Black family are more than mere subjects for academic discussion. They are real, and they are responsible for the survival and growth of Black people in this country for centuries. We must tell them and make them understand that these sources of support are there for them if they are willing to remain connected to them. That means, among other things, being devoted to the family; valuing education and hard work; and remaining connected to the church, the center of spiritual, social, and political activity in the Black community. These are the roots that define who they are and help them form positive images of themselves.

When social scientists today speak about family-life crisis and the breakup of the American family, we have to take their pronouncements with a grain of salt. Forced breakup of families is nothing new to Black people. It has been our lot through slavery and subsequent economic realities. That has been our history in this country. And we have survived it only by drawing on the strengths within our families and our culture.

We are not denying that, as Americans, Black people are facing some daunting challenges. The drug epidemic is a case in point. We are not immune to the maladies that afflict the society as a whole. But as we search for solutions it is helpful to know that one of the strongest resources we have at our disposal is the strength within our own families.

DIVERSITY WITHIN THE FAMILY

If Blacks trace back through their families, most would find a rich heritage that might include not only African but Native American, Asian, or European ancestry. Today that diversity shows up in the variety of skin color, hair texture, facial features, and overall body types in our families. Brothers and sisters in the same family might have such different features that they appear unrelated. How we as parents feel about these differences has a great impact on how our children feel about themselves. The building blocks of who we will become are laid down in our families. That is where self-esteem is born and nurtured, making a person strong enough to face society's challenges.

If our children are to have a high self-esteem, they must first learn to accept themselves. That happens when we show them that we accept them. And we do that by appreciating them regardless of their shade of Blackness, tightness of curls, or thickness of lips. Children who accept themselves can easily accept others. They are much better equipped to function effectively in a sometimes hostile world.

As parents, grandparents, or anyone contributing to the rearing of Black children, we must become sensitive to the variety within Black families. Grandma might prefer straight hair because it is easier to handle when she has to get three girls ready for school. But she has an obligation not to let the child with straight hair come to feel that she has "better" hair than her sisters'. Each family member must feel that he or she is accepted by the family regardless of how different he or she might appear. That is the basic knowledge that will give children the confidence to face adversity.

A grandmother we know demonstrated the kind of Black appreciation we think is desirable. She took her granddaughter to be fitted for braces. The orthodontist told the grandmother that he could fit the braces in such a manner as to downplay the size of the girl's lips. Right there in front of the girl, the grandmother told him that his suggestion was racist. She turned to the girl and told her, "There is nothing wrong with your lips. They are fine just the way they are. I'm not going to let him or *anyone* change them in any way."

The grandmother's action sent a strong positive message to the little girl about her appearance. We all need to appreciate the images in our own families and accept them as worthwhile regardless of how White society sees them.

THE GENOGRAM

Now that you've become more aware of your feelings about race it might be helpful for you to look back in your family to see where some of those feelings came from. One way to do this is to use a *genogram.* Authors Monica McGoldrich and Randy Gerson in their book *Genograms in Family Assessment* have presented this tool as a useful device in exploring the richness and value of family history. A genogram is nothing more than a family tree diagram that can be used to trace a specific characteristic like assertiveness through a family. We encourage you to take the time to design one of your own family. It's not only an excellent vehicle for self-exploration but also a way to involve your children in discovering various characteristics of their family history. And the positive results you find will directly contribute to their self-esteem.

You can use a genogram to uncover the source of some of the images and ideas that have been shaping your family for generations. You might find surprising strengths. For example, you might stumble on an uncle who won respect in the old South by asserting his rights as a human being. Many of us who succeed do so because of such determined relatives who taught us, directly or indirectly, to trust our own worth when the society around us denied it.

On the other hand, you might find that people you loved dearly might have left you with negative feelings about being Black. Was it Uncle John who said you should always look down when you speak to a White man? Did Great-Grandma really say, "I don't ever want you to take me to a Black doctor?"

We should not be upset when we identify relatives who might have been sources of negative influence. We are not looking back to accuse or condemn anyone. Indeed, we should look back with compassion, because our ancestors had it even tougher than we do. The best thing for us to do is to try to break the negative cycle in our lifetime.

As you can tell, a genogram can be a very sensitive tool. You are using it to explore deeply personal characteristics of people, some of whom will still be alive, who are important to you. You will want to be considerate in your evaluation, in how you discuss your findings with others, and in deciding who sees it. Again, your goal is not to humiliate, expose, or degrade anyone who might not have contributed positively toward establishing your racial identity. You simply want to become aware of the impact they might have had on you.

In constructing a genogram, symbols are used to illustrate members in the family as well as relationships (see figure 1 on page 97). A square represents a male relative and a circle depicts a female. A sample of a genogram is shown in figure 2 on page 97. Let's see how it works. Three generations are represented: grandparents on top, parents in the middle, and children on the bottom. The bottom level represents the person we are interested in when tracing a characteristic and its impact. We want to see what influence the other levels have had on that person. Of course, there may be influential members of the extended family who are not blood relatives. These people can be represented by placing their symbols off to the side and noting who they are.

Once you have your diagram set up, the next step is to be clear on which characteristic you are tracing. Is it business sense? Religious orientation? Assertiveness? When you're clear about what you want to trace, it's time to rate the individuals in the diagram. Let's say you are tracing Black cultural awareness. Select six questions like the following that you will ask yourself about each person.

1. Did this person teach me about Black history?
2. Did this person display Black cultural artifacts around the home?
3. Did this person act as a Black role model?
4. Did this person appreciate or wear African clothing, such as a dashiki?
5. Did this person patronize Black cultural events?
6. Did this person take pride in Black cultural expression (speech, hairstyles, etc.)?

The person gets one point for each yes answer, for a maximum of six points. When you're through assigning points for each person it's time to review the results. The people with sixes have *potentially* contributed most to the positive racial identity of the person(s) on the bottom level.

We refer to this process as a Positive Racial Identity Development Exercise (PRIDE).

* * *

Figure 1. Genogram Symbols

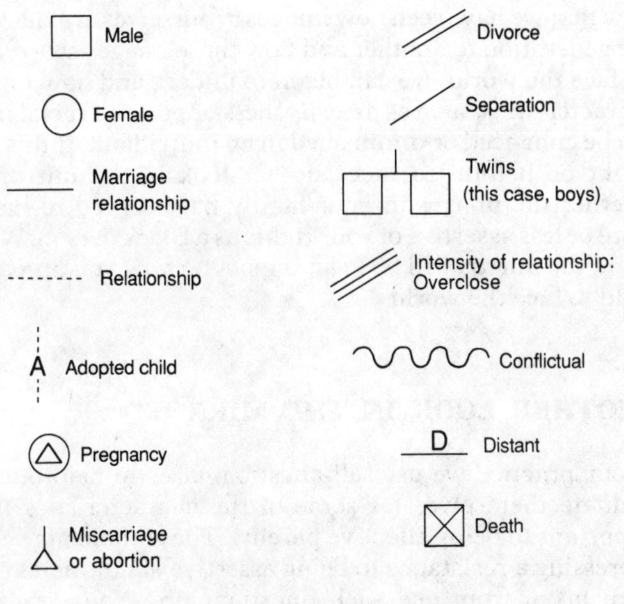

Figure 2. Sample of Genogram Structure with Symbols

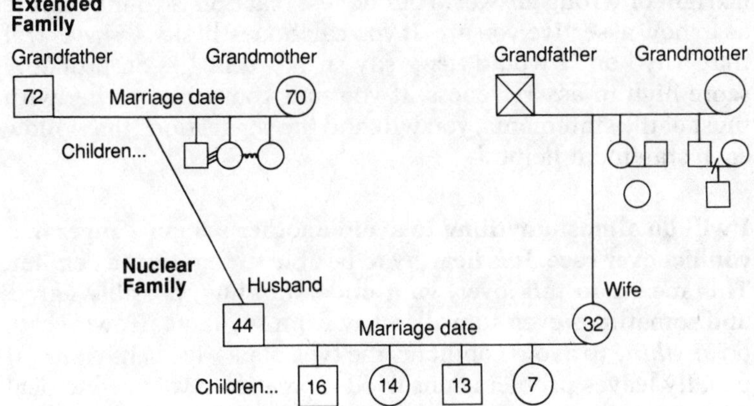

Now that we have seen how images of ourselves are shared from one generation to another and how those images shape the way we face the world, we can begin to understand how important characteristics, such as assertiveness or positive racial identity, can be enhanced or diminished in an individual. At this point it might be helpful to take another look in the mirror to see whether the images in your family have served to make you more or less assertive of your rights as a Black person. What you see in the mirror will have an impact on how you prepare your child to face the world.

ANOTHER LOOK IN THE MIRROR

In our practice we use self-questionnaires to help our clients evaluate themselves for some of the characteristics that are important to being effective parents. The statements below, all expressing a resistance to being assertive about racial matters, were taken from one such questionnaire. Your reactions to them can help you measure your assertiveness in dealing with racial conflict in your own life.

Read each statement and give some thought to whether or not you agree with it. The remarks that follow each statement will give you some insight into your assertiveness level. There is no right or wrong answer. Your honest reaction is your best clue as to how assertive you are. If you can honestly say, "I *never* feel that way" or "I would *never* say such a thing," you probably score high in assertiveness. If you find yourself agreeing with most of the statements, you will find the suggestions that follow each statement helpful.

I will do almost anything to avoid another person's anger in a conflict over race. It is healthy to be able to negotiate a conflict. This means to talk over, gain understanding, possibly agree, and sometimes even to walk away from the issue. However, to do *anything* to avoid conflict is the type of passive behavior that usually leaves problems unsolved. Sometimes we need to deal with people's anger by confronting it, and hopefully resolving the conflict. When we say confronting, we are not suggesting violent confrontation. We simply mean dealing with the situation then and there.

One of the authors took his nephew to a fast-food restaurant. He sent the boy to purchase the meal. After a while he noticed that the boy was no closer to the counter because adults kept stepping ahead of him in line. The uncle told the boy to go to the head of the line and tell the cashier that he was there before both of the people who were served ahead of him. Nervous, the boy did as he was told. Initially the cashier, who had been unaware of what had happened, had chosen to be passive and not correct the situation. After a direct and clear explanation was made by the boy, with the uncle's help, the cashier apologized and offered the boy a free soda. It was a simple instance of assertive action for both uncle and nephew, but the smile of satisfaction on the boy's face showed it was worth it.

The boy's bewilderment and frustration at the rude behavior of the adults in this situation and the lack of support by the cashier were what initially kept him from taking his rightful place in line. Through his uncle's encouragement and guidance he was able to get the acknowledgment and consideration he deserved from the beginning.

I prefer that others not be straightforward with me concerning race. Some Whites and some Blacks are so uncomfortable with each other that they cannot even bring themselves to use the words *black* and *white* in each other's presence. If a conflict develops, they would rather pretend that race is not an issue than deal with it openly.

While on a field trip with his class, a Black youngster, Marcus, had a disagreement with a White child from another school. In the course of the argument the White child called Marcus a nigger. Marcus's teacher, who was White, managed to calm the children. When they returned to school at the end of the day, she met Marcus's mother and reported on the trip.

"We had a great trip today," she said. "We had a minor problem with Marcus and a boy from another school, but everything is fine now." After a few questions the mother was able to determine that the White child had called her son "a name." Neither of the adults wanted to say what the name was, however. Meanwhile, Marcus stood there still angry but now also puzzled as to why the adults were talking in riddles about something that seemed perfectly clear to him.

Both adults were too uneasy about the subject to be straightforward with each other. They just wanted the conversation to be over. If the adults, particularly his mother, had been able to address the issue squarely, Marcus would have felt better knowing that someone possibly understood how he was feeling.

When I am assertive about my race, others are shocked, hurt, or angry, and I feel responsible. If this statement expresses your own feelings, you are taking on an enormous responsibility in your relationships with other people. You are actually blaming yourself for the way they feel when you stand up for yourself.

A young man told us this story. He was the only Black person in a meeting with his boss and some of his colleagues. The subject of religion came up. His boss turned to him and asked, "How come Black people are so religious?" The other people chuckled and turned to him to see how he would react. He felt that the question was totally inappropriate but he could not think of a way to make the point with his boss without creating a scene. Thinking it would be best to keep his response on a light note, he replied, "Perhaps because many White people are not." Everyone laughed except his boss.

After the meeting she told him she was hurt and embarrassed by his reaction. It did not occur to her that he might have been embarrassed by her question. He ended up wondering whether he had reacted too strongly. Instead of feeling good about asserting himself, he began to worry about whether he had "hurt" *her.* Sometimes people will react that way when you assert yourself in a racial context, but it is your right and obligation to stand up for yourself.

Most people are more fragile than I am, so I avoid being assertive about my race. We sometimes believe that other people will not be able to handle a discussion of race openly and directly.

Maryanne is a White woman in her twenties. Having grown up in the Midwest, she has had only television knowledge of Black people most of her life. Now she spends time with her friend Janice, a Black woman she has met since moving East. She still has difficulty relating to other Blacks, however. She is afraid to even say the word *black* in front of them. Out of concern for her sensitivity, her friend Janice finds herself avoiding the use of the word *black* in Maryanne's presence.

Janice would be more helpful to her friend if she told her openly that she need not be embarrassed to use the word *black* in front of Blacks. Instead, she took it upon herself to protect Maryanne.

If I assert myself on racial issues, others will get angry at me. This condition is similar to the one above. When people are afraid to speak up in racial conflicts they are usually concerned with one or both of the following: hurting the other person or making the person angry.

A group of college students, Blacks and Whites, were riding in a car, listening to the radio. One of the songs mentioned looking back in time to when people lived in caves. One of the Black men was deeply offended. "That doesn't apply to Black people," he said. "We never lived in caves." One of his White friends reacted with irritation. "You're too sensitive," he said. "How can you take nonsense like that seriously?" That led to an all-out discussion as to whether Black people should be promoting such ideas in their music, whether seriously or not. The discussion eventually deteriorated into ridicule.

The important point here is that the first young man strongly defended his belief about the subject even though his friend reacted angrily. Being able to do this is good for your self-esteem. It will be uncomfortable when you first try it, but it is worth practicing even with small issues.

I find that I cannot or do not handle other people's anger well when race is involved. Sometimes people overreact in conflicts when the opposing parties are of different races. Blacks in conflict with Whites often assume that race is the cause, but frequently it is not the main difficulty. However, the fact that the people are of different races does create another level of difficulty in the conflict.

Mark is a Black ten-year-old who lives in a largely White suburban town. He is the only Black member of his little league baseball team. When a new coach took over, Mark's parents noticed that their son began to spend more time on the bench and less on the field. They discussed it at home and concluded that the coach was discriminating against Mark because of his race. They planned to bring it up with the coach at the next game.

When they arrived at the playing field before the game, a small group of parents were meeting in the parking area. They invited Mark's parents to join them. They were discussing the new coach's style. The other parents also were concerned that their sons were spending too much time on the bench. They felt the coach was too competitive and was only playing the very best players. They agreed to talk to him about the direction of the team.

Mark's parents were relieved to find out that race wasn't the issue after all. In their anxiety over the situation they failed to notice that the coach was treating some of Mark's White teammates the same way he treated Mark. In the end they came to realize that it is normal for a Black person to have nonracial conflicts with someone who is not Black.

This can be a very difficult issue because it is not always easy or possible to know whether or not race is a cause in a conflict. Even if Mark had been the only player on the bench this would not have been proof that the coach's actions were racially motivated. On the other hand, the fact that there were White players on the bench did not prove that the coach had not taken race into consideration when he decided to "bench" Mark.

The best we can do as Black parents is to pay attention to the whole situation, keep an open mind, and remember that conflicts between Blacks and Whites are not always as simple as black and white. Sometimes other factors are involved, which, ironically, can make the conflict easier to resolve.

To avoid asserting my race, I try to please all of the people all or most of the time. Some Blacks, particularly those who live in integrated settings, often find themselves trying to bridge the gap between Blacks and Whites. They try to please Blacks who may not want to integrate as well as the Whites with whom they themselves choose to integrate.

Michael, a Black attorney, lives in the predominantly White suburbs of a large eastern city. His neighbors and professional colleagues are White and college-educated. His childhood friends all live in the city, an hour away. At home in the suburbs he speaks and dresses like the people around him and gets along well with all his neighbors.

When Michael drives into the city to visit his old friends everything about him changes, from the way he speaks to the shoes he wears. His neighbors would barely recognize him. Likewise, his friends in the city have never seen his suburban side. You can imagine how difficult it would be for Michael to entertain friends from his old neighborhood and his new neighbors at the same time. In effect Michael is living a double life.

People choose to integrate for their own reasons. Some simply want to improve their children's educational opportunities. They do not necessarily have any political motives behind their choice. Other people see integration as a way to promote their dream that all people can live together peacefully. And some might simply want the quiet associated with suburban living.

Whatever your choices in such situations, it is important to make sure that they are consistent with your beliefs. You will not be able to please everyone, but at least you will be at peace with yourself.

I do not ask questions in front of White people because I may look stupid or ignorant. It is surprising how many achieving, educated, middle-class Black people feel uncomfortable asking questions in front of Whites.

Jasmine, one of our clients, is a corporate employee. She told us her coworkers react differently to her questions and suggestions than to those of her White counterparts. Sometimes, she said, moments after her suggestions have been largely ignored, a White person will make the same suggestions and they will be much better received. And when she asks a question, she said, her colleagues react as though they think she is naive or stupid. Jasmine has found it difficult to negotiate in these circumstances.

These experiences are common in corporate settings. No one will argue that corporations have resisted hiring women, Blacks, and other minorities over the years. If it were otherwise, there would be no need for all the legislation passed to help these people to get a foothold in business. By now, however, most companies have adopted the principles of equal opportunity in employment and promotions. Where the difficulty comes up is in the enforcement of those policies. The people who are expected to make the hiring and promotion decisions are often the same people who have resisted minority hiring for years. As a result, they find ways to get around the laws and the company policies that force them to hire women and Blacks. Among the ways they do this is to belittle the contribution of those people, trying to make them look stupid and even to make them fail if possible.

If you find yourself in such a situation, seek out people you can trust, Black or White, explain the problem to them, and ask for their help in dealing with it. Often the solution will depend on the nature of the situation or organization involved. Sometimes the corporations will have built-in mechanisms, such as classes or counseling, that can help.

Being devalued by others has a way of eating away at your self-confidence, and any solution you come up with must eventually involve asserting yourself to the people who are doing this to you. For example, if someone repeats your suggestion, say, "That's exactly what *I* said," or "Isn't that what *I* said?" As with everything else, only repeated practice will make you comfortable doing it, so start now and keep at it.

If I am assertive about my race, people will see me as a cold, calculating, castrating person. It's true that many Whites will feel much more comfortable with you as long as you do not bring up the issue of race or racial differences. In many instances, Whites who accept Black people do so with the conviction that Blacks are no different from themselves. Therefore, they are comfortable as long as their Black friends and associates appear and behave as they do. In fact, they might perceive their Black friends as being different from other Blacks.

The relationship sometimes becomes very difficult for such people when their Black neighbors begin to promote and display symbols of Black culture around their home. Consider the following situation. The Morrisons, a Black family, live in an integrated neighborhood in a large city. On St. Patrick's Day they dress in green, eat corned beef and cabbage, put on a fake Irish brogue, and have as much fun as everyone else at the annual block party.

Jonas, the Morrisons' eldest son, attends a nearby community college. He has been studying African culture. One year he decided to attend Kwanzaa, an African harvest celebration, sponsored by a Black students group. For the occasion, he chose to dress in a dashiki, or African gown, and walk to school, which was near his home.

Jonas had barely turned the corner when his White neighbor knocked on his parents' door. "What's the matter with Jonas?" the neighbor asked. "I just saw him go down the street dressed up like a witch doctor. Is he going 'African' on us, or what?"

The Morrisons were dumbstruck. They were angry and embarrassed, but most of all they were frustrated. They didn't know how to respond to their neighbor without upsetting him.

By remaining silent, the Morrisons failed to assert their cultural validity and to point out that their culture had occasions worthy of celebration. They could have explained that their son was celebrating his African heritage and that the occasion might have been as important to him as St. Patrick's Day might be to an Irish person.

When I go to a party where there are White people, I have a really good time after I get (a) drunk, (b) high, (c) introduced to people, (d) two or more helpings of food. Most people need certain social crutches to feel comfortable, and it can be revealing to identify your own and to determine when you use them. If you require these crutches only when you are among Whites, it might indicate that you are not entirely comfortable with your image as a Black person. It might be helpful to ask yourself exactly what it is that makes you uncomfortable in those situations.

To help sort out the problem, try going through such an event without the usual food or drinks. You can then pay attention to the things that cause you particular discomfort.

Perhaps, if you want to make it easier on yourself, you might practice in a smaller setting. A dinner party for four people might be less stressful to you. If you must attend a larger gathering—for example, an office party—you might want to go with someone with whom you feel more comfortable.

Years ago, one of the authors was invited to a bar mitzvah, a Jewish ceremony. She grew anxious as the date approached because she knew she was going to be the only Black person there and would probably receive more than her share of attention. On top of that, she had no idea what to bring or what would be expected of her. At the last minute she decided to ask another Jewish friend, who had more experience with such engagements, for help. The friend suggested a gift and then explained what to expect during the ceremony. As a result, the author was better able to discuss the ceremony comfortably with other guests and to actually enjoy the event.

Our ability to assert ourselves depends on the image we have of ourselves, and those images come to us *mainly from our families.* You can respond assertively in the above situations only if you see yourself as a worthwhile human being.

If you can honestly say you have been modeling assertive behavior for your children, you are to be commended. Keep up the good work! If your style is anything but assertive, don't worry. You are not alone. Most people tend to react in nonassertive ways. Assertive behavior calls for calm, careful, thoughtful reactions. It is difficult to react that way when you are confronted with racism.

Sometimes the shock of a racial attack is enough to leave you in stunned silence. At other times, you might find it difficult to restrain yourself in the face of an outrage, but only by facing those situations squarely and expressing your feelings in a controlled manner will you be able to walk away with your dignity intact. If that is something that has been lacking in your experiences, begin now to improve the situation for yourself and for your child.

We know and understand ourselves better than we know or understand anyone else. Therefore, no matter what we try to do, we will end up teaching our children to be more like ourselves than like anyone else. That is why it is important to take the time to examine, understand, and change our behavior, if necessary, so that we can project positive images for our children.

Chapter Six

PLANTING THE SEEDS: INFANTS AND TODDLERS

It's never too early to start teaching your children that having black skin is as natural and as good as breathing. Children start learning from the day they are born. They learn some of their most important life skills from birth to five years old—the infant and toddler years. Walking, talking, and toilet functions are just a few of the many complex human activities they master in those early years.

To get an idea of how much children must accomplish during this brief time, imagine what it would be like if tomorrow morning you were to wake up in the middle of China. How would you ask for food, or tell someone that you were ill or frightened?

Your toddler has many urgent reasons to learn quickly, and at this age learning is what toddlers do best. But the language gap alone makes their job of learning an enormous task. Because infants cannot speak or understand speech, you, the parent, must make the necessary effort to find ways to communicate important information to them. They have to learn, for example, that the stove and the iron are hot, and that a full bathtub is no place for a child to be alone.

How do you pass on vital information to children who have not yet developed sophisticated language skills? Parents have to adopt a whole set of nonverbal signals in order to communicate with children at this age. For instance, when you put your hand close to the iron and snatch it back, saying, "Ouch! Hot!" you are telling your child, "It's not safe for you to touch this object." Rocking him gently in your arms says, "It is safe for you to go to sleep now." Therefore, you can take much of the credit for what, how much, and how fast your children learn.

As children get older, they begin to learn about the world around them by matching words to objects. You help them by pointing to things and saying their names. For example, "This is your bottle. Say, 'bottle.' Here is your daddy. Can you say, 'Daddy'?" Little by little a child learns the language, and through that he or she learns what is acceptable or desirable in his or her world.

In this chapter we show you some of the ways you can become involved in your children's learning process, and incorporate positive images and experiences of Blackness into their early lives. Right there, at the beginning, is where you want to start to teach them that they are different and wonderful, and second to none as human beings.

When we say "teach" our children at this age, we do not mean teach in the conventional sense. We are not saying, for example, "Frederick Douglass was important and these are the reasons why . . ." Instead, we are trying to lay down a foundation of experiences that we can build on when our children are old enough to digest more complex instruction. We want them to become so comfortable, so confident, and so positive about being Black that in later life they won't need special occasions like Black History Month to make them feel important.

For your infant or young toddler, this means you will have to work on some additional nonverbal ways to get these positive images across. For example, we started the following practice as soon as our daughter came home from the hospital. In the mornings, while one of us is dressing her, we sing a special song for her. It is a tuneless song, and the words vary from day to day. As our daughter got older she loved to join in and "sing" along. On any given day the words might go something like this:

I love your beautiful brown hair
I love your smooth black skin

What lovely brown eyes you have
You are the most beautiful girl in the whole wide world.

It wouldn't make the top ten, but it serves the purpose.

As we sing we point to her eyes and touch her nose or whatever part of her we are singing about, and shower her with compliments. In the beginning the words meant nothing to her, but she knew that we were happy with her features because we smiled as we pointed them out. She still loves this little exercise, and she often starts to sing by herself if we forget.

Make up activities such as this for your children. You can do them at bedtime or at mealtimes or any time you can find a quiet moment together. For example, if you see a pretty Black child on television, you might tell your daughter, "That's a pretty little girl. Her hair looks just like yours. I bet you are pretty enough to be on television." Look for opportunities to praise and compliment your children. These activities will help them to grow up appreciating themselves as worthwhile and attractive persons.

If possible, try to do these exercises in front of a full-length mirror. Seeing themselves in the mirror as you point out and praise their features will gradually add meaning to the exercise for the children. They will more quickly learn to relate their image in the mirror to the good things you are saying.

AGE MAKES A DIFFERENCE

As parents all know, every child has a mind of his own. "The baby will come when it's good and ready" is something parents often hear. The point is that babies will do what they do in their own time no matter what the calendar says. Although we professionals predict when your child will start doing this or that activity, our calendar is really just a rough guideline. Each child develops at his or her own rate. For instance, when your daughter's leg muscles are strong enough and coordinated enough, she will learn to walk. Until then it doesn't matter how much you steady and coax her, she will not walk.

Forcing information down your children's throats and expecting them to understand it before they're ready is the same as expecting them to walk on the day they are born. Such an approach would be useless. So, as we try get information to our children, we have to keep their age in mind. They might not be ready for some of what we want them to learn, but that is not to say you can't begin to teach them. Just don't expect them to understand everything right away.

From birth to about four months, babies spend all of their time learning about their bodies. Little Jamie might spend hours playing with a mobile hanging above her crib. But in reality it is not the mobile but the sight of her hands moving before her eyes that has her attention. Gradually Jamie is learning that those hands are a part of her. At this stage, the best way that parents can teach their children is to show them all the love and affection they can. Dr. Na'im Akbar, a Florida State University psychology professor, has this to say about the importance of closeness and touching at this age:

> Breast-feeding establishes a bond that can help the [Black] baby get a healthy sense of self. This physical contact with a Black body builds an irreplaceable foundation.

But even if you do not breast-feed your children, you can still give them the warmth and cuddling that helps to build their self-esteem. The way you hold your children and the sounds you make in their presence can convey the love and tenderness you feel for them. Take the time to touch and caress those tiny arms and legs. Whisper kind and gentle words to them as you attend to their needs. Let your children see, feel, and hear how much you appreciate them. Even though they might not understand some of the words, just the pleasant sound of your voice will help to reassure them and build their confidence.

From eight to twelve months Jamie will continue to play with the mobile, but by now her attention moves from her arms to the toy itself. She is starting to develop a curiosity about things beyond her own body. This is the beginning of many wonderful occasions for you to involve yourself with your children's play activity. Take the opportunity to feed their curiosity with the things that you want them to appreciate, namely positive impressions of what it means to be Black.

As you provide your children with dolls and other toys, for

instance, try to find Black-oriented playthings. A good practice to follow when buying toys is to ask yourself, "Can I use this toy to teach my child something good about being Black?" or "Is there another toy that can better teach my child about being Black?" If you can't find something you like you might have to improvise. For example, Flora, unable to find a crib mobile with Black figures, made one for her son LaVar using Black Raggedy Ann dolls she made herself. Finding toys for Black children of any age can be a real challenge. We will go into that a little bit later.

SENSORY EXPERIENCES ARE LASTING

Your young toddler learns about the world on a primitive level. We say "primitive" because children have no reasoned or thought-out understanding of their world. Their awareness of their surroundings is based on what their senses tell them. If little Gregory sees you take an ice cube from the refrigerator, he will not necessarily know that it is cold unless he touches it. He has not yet learned to associate refrigerator with coldness, so he has to rely on his sense of touch to tell him the ice is cold.

These *sensory* experiences are important to the way your child perceives the world as he or she grows up. If most of the experiences are positive, the child will develop trust and confidence in the surroundings. If they are negative, he or she will distrust the environment and the people in it, and resist new experiences. People, including children, shy away from things that make them feel badly, and move toward those that please them. The same is true for relationships with other people. Here is an example that shows how a person's early sensory experiences influenced the way she later approached relationships with other people.

Eighteen-year-old Eleanor is the daughter of a biracial couple. She recalls spending time with both of her grandmothers as a child. Her White grandmother was very strict with her. She was very religious and believed strongly in disciplining the child. She often spanked Eleanor because, she said, the Bible told her to do so. "Spare the rod and spoil the child," her grandmother always said. Eleanor cried whenever she had to visit her.

Her Black grandmother was the opposite. She loved the child and never disciplined her by spanking. Every time Eleanor visited, her grandmother would cook her favorite dishes and bake cookies for her.

As an adult, Eleanor remembers her White grandmother as a sad and bitter person who was always looking for a reason to punish her. In retrospect Eleanor wonders if her grandmother had difficulty accepting her Blackness. She remembers her Black grandmother as a warm and generous person. She thinks of her whenever she smells cookies fresh from the oven. Eleanor is still wary in the way she relates to older White women, but thinks older Black women are nurturing and fun to be around. She is working to develop a more balanced view of the women in her family so that she can have a better relationship with her White female relatives.

Eleanor's example shows that those early experiences can have lasting impressions. That is why it is important to give our children positive experiences with warm, loving Black people so that they will grow up to associate warmth and tenderness with Black people. If they do so at an early age, they will challenge the negative stereotypes that they will face for the rest of their lives. They will be able to say, "My dad was never abusive toward me," or "I know that Black people do not all behave that way."

PROMOTE POSITIVE EXPERIENCES

In many instances you, as a parent, can promote the positive images and encounters that are so important for children to experience. For example, when your parents visit, show them what the children like and encourage them to participate in those activities with them. If David likes to go to a nearby petting zoo, ask your parents to take him once in a while. The experience will add to his positive memories of warm, nurturing Black people. If he likes to be rocked to sleep in a rocking chair, tell your baby-sitter so that she can do that for him while you are out.

SHIELD YOUR CHILDREN FROM THE NEGATIVES

It's just as important to protect your children from negative experiences as it is to expose them to positive ones. For instance, Uncle Gary visits his one-year-old nephew Marvin once a week. As soon as Gary enters the house, he makes a beeline for Marvin. "Where's my favorite boy?" he shouts as he sweeps the child off the floor and into the air above his head. Marvin shrieks, his eyes wide with fright. "Stop throwing the child up in the air like that," Marvin's mother, Debra, says halfheartedly. "You know he doesn't like it." Gary ignores her, and they both laugh at the look of terror on Marvin's face. Eventually Debra takes the boy away and quiets him down.

Soon Marvin begins to cry just at the sound of his uncle's voice. Furthermore, he cries whenever any other man goes near him. Marvin's case is another example of how a child sometimes takes his experience with one person and generalizes it to others. It shows how important it is to guard our children against such negative experiences. A reliable way to reduce such encounters is to make your children off-limits to anyone who deliberately makes them cry. Seemingly harmless behavior can be very damaging to children.

EXPOSE YOUR CHILDREN TO DIFFERENT KINDS OF PEOPLE

We have talked before about the need to make our children feel comfortable with different kinds of people. This is an important consideration in a multicultural society such as ours. Your children, as adults, will certainly have to deal with non-Black people in order to achieve some of their goals. If you want your children to be comfortable with people of other ethnic backgrounds, provide them with positive exposure to such people at an early age. For instance, you can invite White and Hispanic friends to bring their children to play with yours. A biracial couple we know held ice cream parties in their backyard for this purpose. They invited neighborhood children of different ethnic backgrounds so that their son would grow up comfortable with different people. A Black couple who lived in a predominantly White suburb took their toddler to an inner-city play group that had Hispanic, Asian, Black, and White children.

TRUST AND MISTRUST

All young toddlers shy away from strangers. They might even be wary of family members who are not familiar to them. It's natural for Alison to cry when her aunts and uncles try to pick her up if she doesn't see them often enough to trust them. But as Alison gets older, she will develop enough trust to become comfortable with other people. And by watching her parents she will learn when to trust and when not to trust strangers. For instance, Alison will come to understand that if someone is visiting in her home and her parents are relaxed and comfortable with that person, it is probably safe for her to go to the person. In time she will also learn when it is not appropriate to trust. For instance, she will learn that it isn't safe for her to go to a stranger on the street.

Unfortunately, some children never lose their early fear of other people. Long after they should be comfortable with people they know and who are kind to them, they still have difficulty relating to others. Five-year-old Brenda, for instance, still refuses to let her aunt Phyllis hold her, even though Phyllis has tried to be very loving and tender toward the child. Brenda still cries and hides behind her mother when Phyllis comes to visit.

Situations such as Brenda's sometimes develop as a result of the experiences that young children have with the people around them. Again, positive experiences encourage them to trust people; negative ones can make them distrustful. So if your child is showing fear or distrust of people, it might be helpful to identify the kinds of experiences that might be contributing to their feelings of distrust. These experiences sometimes come from the most unexpected quarters. Here is an example of how distrust can begin.

Mary, a single parent, lets her three-year-old son, Jake, spend some time with her brother, Ted. She wanted the boy to have the influence of a man in his life. Ted still resented Jake's father for deserting the boy's mother. Furthermore, he thought the boy was growing up to be just like his father.

Sometimes Ted enjoyed the boy's company and acted "just like a father" to him. But most of the time Ted could not hide his resentment of Jake's father, and he often took it out on the child. Before long, negative statements such as "You are no good—just like your father," "You will never amount to anything," and "You could never be my kid" became familiar to Jake. And although he was not old enough to understand all the words, the negative message was usually quite clear.

The major Black male figure in Jake's life was someone who made him feel miserable. As a result, Jake became more and more withdrawn from his uncle. But even more important, he became distrustful of all Black men who came near him. Jake's experience is another example of how children can generalize from their experiences. If someone treats them badly, there is a strong possibility that they will assume that anyone who reminds them of that person will treat them the same way.

Unfortunately, Jake's problem is not uncommon. Even well-meaning parents and relatives sometimes subject children to such negative programming simply because they do not know the damage that is being done. One way to begin healing those scars is for you to sit down with your children and, if they are old enough to understand, admit that you have made some mistakes but that you're working to change. More important, regardless of their age, begin right away to replace the negative messages with positive, supportive ones. Say things like "You are important to me," "You are a beautiful child," or "Everybody makes mistakes. You will do better as you learn more. You are such a good listener!" These are the kinds of expressions, accompanied by supportive actions, that will build trust in your children. In addition, you will feel better about yourself for having given them the support they need to succeed in society.

CHILD ABUSE

A common reason for distrust in children is child abuse. Children who have been abused become distrustful of other people whom they perceive as being in a position to abuse them. For example, if a child has been physically abused by his father, he will quite likely distrust anyone whom he sees as having authority over him. But the harmful effects of abuse can go beyond the victim. Research has shown that many people who have been abused as children go on to abuse others.

For instance, five-year-old Aaron grew up in a home where he saw his mother being abused by her boyfriend. Aaron was also subjected to frequent beatings. He was referred to us for counseling because he had begun hitting not only the girls in his "Head Start" class but also his female teacher. On a visit to his home, we found he was living under terrible conditions. There was poor sanitation and signs of drug use in the home. (Aaron later told us there was nothing wrong with taking drugs as long as you didn't take too much!) Given the conditions in the home, we felt we had no choice but to recommend that Aaron be removed from it. We suggested that he be placed with relatives who had a more stable and supportive home life.

A Black child in Aaron's circumstances is in danger of growing up to believe that the conditions in his life are normal for Black people. Such experiences can contribute to distrust of Black people in general, and subsequently lead to violence against other Black people—Black on Black crime. Just as Jake came to believe that all Black men might be verbally abusive to him, Aaron was in danger of believing that all Black men abuse women. He had already come to believe that taking drugs was acceptable among Black people. He had no way of knowing that most Black people live an entirely different kind of life, or that some White people have the same problems. As a result of such experiences, Aaron could have developed negative perceptions and negative expectations of himself and of other Blacks.

Everyone condemns intentional physical abuse; however, it is possible to cause the same kind of harm unintentionally. Abuse includes not only the kind of physical torture that gets in the news but also excessive spanking, mental cruelty, and even the type of verbal abuse that Ted used on his nephew Jake.

Some people believe that beating is the best way to discipline a child. For some, it is part of a religious conviction. It's not our intention to challenge anyone's religious beliefs, but we do not advocate "beating." The difference between beating and spanking is not only in intensity and severity but also in motivation:

Beating a child serves to make parents feel better when they believe their children have "wronged" them. The inevitable risk is that it only builds resentment in a child.

Although spanking can work as a temporary painful deterrent, it should be infrequent and done when the parent is in control and not overly emotional. Heavy reliance on physical punishment can have negative side effects in the child. A child who is spanked excessively might become overly aggressive toward others, or fearful and withdrawn in the presence of authority figures.

When punishment becomes necessary to emphasize or enforce discipline, we recommend a less destructive method, such as "time-out." In a time-out procedure the child is sent to a separate area, his or her room, for example, without any entertainment for a short time (usually fifteen minutes). Such punishment must be accompanied by clear explanations of what the child did wrong and what kind of behavior is expected of him or her. Generally, we have found when parents focus mostly on being firm, clear, and consistent about what they expect from their child there is much less reliance on the harsher and potentially more destructive approaches to punishment.

Signs of Child Abuse

How can you tell if a child has been abused? Most victims of abuse give some indication of their private torment. Here are some signs that may suggest that a child is being abused:

- Exhibits a sudden change in behavior. A child who is normally quiet suddenly begins to "act out," or an outgoing child suddenly becomes quiet and withdrawn.
- Reacts with anxiety when you attempt to touch or get close to them
- Appears always fearful and uneasy
- Shows overt signs of abuse, such as unexplained welts or bruises

Aside from outright abuse, just a sum of negative experiences in a child's life is all it takes to build distrust. Jane's experience illustrates this problem. She is one of five children raised by their father after their mother died. Jane's father did his best but never quite learned how to discipline the children. Mealtimes were particularly bad. He would put out their meals in bowls in the middle of the table, but before he could sit down there would be a wild scramble, and the bulk of the food would go to the biggest and fastest children.

As the youngest, Jane seldom got enough food. She often went to bed hungry and angry. As an adult, she distrusted any situation where people were expected to behave on their honor. She always felt someone would cheat her. For example, at the office where she worked the management was going to award bonuses for the best producers. Since it was near Christmastime, they offered to divide the bonus pool among the entire staff.

Although Jane was among the top producers and would receive a large bonus, she voted to have the pool divided equally. Because all the employees were on their honor to count and record their own production figures, Jane suspected that some of them cheated, and she did not want them to get more than they deserved in a merit bonus. She was so consumed by distrust of others that she was willing to forgo a substantial bonus for herself. Unless someone or something intervenes to change her outlook, Jane will probably raise her children with the same level of distrust in other people.

Our children need to trust in themselves and in Black culture as a whole to survive and advance in society. We can help build their trust by insuring that they have positive experiences in their formative years.

SYMBOLIC PLAY

Starting at about age two, children develop what we call *symbolic play*. This is just another way of saying they start to use their imagination as they play. For example, three-year-old Lee arranges all the dining room chairs in a row, and seats his dolls in all but the first chair. Lee then puts on his baseball cap and climbs into the front seat, pretending to be a bus driver. Five-year-old Laura has named all of her dolls. Some of them she considers her friends, and others she considers her children.

She shares advice with her "friends" and discusses clothes and the "children" with them. She reads to the "children," grooms them, and disciplines them when they are "bad." Harold, a third child, has an imaginary playmate, Dennis. Harold spends time talking, laughing, and playing with Dennis. Sometimes Harold's mother worries that her son has too vivid an imagination.

All three children are simply discovering that they can create an imaginary world that can be a source of great enjoyment to them. There they can explore relationships with other people, imitate their parents, and play roles that are impossible for them in real life. We encourage you to involve yourself in your children's play. Tap into their rich imagination and provide them with positive expressions of Blackness.

For instance, provide your children with Black and other ethnic dolls, and take the time to join them in playing with their dolls. Help them dress and groom the dolls while you compliment them both: "This is a beautiful doll. It looks just like you. Look at her hair. It's just like yours. Did you know your nose is as pretty as your doll's? You look so nice together, you must take your doll with you to the birthday party."

Toys, dolls in particular, are an excellent vehicle through which children use their imagination. An experience with one of our therapy groups shows how effective doll play can be in helping children express themselves. The group consists of exceptionally gifted Black children. In one session we discussed some of the images of Black people they see in films. We had provided action-figure dolls that the children could use to reenact scenes from their favorite movies. When we discussed a particular film, one boy, Jay, picked up a tall White doll and used it to knock down all the Black and Latino dolls. "That's the way it was in *that* movie," he said, "but this is how it would be in *my* movie." He then picked up the smallest Black doll and angrily used it to knock down all the White dolls. "This is how it would be in *my* movie and in *my* world," he repeated. Jay was using the dolls to express his anger and resentment at the way he saw non-Whites portrayed in the film.

Doll play is one of the best opportunities for you to help your children exercise their imagination. But it is not the only one. Just about all activities you do with your children, such as reading and storytelling, are excellent ways to involve and expand their imagination.

Your child, using his or her imagination, will hit occasionally on some form of behavior that you might consider inappropriate. It is important to let your child know that you disapprove. For instance, simply say, "Mommy feels badly when you hit your doll," or "It's not nice to shout at someone when they make a mistake." Once you have pointed out the inappropriate behavior, you can then go on to model appropriate behavior for the child.

BOOKS, STORIES, AND YOUR CHILD

Books are perhaps the best ways to stretch your children's imagination. You can stimulate their interest in books long before they learn to read by reading to them. At first they will probably understand only the simplest stories, but there is no need to limit yourself to those. Just reading to them will capture their imagination. Although reading to your children might seem to be as innocent as anything could ever be, however, some caution is necessary.

Prepare to be surprised by how difficult it is to find good books or stories for and about Black children. Just as in movies and television shows, popular children's books and stories feature few if any Black heroes. For example, among the old storybook classics, there are no Black equivalents of Cinderella, Snow White, Prince Charming, or other popular characters in children's literature. The only Blacks you will find in classic children stories will be more along the line of Little Black Sambo or other demeaning images of Blacks.

COLOR-MEANING WORD ASSOCIATION

Color-meaning word association is a technical term that refers to the fact that people associate certain characteristics with certain colors. For instance, white is seen as pure, clean, virginal, innocent, or honest. Black is perceived as dirty, mysterious, devious, ugly, grim, or morbid. Other colors have common associations: green means sickly or envious; red means dangerous, and so on. But black and white carry clear racial implications, because people are often assigned characteristics based on the color of their skin.

Some of the most blatant and simplistic representations of white as good and of black as evil are found in children's literature. There is no shortage of evil Black witches, good White fairies, good guys dressed in white, and bad guys dressed in black. Villages full of innocent White children, who only tell "little white lies," are usually threatened by villainous Black knights, and in the end they are saved by blond-haired, blue-eyed White knights.

Although Black writers have created positive literature for Black children, it is tough to compete with the old stereotypes. For the same reason that Black children reject Black dolls in favor of White dolls, they tend to favor White images in literature.

Showing and reading books about Blacks to your children even before they learn to read is a way to help head off such White preference before it gets a foothold. Again, our goal is to get our children so comfortable with good Black images that they will automatically gravitate toward such images instead of the negative ones.

Customizing Books for Your Children

Spencer, a young father, told us what made him concerned about the books he was reading to his children. One night he was playing an album of children's stories for his daughter. One of the stories told how Cinderella came by her name. According to the story, Cinderella's stepmother made her do all the dirty work around the house, including cleaning out the fireplace. Her hands and face became so blackened by the cinders that her wicked stepmother named her *Cinder*ella. It took magic to transform her into an image that would attract a prince.

The idea of a "blackened" Cinderella started Spencer thinking about positive Black images in children's literature. Unable to find any, Spencer decided he had to somehow change the images in the books he was reading to his daughter. Now, when he reads Cinderella to his daughter, Cinderella is Black. He even colored her black in the book. He changed Snow White's name to Jackie, the same as his daughter's. And throughout such books he removes degrading images of Blackness and replaces them with descriptions that have no color-meaning. For example, "the hideous black creature" becomes "the horrible monster."

Spencer lets his daughter watch as he changes the pictures in the book. He also lets her know exactly what he is doing and why. He tells her, for instance, "All these pictures show 'Jackie' as a pretty White girl, but she can be a beautiful Black girl just like you." He also tells her that there is another version of the story in which the girl is called "Snow White," or in which Cinderella is White. Spencer says he explains all this to his daughter to make sure that she is not caught off guard when someone else reads her the original versions of the stories.

You can change any story you like in this way to make it more relevant to your own children. As a variation, you can let your child be the hero of the story. For instance, you can remove the offensive characterizations from the Tarzan stories and let your son be Tarzan. With a little effort you can have a great deal of fun with your children as you help them create positive Black images by changing these classic stories. (The remake of the film *The Wizard of Oz* into *The Wiz* is an example of a commercial application of this idea.)

We have all heard the expression "You can't tell a book by its cover." Well, this applies to children's books as well. While shopping for children's books one day, we were so pleased to find one that had Black children on the cover that we snapped it up without looking inside. When we sat down to read it to our daughter we noticed something peculiar. There was one Black character in the book. In every instance in which his picture appeared he was shown in a position that was subordinate to the White children in the story.

In a section where they were demonstrating the difference between "up" and "down," the children were on a see-saw. The White child was up, and the Black child was down. When they demonstrated "give" and "take," the Black child gave, and the White child took. In "right" and "wrong," the White child demonstrated right, and the Black child demonstrated wrong. It was infuriating. The next day we returned the book and got our money back. We tried to explain the situation to the clerk, but she looked at us with bewilderment. Many people just don't understand that these subtle messages reinforce negative stereotypes about Blacks. It falls to us as Black parents to guard our children against such images.

Reading Aloud

When you find suitable books or have improvised to create your own, read aloud to your children as much as you can. Let them see your joy and appreciation of the story. It will help them to develop a love of reading if they associate it with happiness. Show interest in the story. Wonder out loud as to what is going to happen in the story. It will get your child to think about that, too. Comment on the characters and their actions as you go along. Tell your children what you like and what you don't like about the story. Tell them how the characters might be feeling about what is happening in the story. Ask your children questions about the story as you read: "Do you like Mary? What kind of person do you think she is? You know, Mary is as smart and as pretty as you are. What would you do if you were in Mary's place?" Do whatever you can to involve your children in the story. Describe the characters. Point out their features. Compare them to your children's and say how lovely they are.

Look for opportunities to broaden the story. For example, look for references to historic figures and take the opportunity to tell your children something about them. Look at background images. Is there a painting on the wall? Is it of some famous historic character you recognize? Take a moment to discuss it. Explain to your child why someone would want to keep that picture in their home: "This a picture of Guy Bluford. He was the first Black astronaut to actually travel in space. The Smiths have a picture of him on their wall because they are very proud of him."

Sometimes the right book can be helpful in dealing with a particular problem you might be having with your child. For example, if your son is having difficulty relating to people of other ethnic backgrounds, it might be helpful to find a book about a child with the same problem, and read it together. Reading and discussing such a story with your child will almost always be more effective than lecturing him on the subject.

Librarians can help you locate books on specific topics. Don't be afraid to ask them for help.

MIRROR, MIRROR . . .

Something as simple as hanging a mirror in your children's room can be a great opportunity to boost their self-esteem. Looking in a mirror is a fascinating experience for young children. They are quickly captivated by the little screen with the "picture" of someone in it—someone who mimics everything they do. It is nothing less than magic in their eyes.

As your child learns to recognize his or her image in the mirror, take the time to compliment his or her features. For example, say to your daughter, "This is your nice Brown skin. It matches your beautiful brown eyes." Run your fingers through her hair and tell her how pleasant it feels. Trace the line of her nose. Describe the shape and compare it to your own or to that of someone in a picture, or in her favorite story. "Your nose is just like Laura's. Remember Laura? She is the pretty girl you liked so much in that movie we saw." Describe skin color differences between people—real and fictional—and explain the beauty and the richness in the variety: "Black people's skins come in many different shades of black. It can be dark like mine, light like your dad's, or anywhere in between—like yours. And they are all beautiful!" Use complimentary words such as *lovely*, *pretty*, or *nice* so that your child will learn to associate them with his or her image. Smile as you do these things to let your child see that you are happy, pleased, and proud of him or her. Your goal is to help your children feel good about the person they see in the mirror.

Some parents worry that spending so much time in front of a mirror might encourage a child to be conceited, vain, or selfish. You needn't worry about that. Children *need* to be self-centered before they can relate to other people in a healthy way. In other words, they have to know and be confident in who they are to function properly in society. Self-confidence, not conceit, is what you are trying to build. And that is what develops when children get a positive sense of who they are early in life.

THE PICTURES IN YOUR HOME

The pictures you display in your home help form images in your toddlers' minds and can have a lasting effect on the way they see the world. Here is an example of how this can work.

Robert is a successful minister with a large congregation. He grew up in a middle-class Black family that has produced several ministers over the years. Robert recalls that one of the most powerful images of his childhood was a large picture that hung in his family's living room all of his life. The picture was of Robert's grandfather standing in a pulpit, looking toward the camera while the congregation gazed at him with upturned faces. "That picture was so alive," said Robert, "it was as though my grandfather were still living in the house with us. And the way the people in the picture looked at him—so much respect! As far back as I can remember, I wanted to be just like him."

Hang pictures of Black people you respect in your home. Pictures of immediate family members, elders, and historic figures can help stimulate your children's imagination and serve as inspiration later in their lives. You don't need fancy formal portraits. All you need are clear pictures of people in a dignified setting. There are different ways you could do this including having photographs made, or even cutting out pictures from magazines. Also use pictures of plants, animals, landscapes, or cityscapes to brighten your home, especially your child's room. Such scenes can help your child to realize that there are other realities beyond what he or she sees every day.

Our daughter, for example, loves the sculptures and colorful African art we have in our home. Of course, she doesn't yet understand what they mean, but when she sees similar artwork in other people's homes, she points to it with pleasure at recognizing something she likes. By helping your children to recognize positive symbols of their culture at an early age, you help them to develop an appreciation for their culture as they get older.

Even though a child might be born in a particular culture, if he or she is not raised among the symbols of that culture or exposed to them, those cultural representations will be foreign to the child. A recent television interview of a Native American boy provided a dramatic example of this. The boy expressed a strong dislike for "Indian" culture. He was born among Native Americans but raised entirely in White society. The boy said Native American culture—religion, art, language, and community—meant nothing to him. In fact, he said he was embarrassed by it. He believed that Native Americans were dangerous and that they raped and killed women and children.

Undoubtedly, the boy's perception of Native American culture comes from films, television, books, and perhaps even his peers. Without positive information to counter the negative views of his culture that are so prevalent in American society, it is not surprising that the boy has rejected his culture.

As in the case of Native American culture, there are many false or misleading images of African-American culture. We talked about some of them in chapter 3. It falls to us as Black parents to ferret out and destroy those images and replace them with accurate ones. The toddler years, when your children have a voracious appetite and a natural instinct for learning, are the perfect time to expose them to accurate images of their culture.

TOYS AND TOTS

We adults sometimes think of toys as frivolous things that children use to pass the time, or as things we use to distract them when we want to do something "really important." Yet toys are essential to a child's development. For example, by manipulating toys children develop their fine motor skills—the ability to perform delicate tasks with their fingers. Toys also help children use and expand their imagination. Their attitude toward their toys, dolls especially, tell us much about how they see themselves and the world in general.

Young children often use toys to build a fantasy world around themselves and give the toys qualities that are important to the child. For example, Tracy has named her dolls after her friends and other people she admires. Deena, who has trouble relating to other children, finds comfort in the friendship of her dolls. Both girls are using dolls to enhance their real-life experiences. Tracy uses her dolls to expand on the good relationship she already has with her friends. Deena relates to her dolls in the way she would like to relate to other children.

Racial Awareness Through Doll Play

Our research, described in the introduction, has shown that children's attitudes toward dolls can reveal their awareness and underlying feelings about racial differences. Many of the children we interviewed chose White dolls over Black ones because they felt that the White dolls were "prettier," "cleaner," or "nicer." Many Black children even chose White dolls when asked to pick out the doll that looked more like them. These results tell us that early in their lives, many Black children learn that Whiteness is more valued than Blackness in our society. Therefore, when they have a choice they will often choose white over black.

If children begin to show preference for White dolls as early as in preschool, we have to work with them even earlier to change their perceptions that Black dolls are less desirable. One way to do this is for us to help our children choose Black dolls and teach the children that those dolls *are* beautiful. For example, if your daughter likes "Barbie" dolls, by all means get her Barbie. But also choose Black characters from the Barbie world. *You do not want your child to grow up thinking that only White dolls, and by extension White people, are attractive and nice.*

If your children have had only White dolls, you will want to be very careful when you introduce Black dolls to them. The last thing you want to do is to buy them all new Black dolls and immediately take away their White ones. The process has to be gentle and gradual. Remember, children form very close bonds with their dolls.

A good way to approach the matter is to buy the Black doll you want your child to have, but before giving it to your child, let him or her see you holding and taking care of the new doll. You might say to the child, "Isn't this a beautiful doll. I love her so much. She reminds me of you when you were a little baby."

Continue to build up the Black doll by dressing it in the best clothes, or having it sit next to you, or doing anything you can think of to make your child see that you prefer that doll. Next, offer the doll to the child on a conditional basis: "Would you like to play with this doll? You can have her, but only for a few minutes, and only if you promise to take the very best care of her. She is my favorite doll, you know. Will you take care of her for me?"

By this time most children would jump at the chance to hold that doll even for a *second.* All you are doing by taking this approach is making the doll seem so attractive the child can't resist it. That is exactly the way children learn to prefer White dolls in the first place. Books, television, and everything around us paint such a rosy picture of Whiteness that children take it for fact that White things—and people—are more attractive than black ones. In our research we found that children began to desire Black dolls after we showed them that *we* thought the dolls were attractive and worth having.

When you are satisfied that the child is interested in the doll and ready to own it, you can offer it to him or her: "I'm glad you like my doll so much. If you promise to take care of it as well as I did, you may keep it." Another variation might be "I'm glad you like my doll so much. If you'd like, I'll buy you one just like mine if you promise to take care of it." Repeat this process as often as you think is necessary to get your child to appreciate Black dolls.

The most important part of this exercise is that as your child is learning that Black dolls are beautiful, desirable, and good, he or she is also learning that the same is true for himself or herself. And that was our real objective in the first place.

DAY-CARE CENTERS

For most of us, a day-care center is the first place our children will spend a significant amount of time away from home. If you consider that this is at a time when they are learning who they are and how to relate to the world around them, you will see why we have to choose day care with caution. There is a running debate as to what it will mean to have a whole generation of children raised in day-care centers. This debate recognizes the fact that, in effect, strangers will be raising our children in their most impressionable years. Considering the additional difficulties involved in raising Black children in White America, you can see why choosing a facility that is sensitive to Black issues is very important. In some ways day-care centers are taking on the role that the extended family has traditionally assumed in the lives of Black people.

You will want to visit several centers before you make up your mind. If you know other parents who use the centers, ask them about the quality of service they provide. Ask all the questions you need answered to satisfy yourself that you are dealing with a facility that is licensed, clean, and safe for your child. But even when you have this assurance, your search might not be over. You still want to make sure that it is an environment that supports a Black child's development.

FINDING DAY CARE THAT WORKS *FOR* YOUR CHILD

Here are some clues that can help you to evaluate a day-care center. When you first walk in, notice the decorations. If the facility is sensitive to ethnic concerns, it will probably have decorations that show people of different ethnic backgrounds doing a variety of jobs. In particular, look for pictures of Black people participating in positive, respectable jobs.

The same thing is true for toys. For a center to be considered suitable for Black children, it should have Black dolls among its toys, and these toys should be valued by the children and the staff alike. Dolls and action figures should be of equal or very similar quality and stature as White ones reflecting positive Black figures. Of course, we do not expect day-care centers to have *only* Black dolls; however, we believe they should have dolls that represent various ethnic groups. Encouraging *all* children to play with ethnic dolls is one way to help them to develop an appreciation for people who are different from themselves.

Books are another clue as to whether a facility has taken its Black clients into consideration. Look for books by or about Black people. And just to be safe, turn a few pages to see how Blacks are portrayed *inside* the books. You are looking basically for the same kinds of books and toys that you would consider bringing into your own home.

Perhaps the most important component of the day-care center is possibly the hardest to evaluate: the staff. It is easy enough to tell if the center has Black staff members, but that's as easy as it gets. Every center director will probably be quick to tell you that his or her facility is sensitive to the needs of minorities. But as we know, some centers can do more harm than good.

For instance, during our research we visited a day-care center in a nearby city. To our dismay, we found that in a class with an obvious majority of Black children, the teacher had a White Cabbage Patch doll as the favorite doll for the children. When we brought to her attention the fact that the only doll in the classroom was White, she said she was sorry but that was the only doll she had and besides, "that's the children's favorite doll."

These types of classroom situations can distort the way Black children see themselves. They learn to groom and cuddle the White doll. They hear the teacher use positive adjectives to describe the doll's beautiful blond hair and green eyes, and soon they come to associate those characteristics with being beautiful.

It is easy to see how children can come to believe that *they* are not beautiful because they do not possess the qualities that the teacher has taught them to associate with beauty. Keep in mind that it is not necessary for the teacher to tell them that brown eyes and black skin are ugly for them to believe this. The fact that there is nothing in the classroom to suggest that *their* features can be considered beautiful is enough to convince them that they are not. If the staff of a day-care center does not convince you that they are sensitive to this issue, you might do better to look elsewhere.

There is nothing wrong with a Black child cuddling a White doll or a White child cuddling a Black doll. In fact, we think such exposure could help them to appreciate each other's physical differences. Children in these settings need to have a choice of dolls of different ethnic backgrounds. They also need someone who is sensitive enough to the issue to tell them that Black and Brown dolls have different features and that they are beautiful, too.

We enrolled our daughter in a weekly play group at a day-care center. The center's director had a reputation for being sensitive to children's individual needs. Unfortunately, she left shortly after our daughter enrolled, and a new director took over. When we subsequently visited the center, we noticed that they had no representations of Black people. All of the books, dolls, and other toys were White-oriented. When our daughter took her Black doll to the center, there were some smiles but mostly puzzled looks from the staff. The center's director told us she was writing a paper on the importance of using multi-cultural materials in day-care centers. She offered no support to our daughter when she brought in her Black doll, however. In spite of the director's professed sensitivity to the issue of ethnic representation in toys and pictures, we subsequently saw no change in the center's materials. We eventually moved our daughter to another center.

Some people, even professionals such as teachers, appear to feel that the issue of ethnic toys and dolls is frivolous. But we know that it is quite serious. If you doubt the seriousness, consider this: What would happen if all over America someone offered free Black dolls to all families, schools, and day-care centers in exchange for their White dolls. Imagine that all the schools accepted the Black dolls and threw out their White ones. We would find that people *do* feel strongly about the color of their dolls.

One Christmas we hand-colored Santa Claus brown on our daughter's sweater because we couldn't find any sweaters in the stores with Black Santas on them. When our daughter wore the sweater to her day-care center, the staff made a few nervous comments, such as "Who is that on your sweater?" or "Isn't that a lovely sweater." No one used the word *black,* but several staff members looked at the Black Santa Claus with surprise, if not shock, on their faces.

What we learned from our daughter's day-care experience is that when it comes to providing Black children with positive images of Blackness, many people are willing to discuss and intellectualize the issue, but too often that is as far as it goes. Addressing the needs of Black children is seldom a priority for many day-care centers, especially those located in the suburbs.

Suburban Black parents who are looking for day care have to make locating suitable facilities *their* priority.

PLAY GROUPS

If you choose to stay home with your preschooler, instead of enrolling him or her in a day-care center, you face another problem: finding appropriate playmates for your child. A play group could be the solution to your problem.

A play group is a group of preschool children whose parents meet at least once a week to give the children a chance to play together. It is an excellent way for parents to get playmates for their toddlers. They cost nothing to start. All you need is a meeting place that's big enough to accommodate all the people, with comfortable seating for the adults.

It would also be helpful to be able to store toys at the site. Church halls and community centers are good places, but if someone in the group has a large enough space in his or her home, that can be just as good. We recommend a neutral space, however, so that one child doesn't have an advantage over the others because the meeting is held in his or her home.

If you have the time, we highly recommend joining or starting a play group. In addition to providing your child with playmates on a regular basis, it is a way to expose him or her to other cultures. You can do this by inviting people from other ethnic groups to join your play group.

Just as in day care, children in play groups can use dolls, pictures, books, and photographs of one another to learn about racial difference and similarities. Parents can help them by pointing out differences in hair texture and color, eye color and shape, and skin color. Learning these characteristics early helps children to understand their racial identity.

A play group with other Black children can be an opportunity to reinforce the children's racial identity. William Bumpus, a college professor and attorney, and his wife, Gayle King, a local television newscaster, have two lovely children, Kirby and William. They both play with our daughter Dotteanna and occasionally exchange ethnically oriented gifts. One day Bill brought his children over with two black dolls for our daughter.

It was a joy to see the three of them hold, cuddle, care for, and play with the dolls. The positive feelings and sense of ethnic pride the children experienced help foster healthy self-esteem and positive racial identity.

Black professionals must make time in their busy schedules to ensure that their children are exposed to other Black children and to positive cultural experiences.

BLACK IMAGES IN THE MARKETPLACE

Even grocery shopping provides opportunities for you to expose your child to positive Black images. It has been a long time coming, but today it is possible to find a few household products with pictures of Black people on the labels. Choosing these products can help boost your children's self-image. If this seems to be stretching the point, consider this: Why do manufacturers put pictures of people on their containers? Because they hope people will identify with the images and buy the products. And that is exactly what happens. People *do* identify with those images.

From the first time we took our baby girl shopping with us, we looked for products with pictures of Black people on the containers. Now, at age two, our daughter still looks for the brand of toilet paper we usually buy because it has a picture of a cute Black baby on the wrapper. Cereals and diapers are among the products that often feature Black models on their containers. All things being equal, we urge you to favor such products whenever possible. It can serve as positive reinforcement to Black children that their image is attractive.

Finding products with appropriate Black images is only part of the problem. Using such products in this society sometimes demands considerable courage, especially for small children. The way our daughter's day-care staff reacted to the child's Santa Claus sweater shows what children can expect when they choose Black images. It takes as much courage to have the only Black doll in class as it does to *be* the only Black child in class. It is important to remind our children that they and their Black dolls are attractive in spite of what anyone might say or imply.

It is all part of helping them to face society confident in the knowledge that they are *different and wonderful.*

A GREAT OPPORTUNITY

It's easy to be overwhelmed by your infant or toddler. After all, you are completely responsible for the survival of a human being who, in the beginning, doesn't even know how to speak. And with all there is to teach him or her, it is tempting to panic and leave everything to chance. But here is a reassuring fact: Infants and toddlers present us not only with enormous responsibilities but also with equally impressive opportunities. For instance, as we said earlier, they have a lot to learn, but they are naturally great learners. As Black parents, we can take advantage of their natural learning process to mold them into self-respecting Black people. The toddler years offer the best opportunity that we will have to teach our children that they are indeed different and wonderful and have them accept it for life as an undeniable fact.

PART II

Outside the Garden Gates:

THE WORLD AT LARGE

Chapter Seven

FERTILIZING THE SOIL FOR GROWTH: RACIAL IDENTITY IN THE SCHOOL-AGE CHILD

As your children reach school age, you need to be aware that there is a direct connection between their self-esteem, their racial identity, and their academic achievement. Simply put, the better your child feels about himself or herself as a Black person, the more likely he or she is to succeed in school. Negative feelings about being a Black person can rob your child of the concentration necessary to succeed academically. Frank's case illustrates just one of the forms this problem can take.

Ten-year-old Frank is the only Black child in his class in a private school. His parents have blue-collar jobs and work hard to keep their only child in a private school where he can get "the best" education. All of his classmates are middle- to upper-middle class. Most have computers at home, many spend summers in Europe, they dress in designer clothes, and they always have plenty of money to spend.

Frank believes that his classmates are wealthy because they are White, and that he is poor because he is Black. He expresses strong negative feelings about being Black. Feeling alienated from his peers, he is unable to relate well to them or to concentrate on his work. Although he has tested as "gifted," his work is not up to his potential, and his teachers are considering putting him in a learning-disabled class. He was brought into therapy because he had started to steal money and other belongings from his classmates.

Frank's case offers an extreme and visible example of the kind of pressures that Black youngsters encounter when they face American society through school. Usually the experiences are more subtle, but their impact is just as great. In this chapter, we want to help you identify these negative elements or influences and to show you how they work on your children, how you can help them to face the challenges, and what you can do to reduce some of the threats.

FRUSTRATION TOLERANCE

There is a certain level of frustration associated with learning. Even the most intelligent child finds some new information harder to grasp than do other children. Success depends on the child's ability to tolerate and overcome the frustration that arises when things do not come as easily as he or she would like. To put it another way, if children feel confident about their abilities, their *frustration tolerance* is higher.

Eva has to be able to question her teacher without feeling stupid in front of her White peers, or appearing "uncool" in front of her Black classmates. Earlier we talked about the fact that many Blacks go through life unable to ask questions in the presence of Whites for fear of looking stupid. School is where this fear usually begins. It takes confidence and high self-esteem for a child to admit that he or she did not understand what the teacher just said. Fellow students, and some teachers, often treat such admissions as signs of stupidity. For example, one teacher had a reputation for saying, supposedly jokingly, "Okay, once more for the retarded ones . . ." before repeating anything.

Ray has to realize that because some of his classmates might be able to do something better than he can, it doesn't mean that they are better than he is. It might simply mean that they were better prepared at home or are better able to perform a certain task. In the course of learning and discovering new things, Ray will likely find things at which he can excel and feel good about.

As we have stressed in previous chapters, children learn the qualities that contribute to high frustration tolerance from their parents' examples. Compliment your children on their *efforts* as they begin to master tasks more easily. Knowing that their efforts are recognized and appreciated gives them the incentive and the confidence to continue striving, which leads to improved results. Children then take these positive experiences and attitudes with them to school.

RACIAL IDENTITY

Your child's racial identity—the knowledge and appreciation of the fact that he or she is a Black person—contributes to self-image and self-esteem. Because frustration tolerance, which affects academic performance, is tied to self-esteem, racial identity can also play a part in academic results. All of this is influenced by the competition that children encounter in school.

Nine-year-old Malcolm related this story to us. He had just finished his work and was taking it up to his teacher, when at the same time, another child, whom Malcolm described as "blond," approached the teacher. The teacher told Malcolm, "You couldn't be finished with your work already. Go back and check it over." The teacher then took the White student's paper and began to check it. Malcolm felt that the teacher trusted the White student more than she trusted him. His level of motivation declined, and he subsequently began to turn in incomplete work and had to finish many of his assignments at home. This in turn prompted his teacher to send complaint reports home to Malcolm's parents.

Because Malcolm felt that his race was a factor in the teacher's response to him, his racial identity and, thus, his self-image were being subverted, consciously or unconsciously, by his teacher. The result was his diminished academic performance.

Black children enter school with a dual burden: to succeed academically, and to sustain a sense of self-worth as a Black person in a largely White culture that is often inattentive to, or disapproving of, their culture and their Blackness. Only a deep confidence in who they are will allow Black children the freedom to concentrate on academic endeavors. Let's look at the school experience in more detail to see how it can actually work against Black children.

THE SCHOOL EXPERIENCE FOR BLACKS

In school, Black children will come in contact with other children with whom they will begin to formally learn about their world—how they fit into it now, and what their future place in it might be. We would all like to think that the experience will be equal for Black and White children, but in fact it will be quite different. Whereas school will probably serve to affirm and build White children's self-image and self-esteem, Black children risk having their perception of themselves lowered by their experiences in school.

For instance, when Mark, a White child, enrolls in school, the quality of education notwithstanding, over the years he will learn something about the great founding fathers of his country and the society they created. He will see the images and learn the names of great men, such as Columbus, Washington, Jefferson, Franklin, and a galaxy of luminaries through the present. He will be able to look in the mirror and, even without thinking about it, feel good about himself because he can *see* the connection between himself and his illustrious ancestors.

For Arthur, a Black child in Mark's classroom, the experience will be entirely different. When he looks in the mirror, he will probably not think of great statesmen, explorers, or scientists. Instead, he will probably recall that his ancestors, in all likelihood, began their history in this country as slaves, and that for centuries his people have occupied the bottom portions of society. He will come to hear people who look like himself referred to as "minorities," "the Black underclass," "lower class," or "underprivileged." And those are just the *benign* terms.

Worst of all, Arthur will probably grow up believing that the perceived differences between his past and Mark's are objective differences that reflect historic fact. It will be years, if ever, before he comes to realize that the "history" he is learning is at best subjective, often distorted, and in some instances outright false.

Just as important as what Arthur will hear about himself as a Black person is what he will *not* hear. For example, the many Black American contributions to this country's scientific discoveries, cultural development, and exploration, if mentioned, will be as little more than footnotes to the rest of American history.

Much of the racial bias that Black children sense only vaguely when they are young will begin to be articulated and demonstrated in school in ways that become clearer as children become better able to understand them. In other words, in school Black children experience firsthand the problem of institutionalized racism.

For example, eleven-year-old Stewart returned from a class trip to Washington, D.C., glowing about all that he had seen and learned. He was disappointed, however, about his teacher's reaction to a question he had asked about Benjamin Banneker, the Black mathematician, astronomer, and inventor who made significant contributions to the plan of the city including assisting in surveying the site. In preparation for the trip, Stewart's father had told him all about Banneker, and Stewart was proud and anxious to relay the information to his teacher and his class. The teacher's response was to dismiss Stewart with a remark to the effect that there was nothing in Washington, D.C., about Banneker. If Benjamin Banneker had been given the prominence he deserved in American history, no school trip to the nation's capital would be complete without mention of him. Stewart was denied an opportunity to participate in an important part of history that truly interested him, and to express his pride in the accomplishment of a Black American.

Because our children enter school at such a disadvantage, we need to explore ways to prepare them for the experience and to help them find ways to overcome its negative effects.

THE SCHOOL ENVIRONMENT

For a school to effectively serve the needs of students from a variety of racial backgrounds, it must give those children a chance to integrate those things that are important to them and to their racial identity into their learning experience. Black children can only be helped by learning about the significant contributions that Blacks have made to society. For instance, the following Black Americans either invented or made major contributions to the development of some everyday conveniences and entertainments we take for granted:

John Love: the pencil sharpener
Thomas J. Martin: the overhead sprinkler
Lewis Latimere: a type of electric lamp
Granville T. Woods: the roller coaster
Leonard Bailey: the baby crib
Joseph Hunter Dickenson: the phonograph
William Purvis: the fountain pen
W. Johnson: the eggbeater
Alexander Miles: an elevator door operating mechanism
Joseph Smith: the lawn sprinkler

It would be a simple matter to look around a classroom or a school, identify examples of Blacks' contributions, and incorporate those facts into the children's lessons.

If a school is to be conducive to learning, it must focus on the children's strengths, not their shortcomings, and reward their positive behavior. Think back to what we said when we discussed reinforcement. The same things apply here. It's all too easy to become so obsessed with "how bad kids are today" that we fail to see when they do good. Here is an example in which a school's administration missed an opportunity to promote something positive among their students.

In a small suburban town with a growing Black population, many White families have either moved away or sent their children to private schools. As a result, the majority of students in the school system are Black, but the teaching staff remains predominantly White. There is a great deal of tension in the town and the school about the situation. Some of it shows up as an uneasiness between teachers and students.

The junior high school held a talent show, but several of the Black students were not allowed to perform because of a rule that students under any kind of disciplinary action could not participate. Naturally this ban only contributed to the tension in the school.

What the administration failed to understand was that the performance was an opportunity for some of the children who were not doing well academically to do something that would make them feel good about themselves. They could then build on that experience in the future. Instead, for that entire year, those youngsters had nothing to feel good about. For many who felt their culture was being undermined, this would have been a great occasion to express their cultural validity. Denying them permission to perform was an unproductive and punitive approach to teaching them about responsibility.

Compare the preceding example to the following one, in which a school system stresses the positive in their students. In New Haven, Connecticut, Dr. James Comer of the Yale University Child Study Center has developed and incorporated a system in the city's schools whereby teachers and students welcome new students and accentuate their positive behaviors. For instance, existing students introduce themselves to new students and try to make them feel at ease. This is only a small aspect of the program, which is intended to facilitate overall academic achievement. Results have been encouraging. Academic achievement scores at the schools that implemented the program have steadily improved. In Chicago, Marva Collins has brought national acclaim to Westside Preparatory School and in New Jersey, principal Joe Clark used discipline to create major changes in Eastside High School.

Even the most well-adjusted child needs a supportive atmosphere in order to achieve the best he or she can. But we all know that some children will forever be square pegs in round holes. A child's strength might lie outside the mainstream. For such children, it might be necessary to find some form of alternative education, such as the Montessori method, which is geared toward preschool children. Instead of following a rigid routine, children are allowed more freedom to pursue their own interests. There are private schools at all grade levels that focus on helping a child to discover his or her strengths and to use those strengths to facilitate learning.

In New York City there are private schools that focus on Black history as an integral part of the curriculum. The Muslims in particular are to be commended for their emphasis on building self-esteem in their students. If your child has difficulty in a traditional school environment, it might be helpful for you to look into some form of alternative education.

Your local board of education probably has a list of schools called "Out of District Placements." Many of these schools have more structured programs for children with severe conduct problems who have difficulty adjusting in public schools. They tend to serve children with emotional or behavior problems, and they are usually free. The list might also include private schools that charge tuition fees; however, in some instances subsidies are available. By law, if your child is having difficulty, and the public school isn't meeting his or her needs, the school system is responsible for placing your child in an alternative education setting that meets those needs—more about this later.

PREDOMINANTLY WHITE SCHOOLS

Black Americans who become economically successful face a unique dilemma when it comes to their children's education. The homes that sometimes come with their improved economic status are usually in predominantly White neighborhoods or towns. Consequently, their children become part of a tiny "Black minority" in otherwise all-White schools.

Occasionally you will find an administration that is sensitive to the children's needs. For example, a suburban junior high school has a rule that only students of the school can attend school dances. The parents of one of two Black girls who were students there (no Black boys attended) informed the principal that this rule could create a difficulty for the girls. The principal agreed to waive the rule for those two girls. It is important to communicate with school officials about whatever concerns your children have. Because so many problems stem from lack of awareness, sometimes just raising an issue is all it takes to generate potential solutions to a problem.

In many instances, however, there is so little concern or awareness about Black culture or the needs of Black students in predominantly White schools that Black children come under a great deal of pressure to conform to cultural standards that are foreign to them.

The clear advantage of most predominantly White schools is

that they usually have a larger resource base and consequently can offer a higher quality of education. Some school systems unofficially perform studies to determine what constitutes an "average" student to insure that their schools produce no average students. This might not be fair, but it's done to give their students a competitive edge.

Parents who wish to take advantage of above-average quality education must also find ways to provide the Black cultural ties and role models that their children need to affirm their racial identity in such an environment. We talked about finding role models for your children in chapter 3.

Predominantly Black Schools

The chief advantage of predominantly Black schools is that children who attend them are surrounded by elements of Black culture that can affirm their racial identity. Music, dance, speech patterns, hairstyles, and dress styles all reflect familiar cultural values. The children see role models in principals, teachers, and other school professionals, and the racial component often seen in integrated settings is usually absent from academic competition.

Unfortunately, most predominantly Black schools arise out of negative rather than positive circumstances. Most of them are in blighted urban areas abandoned by the White population. Starving for resources and beset with the problems of urban decline, these schools seldom manage to realize the benefits of their integral Black environment.

Another negative associated with predominantly Black schools is that children who attend them might not learn to function and compete as they must do in an integrated society. We believe, therefore, that children need to be exposed to an integrated environment to learn to cope with our diverse society.

Integrated Schools

The average Black child is bicultural and bidialectical. This means that he or she is equipped to function in two cultures that are so different from each other that they exhibit linguistic differences. This ability is a strength and a gift. A Black child's inability to adapt to the so-called White mainstream and his or her preference for a Black environment should not be seen as a deficit. After all, would we say that the average White child is at a deficit if he or she cannot adapt to life in Watts or in Harlem? Probably not. Most Blacks and Whites are naturally more comfortable in their respective cultures. But integration is necessary if American society as a whole is to function effectively. Schools are still our best hopes for effecting integration in society.

Research and clinical findings have shown that when Black and White children work toward a common goal with adequate and equally supportive supervision they tend to respect one another's differences. Cooperative learning teams can also be helpful in fostering friendship and cooperation, and in relieving racial tension in integrated schools. A cooperative learning team is a group of students assigned to work on a task; they must cooperate in order to complete it successfully. For example, let's say a teacher gives each of five children ten pieces of a fifty-piece puzzle and instructs them to cooperate in solving the puzzle. A group of Black and White children given such a task could discuss what it was like to have to cooperate, and perhaps gain some appreciation of one another's strengths.

The main advantage to integrated schools is obvious: They give both Blacks and Whites a chance to learn to understand one another and improve their chances of being able to function together as adults. Of course, keep in mind that in order to obtain quality integration, including a culturally relevant curriculum and experiences, you'll need to make your interests and desires known. Again, if you feel that this is a desirable goal for your children, then it's worth pursuing school integration. Of course, your financial situation will partly determine whether integration is an option for you. We live where we can afford to live, and that determines where our children will go to school. But if you have occasion to change residences, you might want to seek opportunities to get your child in an integrated setting.

Another way you can approach integration is to give your political support to magnet schools (schools established to be multicultural). Located in areas where they attract good students from different areas and different ethnic backgrounds, these schools are particularly well equipped to offer your child a quality education.

It bears repeating that as we evolve in an integrated society and in integrated schools, it becomes increasingly important that we make sure our children receive sufficient exposure to their Black cultural roots. A Black child who has a strong positive home environment and extracurricular support is able to go into an integrated environment and retain his or her positive racial identity and self-esteem.

Ten-year-old Lewis is such a person. He has a strong sense of ethnic identity. He has good rapport with all his neighbors—Black and White. He goes out of his way to stop in and say hello. Lewis also demonstrates leadership potential. One summer he arranged a nature walk for neighborhood families. It was well organized. He had maps, displays, games, and reading material. He made the afternoon interesting for children and adults alike. They were more than willing to pay the small fee he charged. His confident interaction with a variety of people is a joy to see.

ACADEMICS

Eight-year-old James came home from school angry. "How come Black people never do anything important?" he asked his parents. In a class discussion that day, the teacher had listed some of the contributions of different ethnic groups to American culture. There was no mention of African-Americans' contribution. James's parents were appalled. They lived in what they thought was an enlightened community, and they had taken it for granted that James was learning about Blacks in school.

In a meeting with the school's principal, James's parents discovered that there was little representation of Blacks in the curriculum. A tour of the classroom revealed no images of Black Americans anywhere. The teacher's explanation was that Blacks were "fawned over" in February—Black History Month.

James's parents calmly informed the principal that they believed that their son needed exposure to information and other representations of his culture in school in order to optimize his learning experience. They recommended books and provided posters for James's classroom to begin to enhance the image of Black Americans.

As reflected in textbooks, many schools' curricula contain few representations of Black Americans and their contributions to history. There has not been a sufficiently deep exploration of Blacks' achievements to fully offset the misrepresentations and omissions that enshroud them. This condition prevents our children from learning about their own heritage, and it also prevents non-Blacks from learning the truth about their Black counterparts. Myths and stereotypes thus flourish.

In this atmosphere, a child who chooses to study, discuss, report on, or even mention a Black figure in American history is at considerable risk of not being taken seriously by his peers and his teachers. A sensitive teacher who is aware of the risk the child is taking will use such an opportunity to introduce other figures from Black history. For instance, people such as W. E. B. Du Bois, poet, author, and historian; Madame C. J. Walker, a successful Black businesswoman; Mary McLeod Bethune, educator and presidential adviser; and Asa Philip Randolph, labor leader and civil rights advocate, all present fascinating portraits of Black Americans who accomplished great things.

James was lucky. He had parents who were alert to his needs and conscientious enough to do something about them. They were also knowledgeable and comfortable enough to approach the school and *assert* James's right to have his culture represented in the curriculum.

You don't have to be an expert to make a difference in your child's education. We can't overestimate the value of parental involvement. As indicated earlier, this might mean providing input to fill the gaps that frequently exist when it comes to educating Black children about their culture. This need can be identified by staying informed. Simply ask your child about his or her school experiences. Only by communicating with your child can you find out whether the school is meeting his or her needs in a progressive and sensitive way. For example, you can look at how the teacher presents in class the value of having a variety of ethnic groups that contribute to our society.

Eleven-year-old Keith came home from school and said his

teacher had asked him to cut out newspaper stories and pictures about recent drug arrests in the area. Because Keith is the only Black child in his class, his parents are always careful to find out from him how certain material is presented to the class. The drug assignment raised a red flag in their minds. They questioned Keith about the class discussion. He said that the teacher had mentioned that there is a lot of drugs in the big cities where Blacks and Hispanics live.

Keith's father sent the teacher an article dealing with anti-Black bias in the press. In a subsequent discussion, the teacher denied making the remark. She was offended because she felt that Keith's father, by sending her the article, was implying that she was biased. Keith's father explained that the article was just a way to remind her that whatever the children collected in their clippings should probably be viewed with reservations. The teacher eventually came to see the father's point of view. She offered to read the article to her class when they discussed the ones the children had collected.

The simple act of asking your children, "What did you do in school today?" can be one of the most effective ways of keeping in touch with their learning experience. To be effective, it has to be more than just a rhetorical question. You have to sit down with your child, ask questions, listen to the answers, and be prepared to take action if you hear something that disturbs you.

CULTURAL EVENTS

Another important component of the educational experience for Black children is the way Black cultural events are celebrated in school. For Blacks, perhaps the only significant cultural celebrations recognized by their schools are Black History Month and the birthday of Dr. Martin Luther King, Jr. And in a few states, the latter is not yet celebrated as a legal holiday.

These events are extremely important to the racial identity and self-image of Black children, rare occasions when they can experience the pride of seeing the accomplishments of Black Americans spotlighted. Therefore, how a school observes these events can make a difference in how Black children learn.

Black History Month, for example, can serve as a *beginning* of the recognition of Black contributions to American society. It can be the spark from which interest expands to the entire school year. Unfortunately, this does not always happen.

For instance, in chapter 3 we mentioned the student teacher who was observed pulling down pictures of Black people in her classroom at the end of Black History Month and replacing them with images of spring. None of the pictures of White heroes was touched.

As a parent, make a point to contribute something to enhance the celebration of Black culture in your child's school. You can help by providing posters, books, artwork, or anything that appeals to you to the celebration. You can even loan something from your own collection of family heirlooms.

Most schools are happy to have parents assist in the classroom. Make your presence felt regularly if you can. It will encourage teachers to include Black images in their permanent classroom displays. (Just imagine what would happen if every parent who reads this book decides to go to their child's teacher and offer literature about Black history. We would probably have the beginning of a movement to integrate Black history into the curriculum!)

BEHAVIOR PROBLEMS

A common situation that Black parents have to contend with is the perception among many school officials that Black children usually have behavior problems. It's not unusual for parents to be told that their child is *hyperactive*. Your child might bring home a report that describes his behavior as any of the following:

Runs around classroom
Inattentive
Easily distracted
Aggressive or impulsive
Hits others
Breaks materials
Overly dependent
Seeks excessive approval or attention

Needs to be close to adults—clingy
Temper tantrums
General disruption
Curses
Teases
Speaks out of turn
Daydreams
Withdrawn
Unable to join group activities
Negative
Oppositional
Refuses to participate
Cuts class
Apathetic
Passive

These symptoms all indicate that a child is having problems in school but might also be associated with a child's reaction to racism. Many children respond inappropriately to racism because they simply do not know how to react or that they have a choice in how they react.

For example, twelve-year-old Lawrence frequently went to school wearing a shirt that had a red, black, and green map of Africa across the front. On more than one occasion, one of his teachers, who happened to be White, made comments that Lawrence perceived as negative about the shirt. For instance, she would ask, "Why do you wear that shirt so often?" In a subsequent class, the teacher chose to show a film about Africa that depicted bare-breasted women and men with spears. When the mostly White class laughed at the scenes, Lawrence became upset and started to leave the class. The teacher told him he could not leave without a pass, but he left anyway. He was later disciplined for his conduct.

It was never determined whether the teacher's intent was malicious. Lawrence, however, connected the teacher's comment about his shirt and the fact that there was no academic reason for showing the film (this "class" was his homeroom), and he was embarrassed and offended by the experience. He accepted his punishment in silence, because he did not know how to express his feelings about the racism he perceived. He was finally able to discuss the incident openly after spending some time in therapy.

Non-Black school officials seldom appreciate or acknowledge how prevalent racial discrimination, even racial attack, is in their schools, and how deeply such discrimination can affect the victims. Often these incidents remain buried due to the victims' own desire to ignore racism because dealing with it can be so uncomfortable. As a result, school personnel do not always explore the racial angle as a credible factor in children's behavior problems. Therefore, it is important for you to ask certain questions if your child exhibits the symptoms mentioned above. For instance, school officials should answer the following questions for you before any drastic remedial action is attempted:

1. How long has this behavior problem existed?
2. When does the behavior usually take place?
3. What events usually lead to the behavior?
4. Is another person part of the problem?
5. What solutions have been tried?

The answers to these questions can be helpful in identifying possible racial aspects of the problem. Obviously, the sooner the situation is brought to your attention, the better your chances for dealing with it effectively. Therefore, schools should notify you promptly when there is a problem.

After a problem has been pinpointed, you can begin to address it. If racism proves to be a factor, you already have the tools to help your child. Think back to our discussion of assertive behavior in chapter 3. Remind your child that *assertiveness* is the most effective way to deal with an interpersonal problem. It might be helpful for you to *model* an effective response and to *reinforce* the behavior whenever the child exhibits it.

Athletic competition is a popular outlet for Black children who become overly competitive with non-Blacks in the classroom. It is particularly effective because when children participate in cooperative endeavors, such as in the attempt to win a game, they almost automatically develop greater respect for one another.

For example, John showed a great deal of anger and resentment toward Asians. He began to talk admiringly about hanging out with a neighborhood gang that competed strongly with an Asian gang. Alarmed, John's parents felt an urgent need to find something to take his attention away from gang activity. They enrolled him in a soccer program at a local boys' club. The program included children from Black, White, Hispanic, and Asian backgrounds. John developed a much greater tolerance for the non-Blacks on his team. He tended to generalize less about Cambodians, whom he once distrusted, and eventually became quite friendly with a Cambodian on the team.

Of course, positive behavior should be reinforced as promptly as possible. Anything that the child likes or appreciates can be a reward, even something as simple as a surprise pizza party, as long as the child gets the message that what he did was appreciated.

STANDARDIZED TESTING

As long as standardized tests have been in use, they have been a source of concern to Blacks. These tests have been used by biased, self-serving mental health professionals to suggest that Blacks are less intelligent than Whites. Even in the absence of such overt attempts to discredit Blacks, standardized tests are still suspect in what they tell us about intelligence. Furthermore, their effects on Blacks are still considered to be negative.

Specifically, the tests are considered to be biased toward White middle-class values. A child's results might reflect his or her practice, motivation, or reading levels. The test taker's rapport with the examiner has also been shown to impact scores. If Sara comes from a middle-class home, reads well, has been taking practice tests in areas related to IQ, and has been promised a new bike if she does well on the test, she will probably appear to be exceptionally intelligent! A child without these advantages wouldn't fare as well.

Of course, none of the above factors *proves* intelligence. Standardized test scores indicate past or future achievement, but they do not indicate *innate intelligence.* Yet they are often used to "track" Black children and place them in special education classes that do not provide an adequate education. Children often come to believe that because they are in such classes they don't have to achieve on a high level. Nothing is expected of them and, naturally, underachievement becomes a self-fulfilling prophesy.

In response to this situation, the Association of Black Psychologists has supported parents who do not want to have their children tested. In one California case (Larry P. vs. Wilson Riles), a court ruled that IQ tests could no longer be used to place children in special education classes.

Sometimes testing and special placement are necessary in order for children to receive the individualized instruction they need. The goal should always be to build on the child's strengths, work on areas of need, and "mainstream" the child back into regular classes as quickly as possible.

If testing becomes an issue in your child's education, you have the right to obtain independent outside testers. You can also choose in-school advocates who will insure that the process works best for your child.

TEACHERS

A teacher, Black or White, who is going to teach Black children should first examine his or her own attitudes about race. He or she should be comfortable enough with the child's race to be able to communicate a genuine sense of feeling and caring.

A teacher who comfortably and routinely refers to Blacks as "second-class citizens" is an example of someone who is not suitable to teach Black children. It is difficult to imagine how someone with such a perception of Blacks can avoid having a negative impact on Black students.

A teacher's *perception* of a student leads directly to an *expectation* of the student. If the teacher perceives the child as intelligent, then he or she will expect above-average work from the child. A child's *performance* tends to mirror the expectations of his or her teachers.

For instance, a young woman recalled her childhood in the segregated South. She told of her Black teacher pointing to a group of White children and saying, "See those smart White kids? Next year [integration] you'll have to compete with them. They're going to beat the pants off you." The woman said that the next year she started school terrified and received poor grades. Later in the year, when she discovered that the White children were not geniuses, her grades recovered and she was able to excel.

As we've said before, your child's teachers can be most effective if they have some sensitivity and awareness of the stresses your child experiences as a Black person in an education system that emphasizes White values. It is surprising how often that awareness is lacking.

One of the authors was consulting at an exclusive private school. Dr. King's birthday was approaching, and she was pleased to hear a predominantly White choir practicing a song for a program in his honor. Then a line of the song caught her attention: "He helped all the chocolate people . . ." The author walked up to the door and peered in. The teacher turned around and saw her. The next time the choir came to the line, the teacher tried to say something other than "chocolate," but the children, not knowing what was happening, kept singing "chocolate." Embarrassed, the teacher looked helplessly from the door to the choir until the song ended. The incident would have been amusing if it were not so sad.

It was sad for two reasons: Until the moment the author looked in, the teacher did not seem to have considered the implication of singing those words to an audience that included Black children. Second, she did not seem aware that Dr. King's contribution was to *all* people, not just to Black Americans. Both sensitivity and awareness were lacking.

In the classroom, this lack of sensitivity can have a more immediate impact on your child's academic success. A common complaint we hear from Black children is that teachers fail to call on them even when the children think they have the right answer. Often the child will resort to blurting out the answer, thereby compounding the problem because the teacher now feels he or she has a good reason to ignore or to punish the child. Marcia's experience illustrates this lack of sensitivity.

Marcia brought home a note from her teacher explaining that she was "overenthusiastic" in class. Essentially, if Marcia saw another student having trouble with his or her work, she would sometimes leave her desk to help the person. In all likelihood the same actions by a White child would be seen as supportive or leadership behavior, not as disruptive as in Marcia's case.

This type of reaction to children who are creative and enthusiastic can stifle their creativity. There are many constructive ways that a teacher can accommodate a "overenthusiastic" child, or one who is so bright that he or she is bored by the class routine. For instance, Marcia might have been assigned to work with children who were having trouble. A child who tends to blurt out answers might be allowed to write the answers on the board as they are called. Teachers who are sensitive to the predicament of Black children in school look for such opportunities.

It is very painful to see a teacher resolve a conflict between a Black and a White child against the Black child even when there is evidence to support the Black child's position. Black children often complain about this injustice. One of the authors witnessed such an incident when she was in a classroom to observe one of her clients, Cheryl, a gifted child who was having serious conflicts with Kay, a White girl in her class. At one point, during the observation, the author called Cheryl over to provide some feedback on her behavior. As soon as Cheryl got up, Kay took her seat. When Cheryl returned, she asked assertively for her seat back, as the author had instructed her to do. Kay snapped, "What did you say? You can't talk that way to me." The incident took place at the back of the room.

The teacher, who had seen nothing of what led up to Kay's remark, called Kay up to her. "Why don't you come and sit up here next to me," she said and put her arm around Kay. It took a lot of coaxing and angry denial before the teacher acknowledged that her actions were unfair to Cheryl.

Children have a deep sense of fairness, and if they feel that they are being treated unfairly, particularly by authority figures such as teachers, they develop a distrust that makes it difficult for them to relate to such people. Obviously a situation like the one Cheryl faced would inhibit their ability to learn effectively.

PEER RELATIONSHIPS

For better or for worse, children learn from one another almost as much as they learn from their teachers. We have already discussed the power of peer group influence and how you can use it to help you model appropriate behavior for your young child. As your child gets older, it becomes increasingly difficult for you to influence his or her peer relationships. But there are some peer group facts you'll want to keep in mind because they directly relate to racial identity and academic performance.

Peter recalls that as a boy he used to be embarrassed to be seen taking books home. He would leave his books at school, walk home with his friends, and then hurry back to get his books before the building closed. When this became impractical, he undertook a successful campaign to convince his friends that a person can enjoy books and still be "cool." Like all children, Peter needed to feel that he "belonged" in his peer group. The value of his education was never far from his mind, however.

Among Black children, boys in particular tend to be reinforced for excellence in athletics rather than in academics. If they are good in both athletics and academics, their academic excellence is often ignored or played down in favor of athletics. This is particularly true among peer group members. It is often a challenge for parents to keep their children focused on academics when the peer group's focus is elsewhere, but there are some steps you can take to increase your influence in such cases.

For instance, try to identify other children in the peer group that you can point in the desired direction so that your child doesn't feel isolated. Have your child and other children from the peer group participate in some projects together, and incorporate some academics. For example, invest in educational games that they can play together. Encourage them to read books on subjects that you know interest them, such as sports. Get a book about their favorite athlete. Ask them questions about the athlete. If they know the answer, reinforce them with small rewards. Be flexible. Allow your children time to "hang out" with their groups, and at other times insist that they focus on their studies. Parents can provide space in their home for their child and his or her peer group to meet. A den or even a clubhouse in the backyard would be a good meeting place.

THE PARENTS' ROLE

In the end, as parents you still have more to do with your child's success in school than does any teacher or even the child's peer group. This is true because your child develops the self-esteem and positive racial identity that will contribute to academic excellence at home.

Thus, you always want to avoid situations such as the following: A young man recalled that his father often said, "I always got punished more than any of the other kids in my family because I was the darkest of them. That's why you are going to catch hell—'cause you're the darkest in this family." Though still embarrassed to talk about it, the young man admitted he put "bleaching" cream on his face to lighten his skin. He would then play ball in the sun and end up with even darker skin.

More appropriate is the action of the mother who collected poems by Black poets, such as Langston Hughes, that present positive, supportive images of Blackness, and gave them to her daughter. Another effective exercise that you can practice with your children is to have them complete in writing the statement, "Being Black means . . ." in as many ways as they can. The exercise will reveal to you and to your child areas where he or she is particularly weak or strong in his or her racial identity.

ADVOCATING FOR YOUR CHILDREN

Even if you succeed early in giving your children the self-confidence they will need in school, your job is not done. Even under the best circumstances your child will still need your continuing support to do the best he or she can academically.

To many Black parents, the administration of a school is a mysterious and intimidating process. Some administrators like that perception. It makes their lives much easier if they don't have to deal with dissatisfied parents. But from everything we've said so far, you can see that your Black child's success in school depends very much on your intervention in the process. Therefore, it is essential that you overcome the intimidation. Here are some steps to take.

Know your rights. In most states literature is available to inform you of the rights of you and your school-age children. For example, the New York State education department publishes a booklet titled *Your Child's Right to an Education: A Guide for Parents of Handicapped Children in New York State.* It states that any child who receives special education services, whether for speech, mental retardation, or learning disability, is classified as handicapped. This sounds a bit extreme, but don't let such terminology deter you from obtaining the assistance that is your child's right. Most states have a similar resource guide.

If your child is having difficulty and such a program becomes necessary, there are steps you can take to make sure he or she receives the proper attention. First of all, make sure your child is evaluated properly by someone who is able to establish a rapport with him or her. Second, make sure an Individualized Education Program (IEP) is developed for your child. An IEP should at least do the following:

- Evaluate your child's present circumstances (social and emotional status in the classroom, performance level in different areas)
- Describe the areas in which your child needs assistance; state specific problems to be addressed and how they will be resolved
- Set goals and state when they should be reached
- State what kind of regular classroom experience the child will have if he or she is removed from the classroom
- Specify when the child should be able to return to the mainstream
- Provide that you be informed about your child's progress

The purpose of the IEP or any similar program should be obvious: It can prevent your child from being pushed out of sight and out of mind. By getting involved at the beginning and staying informed about what is happening to your child, you can make sure such a program is working for him or her.

Familiarize yourself with the following rights that may be available to you and your children wherever you live:

1. If your child is unable to attend school for some reason, the school district must provide education for him or

her in the home. The same is true if the child is confined to a hospital.

2. If your child is suspended, you have a right to know why. What behavior led to the suspension? (The behavior must have endangered the health and safety of the child or others in the classroom.) As a parent, you are entitled to a hearing concerning the suspension. If your child is suspended too frequently to receive the minimum instruction required by the state, the school system must provide alternative education for him or her.
3. You have the right to confidentiality. The school should not show your child's record to anyone without your permission. They must keep a list of all staff members and outside agencies that have had access to the records.
4. Records are available to you upon request. They are also available to the child when he or she reaches age eighteen.
5. You can challenge any decision made about your child.
6. All children have the same rights and those rights are to be protected by the school.
7. If necessary, you have a right to an impartial hearing with the commissioner of education if you don't agree with a decision made at a lower level.

It would be difficult to list all the rights of parents and children in all states. Please take the time to obtain specific information about your state and local board of education policies and familiarize yourself with them. They can make a difference in whether or not your child receives a good education. A good place to start is with a teacher with whom you are comfortable.

Talk to someone who has been through it. Talk to other parents whose children have gone through your school system. Find out what problems they had and how they overcame them. Find out which teachers are sensitive to the needs of Black children and which are not. In many instances you have the right to choose your child's teacher if there is more than one for the same grade.

Consult with an outside professional. If your child faces a situation, such as disciplinary action, that is more than you are capable of handling, consult with a professional. Psychologists, school counselors, and social workers, for example, can advise you on how to deal with problems. If the situation is serious enough, you have the right to have a professional appear with you at important school meetings.

Develop a rapport with the school officials. Nothing beats open communications to enhance the education process. In many instances, you will find that teachers and administrators are quite responsive to your child's needs. As we have said before, one of the biggest problems in education is lack of awareness. When reasonable people become aware of your needs, a reasonable accommodation can result.

Make your presence known around the school. It will directly influence the way teachers as well as other children perceive your child. For instance, a mother, noting the lack of Black images in her son's classroom, took it upon herself to find pictures of Black people who had made major contributions to American history. The teacher subsequently noticed a distinct difference in the attitude of White children toward Blacks.

Get involved in school programs or organizations. Join organizations such as the PTO (Parent-Teacher Organization) or PTA (Parent-Teacher Association). They are good places to meet people who are active in education issues and aware of those that might be important to your child. Find out how these organizations work and make your influence felt in them. You can learn a great deal from participating, and at the same time teach your child about responsible citizenship.

Chapter Eight

AT THE CROSSROADS OF THE GARDEN PATH: ADOLESCENTS AND RACIAL IDENTITY

WHAT IS ADOLESCENCE?

Adolescence is the transition period between childhood and young adulthood and covers roughly ages thirteen through seventeen. Young people at this stage of development experience biological processes that subject them to considerable emotional and physical changes. The appearance of facial and pubic hair, breast development in girls, voice change in boys, and sexual responses are just a few of the powerful transformations that take place in adolescents. Confusion and insecurity about their changing identity—who they are and who they're going to be—are common feelings among teenagers.

Along with the physical and emotional changes, young people face outside pressures to conform to the adult world they are about to enter. They are expected to take on adult responsibilities: play less, work more, be serious, show sexual restraint, and plan for the future. They are expected to learn to cope with the world around them more independently, while oftentimes dealing with clingy parents who are slow to acknowledge that their "babies" are becoming adults with rights similar to their own. In addition, the adolescent's peer group expects him or her to conform to its own standards of dress, speech, and behavior.

With this flood of conflicting capabilities and expectations, it's no surprise that adolescents are frequently beset by inner turmoil and interpersonal struggle. For instance, questions about dating—with whom, when, and whether to engage in sex—tend to be foremost in their minds. Conflict between peer group loyalty and the expectations of authority figures, such as parents, teachers, or the law, commonly takes the form of rebelliousness. These experiences help to shape the adult that the adolescent is becoming. For Black youths, these experiences also help to shape their adult racial identity.

In American society, where race is often a volatile factor in issues such as dating, sex, and conflict with authority, Black adolescents face a difficult predicament: Many of the characteristics that define adolescence—rebelliousness, sexuality, peer group activity, and the crystalizing of an adult racial identity—are perceived by a disapproving White society as a challenge when expressed by Black youths. To put it another way, just by doing what comes naturally to *all* adolescents, Black youths find themselves in an "outlaw" position. In this chapter we look at how adolescence can be different and more challenging for Black youths in White America, and how you can help to smooth the passage for your youngsters.

RACIAL IDENTITY

As we've said before, the job of raising children to become self-respecting Black adults begins in the child's infancy. The sooner you begin, the better your chances of success. By adolescence, the impressions, positive or negative, your child has of Black people are about to become a part of his or her adult mentality. Adolescents are forming the racial attitudes that they'll pass on to their own children. But don't be discouraged if you are late coming to the task. You can still make a difference in your child's life.

SELF-CONCEPT IN ADOLESCENCE

As adolescents develop, their self-concept, including their racial identity, can change drastically. Different factors, issues, and people in their lives become more or less important in defining who they are.

Take dating, for instance. If your son says, "I would never date a White girl," perhaps at that time he sees choosing a Black mate as an affirmation of his racial identity. If later he should see hairstyle, speech, or fashion as a more direct expression of ethnicity, dating someone of a different race might not seem as big an issue.

Michael, a youngster attending one of our racial awareness workshops, said that when he started dating he became acutely aware of the racial attitudes around him. His parents told him he was free to date whomever he wished, but his older sister told him that if he dated a White girl he could no longer call her "sister." None of Michael's male friends socialized with White girls, and he felt they would not approve if he did. He therefore chose to date only Black women. At that point Michael identified dating choice as an expression of his Blackness.

In early adolescence youngsters are also trying to formulate their own life goals. Those goals contribute to their perception of themselves. "Should I be a lawyer, a businessperson, or a scientist?" It's possible your daughter wanted to be each of these at one time or another. Good or bad grades might easily influence a change from one career idea to another. It's quite natural for adolescents to vacillate in their interests, attitudes, and views. As goals and expectations change, self-concept might also change.

As your youngster weathers this period of rapid and drastic change, it's best not to forbid them to do something even if you disagree with their choices. It's a sure way to create rebellion. Instead, make it clear that you disagree, and state your reasons, but leave the choice up to them. Reinforce the positive, for example, the fact that they are even thinking about a career, and offer support in the rough spots.

IMAGES OF WHAT'S BEAUTIFUL

Beauty is indeed in the eye of the beholder. As Black people, we have to start taking that fact very seriously. Much of what our teenagers see as attractive—long blond hair, blue eyes, and thin noses—are characteristics of Caucasians. As a result, we often find Black youngsters making cosmetic changes in their appearance that give them a more Caucasoid appearance.

Seventeen-year-old Chelsea saved her money for a hairweave. She had also planned to get green contact lenses, but a girlfriend talked her out of it. Chelsea's mother was upset about the weave, fearing that Chelsea might be having a problem with her racial identity. (As a young girl, Chelsea was disappointed that she didn't have long blond hair.) Under the pretext of preparing her for college, Chelsea's mother persuaded her to come in for counseling. We discussed racial identity openly and told Chelsea why she was brought to see us. She insisted that she didn't have a problem with her racial identity, and said she merely wanted to look the way boys, Black and White, wanted girls to look. "Don't you want me to look attractive?" she asked.

We talked about Chelsea's childhood fantasies of blond hair and how they might have led to the choices she was making. We also helped Chelsea's mother to understand that the choice was her daughter's, and that Chelsea had to make the final decision. (It's always important to remember this when dealing with adolescents in these situations.)

Over several sessions Chelsea was able to admit that she had a problem with her ethnic identity. She cried and expressed anger at a society that did not value her physical characteristics. She continued to wear the hair weave as we worked through ethnic identity issues in counseling, but when she entered college, she decided to put extensions into her hair rather than use an actual weave.

Chelsea's experience is not unusual. It's common today to see young Black women putting even blond extensions into their hair. Not all Black women who use colored contacts or hair weaves are trying to look like Europeans. If your youngster uses cosmetics to alter his or her ethnic appearance, however, you might want to ask yourself whether racial identity issues might be at the root of the matter.

For Black youths to consider themselves attractive, they need to see us appreciating images of Black people. Black skin, curly hair, and broad noses are beautiful. We only have to learn to appreciate them. The way we foster this appreciation is by promoting Black role models of beauty in our community.

For instance, if we are going to have so-called beauty contests and debutante balls, we must define beauty based on our own perception, not European standards. This way we won't perpetuate the myth in the Black community that to be beautiful one has to have light skin and long hair. Does this mean that we are "settling for less"? Definitely not! *Beauty is not absolute.* European standards of beauty are accepted because American society is controlled by people of European descent. African standards, or Asian ones for that matter, are no less valid. Until this idea is widely promoted in our culture, it falls to individual parents to relentlessly remind young people that they are beautiful just as they are.

WRESTLING WITH STEREOTYPES

When Blacks, particularly adolescents, appear or act in ways that are not stereotypically "Black," they are often alienated by both Blacks and Whites.

Seventeen-year-old Guy, who is very intelligent and academically successful, attends a predominantly White school. He describes his dilemma: "When I go back to the neighborhood," he says, "my friends don't think I act Black because I do well in school, and I don't talk like them all the time. When I'm in school, I don't mix with the White kids because although I have very light skin, I'm obviously not White." Guy is paying a price because he does not fit the stereotype.

At the same time, stereotypical behavior, such as "bopping" or certain hand gestures, is both accepted as normal for Blacks *and* seen as a challenge to authority. For instance, Black male adolescents "bopping" down the school hallway, gesturing to one another, are almost automatically presumed to be "up to no good" and are likely to be challenged by teachers. Yet, White youngsters who wear "punk rock" clothes and hairstyles are viewed as going through a normal phase of development and are tolerated.

To foster a constructive relationship between Black adolescents and authority figures such as teachers, it's essential that such figures look beyond the stereotypes and deal with Black teenagers as expressing another way of being. By responding to them at that level, it's possible to exert a positive influence on their development.

ACCEPTING DIVERSITY AMONG OURSELVES

Black adolescents must also be taught to shun the stereotypical idea that as Black Americans we must all behave in a certain way in order to be seen as acceptably "Black." This idea gives rise to the lack of acceptance experienced by Guy.

Among Black teenagers in school, we often see a split based on not only socioeconomic differences but also stylistic differences. In one high school there are two Black groups with distinctly different orientations. One tends to be conservative and noncontroversial in their conduct. They receive a great deal of positive feedback—awards and citations—from the school and teachers.

The other group consists of youngsters who strongly emphasize their ethnicity. They pay less attention to school expectations despite their teachers' efforts. Teachers find them more challenging and more outspoken. They dress and act in ways that identify them with their group. For instance, some of them wear a colorful map of Africa on their shirts. Others wear decorative African carvings. This group sees ethnic loyalty as the main issue. They see the way they walk, talk, and relate to one another as important to being Black. In their view, the conservative group has sold out and has lost their identity. They call them wimps, nerds, and in the authors' day "oreos."

As might be expected, the "ethnic" group seldom gets any positive recognition from White teachers because they don't behave in ways that make the teachers comfortable. The teachers don't understand them, and many don't think it's their responsibility to understand them. So those youngsters get a lot of negative messages about themselves. As far as school goes, they are held in low esteem.

Ann, a girl from the conservative group, expressed discomfort about being with the other youngsters, whom she described as "those very Black kids." She seemed to be afraid that if she became identified with them she would lose friends who were not Black, or who may be less ethnically oriented.

The young people in both groups are in conflict within themselves and with one another. They don't seem to understand that it is possible for Blacks to have different perceptions of themselves and still be considered legitimately "Black." And as usual, Blacks who embrace their traditional African ethnicity are the least accepted by those around them.

Whatever difficulty we have accepting the differences between Blacks probably began in the home. Valerie was the darkest child in her family and was always teased about it. Luckily her mother was alert to the need to make her feel good about herself. She taught Valerie to react with the remark, "The darker the berry, the sweeter the juice." She used it with a smile to blunt the attack from her brothers and sisters.

Fifteen-year-old Wanda, who grew up in Massachusetts, finds her maternal grandparents embarrassing because of their Southern dialect. She goes so far as to pretend not to want birthday and graduation parties because she doesn't want her friends to visit her home and meet her grandparents. Her parents were alarmed and disappointed when they learned of her feelings. They subsequently came to understand her feelings even though they did not accept them.

Sixteen-year-old Jennifer came to us for therapy. She had dark brown skin and "natural" hair cut short. She was very attractive but sought therapy because she felt she had a poor self-image. She was being ostracized by her Black peers because she spoke "proper" English and had many White friends and a taste for "White" music groups such as The Who. She grew up in an upper-middle-class family that socialized with neighbors of different races. She identified herself strongly as a "Black American" but saw herself as "elite" and "multicultural." What Jennifer saw as a social class difference her peers saw as denial of her racial identity. They could not accept her.

We can't expect all "upper-class" Black youngsters to automatically feel comfortable with Black youngsters who live in an inner-city impoverished area, and vice versa. We have to teach our children to be comfortable with Blacks from different socioeconomic classes and environments.

Rosemary recalls that as a child living in the suburbs her father would take her into different neighborhoods and encourage her to relate to Blacks in those settings. For instance, he would take her to his old neighborhood and have her put on a bathing suit and play with the children in the fire hydrant spray. "I want you to be as comfortable with these young people as you are at the pool in your backyard with our neighbors," he would say. These experiences helped Rosemary to develop a sense of community with other Blacks who did not have the advantages she enjoyed.

THEIR TIME TO DREAM

Adolescence is a time when young people begin to think about the future. Decisions about college and career must be made. But college is not for everyone, and there is nothing wrong with vocational education if that is what your teenager wants. Should youngsters who opt for college consider predominantly White schools—perhaps Ivy League? What should the racial makeup of the college be? Would a Black college be more suitable? Among the factors that have to be considered is the present climate of racism on many college campuses. Just as in elementary school, having to deal with racism constantly in college detracts from a student's academic commitment.

Talking about careers and goals with your youngsters at this time is essential. They should be able to sensibly discuss different career options. You can talk to them about what type of work they are interested in and help them explore careers that involve the things that interest them. This discussion will help them decide what kind of higher education or vocation to pursue.

If this is more than you can handle, try talking to the school's guidance counselor about different colleges, career options, and financial aid, if necessary. Some schools and colleges have career days when they invite professionals to talk to students about possible choices. Attend such events with your adolescent if you can. With your help, your adolescent can explore fields that interest him or her.

Be careful not to let "professionals" discourage you or your adolescent from pursuing a field that interests the youngster. It is far too common for educators to deliberately or inadvertently discourage Black youngsters from careers that they think are not suited for Blacks. Steven's experience recounted in chapter 5 is a good example of a so-called professional discouraging a Black youngster from a career she didn't think he was suited to pursue. Fortunately for Steven, his mother was attentive to his interest and pursued college for her son despite the teacher recommendation.

Be an active listener and help your youngsters make intelligent choices. Then be prepared to support them in pursuit of their goals.

INDEPENDENCE

Adolescents have a strong need to affirm their independence. They often feel they have all the answers and that they don't need anyone's help, least of all their parents'. If parents try to help, they will often be rebuffed with, "Stop treating me like a kid!" This is the adolescents' way of asserting their new sense of personal power. They are learning to make their own decisions. As parents, we have to remember that our children have the same rights that we demand for ourselves, and allow them the room to at least contribute to decisions that affect them. Young people's sense of independence is closely tied to their need for privacy. Their doors or desks are likely to be locked now more than before. Many adolescents, especially girls, will begin to confide in diaries more than they do in parents. It's important to respect this desire for privacy. To violate it is to threaten their sense of independence and is a sure way to create conflict.

Althea's mother read her daughter's diary and discovered, among other things, that the young lady was sexually involved with a White classmate. Alarmed, she confronted Althea. Althea became enraged at her mother for reading her diary. Their conflict grew and eventually they came in for therapy. After some time, they were able to discuss issues of trust, and eventually began to talk about what really bothered Althea's mother—the White boyfriend.

Showing that you respect your youngster's privacy can spare you a lot of conflict. But when conflict occurs, it's important to remain open and willing to talk about the issues that are revealed.

THE NEED FOR THE PEER GROUP

As Black parents, when we find out our teenagers are "hanging out" with a group, alarms go off in our heads: Gangs! Drugs! Guns! Violence! Our first reaction might be, "I don't want you hanging out with those kids." This would probably be a mistake. *The majority of Black youths have nothing to do with gang-related activity in their peer group.* Any perception to the contrary is the creation of a biased and insensitive press.

All adolescents relate in a special way to a particular group of their peers. They will usually have spent their *latency period,* roughly the elementary school years, together. They share common experiences. They have their own ways of looking at things. And they've come to understand and trust one another.

A group of Black males might wear their caps backwards, wear identical pendants or medallions, sport identical haircuts, or use catch phrases, such as "word up" or "homeboy," when they talk to one another. These characteristics help them feel that they belong to a group that understands, accepts, and supports them for who they are. This kind of group attachment is one of the ways Black adolescents affirm their racial identity.

Such a group might have *implied* rules of conduct. That is, the rules are simply understood—they don't have to be stated. Other groups systematically set up rules to govern behavior. For example, one group has specific rules about racism and how they will deal with it. They feel it's important to learn to deal with Whites in general, but they object to any member dating White girls.

For Black youths, male and female, the peer group is more than just a group of kids. They rely on one another to *authenticate* and *affirm* their identity as members of a Black culture that's separate and different from the dominant White society. It's a necessary step in becoming a mature Black adult.

Peer Group Risks

It would be naive to think that adolescents are not sometimes led astray by peer relationships. Sometimes the peer group activity can be plain destructive. For instance, if an influential group member decides that it's cool to smoke a "joint," carry a gun, declare war on another group, or make some money by selling drugs, it might be tough for an individual member to resist because of what the group means to him or her.

As a parent, the best way to put your mind at ease about your adolescent's peer group is to get to know them and influence them as much as you can. Welcome them into your home. That way you can learn about their values and their attitudes and keep informed about what your youngster is involved in.

Rob enjoyed playing pool, so his parents installed a pool table in the basement. They also set up a basketball court in the backyard. These attractions made Rob's home a meeting place for many of his friends. Although most of them came over for the games, the stereo, and the snacks, they also found Rob's parents to be sympathetic listeners. The youngsters respected them and usually took their advice. For some it was the only open communication they had with adults. As a result, Rob's parents had considerable influence on his peer group.

Deana brought her new friend Peggy home to spend the afternoon. After Peggy left, Deana's mother told Deana she didn't think Peggy would be a good influence on her. The mother pointed out the way Peggy was dressed. (She wore her sweater tied around her waist, a tube top without a bra, and shorts that couldn't be seen under the sweater.) Deana's mother mentioned other things about Peggy's attitude that bothered her: Peggy hadn't spoken to Deana's mother when she came into the house. She went into parts of the house that were closed off to her, and she handled things that most youngsters would see as off-limits.

Her mother didn't forbid Deana to see Peggy, so the girls got together a few more times. On one visit to Peggy's home, Deana discovered that Peggy's brothers were involved with drugs. Deana decided to limit her contact with Peggy. She subsequently found out that Peggy was also using drugs.

The trust between Deana and her mother allowed Deana to avert a potentially dangerous friendship. This is where the early foundation of trust that we lay with our children can pay off. Although your adolescent may be confused about how to act, he or she will at least feel comfortable discussing a problem with you, and trust your judgment in the matter.

When adolescents do things we disapprove of, we have to find some way to make that clear to them. It's acceptable to temporarily deprive them of something that's important to them, such as an allowance, car use, or participation in sports. The kind of penalty you impose in these situations should depend on your child and what's important to him or her.

FLEXIBILITY

Adolescents often believe that what their peer group thinks, wants, and values are the most important things in their lives. We have to help them understand that there are other important things that require serious attention, such as education and career decisions. Peer group behavior may not be appropriate in those arenas; therefore, adolescents need to be *adaptable* if they want to make it in society.

Sixteen-year-old Chuck walks into a fast-food restaurant near his school. He has gone there to eat many times. His shirt is open to the waist to show off his chains against his bare chest. His cap is on backwards. He approaches the manager and asks, "Yo, can I have a application?" Chuck fills out the application, but a week later he is told he didn't get the job. The way Chuck presented himself probably influenced the manager's decision. Chuck's speech and dress, while prized by his peer group, would not impress a potential employer.

It's essential to have peer group acceptance, but it's just as important to know when and how to adjust behavior and to adapt to different circumstances. This is one of the most critical lessons we have to teach our youngsters.

ROLE MODELS

Role models are critical at this age. They help youngsters form images of the kinds of people they can become. Someone like Arsenio Hall is an excellent role model for Black males. Many teenagers truly admire him because he has an appealing personality, he is friendly with many people they respect, and he has material success. He also shows the kind of adaptability that's essential to success in this society. He projects a sense of ethnic brotherhood with his Black friends. Yet, he expresses himself in a way that mainstream White America can understand and respect. Other Black males that command such respect include Jesse Jackson, Eddie Murphy, and Malcolm Jamal-Warner. All these people strongly oppose drug use.

Successful athletes such as Michael Jordan, Carl Lewis, Jackie Joyner-Kersee, and Florence Joyner are also good role models. Remind your adolescents that people such as these could not earn the money and the respect they do if they abused their bodies with drugs or gravitated toward violence. You can point to many examples of celebrities who failed because they lost sight of this fact.

Role models don't have to be television personalities or big-name athletes. Anyone your youngster can identify with or respect and who behaves in constructive ways can be an effective role model. We asked a group of adolescents, "Who are your role models?" Several cited their fathers. One mentioned a "street counselor." He thought the man was a positive influence in the community because "he's someone who does things with you and [doesn't] just tell you what you should do."

It's not uncommon for youngsters to use their peers as role models. Neil and his friend Lyle were taking part in an exchange program for inner-city Black youths. Neil became aware that their White suburban hosts saw Lyle as aggressive and would probably put him out of the program. Neil explained the situation to Lyle and coached him on how to present himself in a less threatening manner. Neil is obviously a good role model.

High school students who tutor their peers are setting a good example for them. Young people who are able to involve themselves in Black cultural organizations and at the same time participate in integrated organizations, such as student councils, are also setting a good example. Too often young people feel that they have to choose between Black culture and White society. They feel that if they participate in integrated organizations they are compromising their Blackness, and if they take part in exclusively Black organizations they are being anti-White. The key is to be able to function well in either environment by learning what's appropriate in each.

One thing that's clear from the comments we get from youths is that even while they are highly influenced by their peer group they still want communication with adult authority figures.

Youngsters need adults to tell them what's acceptable behavior. As parents, we have to recognize this and make ourselves accessible to them.

A word of caution: Be careful of the role models that you use to inspire your children. Sixteen-year-old James lived in an inner-city housing project. His mother had succeeded in helping him to build a good self-image. He was on the honor roll in high school. One year, his mother enrolled him in a program that placed him with a White family for the summer. The program's purpose was to expose urban youngsters to a different way of living and to motivate them to do well in school. But for some reason, James ended the summer extremely bitter about the experience. He saw it as very patronizing. He said he would have preferred being placed with a successful Black family rather than a White one. He was disappointed that after all his mother had taught him about Black pride, she chose to place him with a White family.

Fortunately, James and his mother had an open and positive relationship. They quickly overcame the experience, and his mother subsequently placed him with a Black attorney's family, who provided the role modeling he wanted.

REBELLIOUSNESS

The word *rebelliousness* is almost synonymous with adolescence. Mark Twain wrote that he left home (about age nineteen) because he couldn't put up with his father's stupidity. When he returned home years later, he was amazed at how much smarter the old man had become! This is how most adolescents see their parents. It's only natural that they rebel. This is their way of *separating* and *individuating;* that is, they are beginning to formulate and separate their own adult identity from that of their parents.

DISRESPECT

All parents would probably agree that one of the biggest problems they have with their adolescents is what they see as a lack of respect. Teenagers talk back, they shout, they ignore, they disobey, they stay out too late. . . . The list goes on. But this apparent disrespect is often just a clue to conflicts within the youngster. Often teenagers just aren't aware of how they come across to their parents at those times. They are not in control of the emotions they feel, and when they "go with the feeling" it comes across as unacceptable behavior.

Rachel and her friend Diane went shopping with Diane's aunt, Gloria. Shortly after Gloria refused to purchase an item for Rachel, Gloria overheard Rachel telling Diane, "You know, sometimes I'd just love to go upside your auntie's head." Gloria felt angry and offended that this young woman, whom she liked, would say such a thing about her. She took Rachel by the arm and told her, "I want you to go and wait for us in the car." The rest of the group continued shopping.

When they returned home, Rachel explained the reason for her anger. Apparently her parents were going through a divorce, and Rachel had been keeping her feelings about the divorce bottled up inside. The shopping experience triggered her anger because her father usually took her shopping and bought her whatever she wanted. With her parents separated and her mother on a tight budget, Rachel had recently been fighting with her mother about shopping.

Gloria explained, "I know this is a difficult time for you, but you have no right to take it out on other people." She suggested that Rachel sit down and talk to her mother about the problem and work something out. Gloria also discussed the matter with Rachel's mother.

Again, the way to deal with this kind of inappropriate behavior is to make the youngster understand first of all that his or her behavior is unacceptable. Simply say, "Helen, I won't deal with you when you talk to me in that tone of voice." "Michael, we have to treat each other with respect if we're going to solve these problems," or "I know you're *becoming* an adult, but I *am* the adult here, now." Remember, to them adulthood is a great unknown. They're actually testing you to see what the boundaries are. They need you to set limits on their behavior.

PARENTAL TRUST

One of the things adolescents have to learn on the way to becoming independent adults is to make their own decisions. As parents, we have to let them go and *trust* them to make the right decisions. That's not to say they always will, but if they have no practice in decision making they'll never learn.

Peter talked to us about his parents' suspicion about the relationship he had with his White girlfriend. He admitted to them that he had a sexual relationship with the young woman but insisted that he always used birth control. Still, his mother seemed obsessed with the relationship. Whenever Peter was out with his girlfriend, the mother accused him of engaging in sex with the young woman even though, he said, most of the time he had not. "My mother never listens to what I have to say," he complained. "She just stands there and calls me a liar."

Peter's parents need to give Peter the opportunity to *earn* their trust, and to let him know that's what they're doing. For example, Peter's mother could have said, "Peter, you know that having sex is a serious matter. We've already talked about it. When you spend time with your girlfriend, I'm trusting you to use your good judgment. I'm not forbidding you to date a girl who is White, but I don't want to have to deal with a pregnancy. Also, mixed couples and their children have a tough time in this society." After the parent has expressed her views, she has to trust the youngster unless she finds evidence not to trust him.

Another way to help youngsters earn trust is to tell them outright that the way to earn your trust is to obey your rules. Expect them to disagree with your rules and to argue with you about them. For instance, you might want to set curfew at 10 P.M. Your son might feel that midnight is more reasonable. You can perhaps settle on 11:30, provided he calls in at 10:30 to let you know where he is. *Negotiating* and *compromising* are critical; they allow your adolescents to see and feel that they have some degree of control. Again, the adult that's growing in them needs this.

TEENAGERS NEED RESPECT, TOO!

Whenever a Black adolescent, especially one approaching early adulthood, senses that an authority figure has a lack of respect for him or her, the situation is headed for disaster.

Ron began college at a prestigious predominantly White university. Within the first two weeks, he had a disagreement with a White student. Someone called campus security. When they arrived, they asked to see his ID, but they didn't ask the White student for his. Ron took offense. He felt that the security officer assumed that because he was Black he was either not a student or he was in the wrong. Ron complained to the university administration. They called us in to provide training and support services to the school about these issues.

This is one of those times when a negative event had a positive result. Although Ron was angry and hostile, he didn't let himself be provoked to violence. He responded in a positive and assertive manner that resulted in constructive steps being taken by the school.

Authority figures have to let Black adolescents know that they understand that what they have to say is important, and that they are willing to listen, even if they don't agree. Listening is the key. Adolescents want very much to feel comfortable sharing what they feel.

DANGEROUS PITFALLS

Black youngsters are particularly susceptible to the twin hazards of teenage unemployment and drug dealing. Because unemployment is high among Black adolescents, drug dealers know they can find a ready pool of youngsters to sell their products on the streets. If we fail to rescue young people who live in communities where drug selling is prominent, we could lose them forever.

A gang member told one of the authors that by selling drugs he makes in one week what she makes in a year. "Where else am I going to find an opportunity like this?" he asked. "How am I supposed to give this up?"

It's very hard indeed for him to give that up, even though he knows it will probably cost him his life. Young drug dealers not only think they are better off personally but also see dealing as a way to help their families.

Robert's mother tells him she is going to kick him out of the house for dealing drugs. Yet, when he pays her rent and buys her new furniture, she accepts it with pleasure. The youngster gets a mixed message from the parent. The parent, in turn, is subject to the sense of hopelessness that affects people in poverty. So, if her son can provide for her by selling drugs, she can pretend not to see the connection between the gifts and the drugs.

This is an extremely difficult problem. There are no easy answers. One thing we can do for the future, however, is something we've stressed all along: We have to continue to help our children build positive self-esteem and to learn to respect their own bodies as well as their culture. Drugs destroy people—users and dealers. If our children learn to love, respect, and value themselves, they won't make self-destructive decisions. Adolescents who are caught up in drug use can often be turned around if they want to be. But it's almost always necessary to get professional help.

Frank grew up in Bedford Stuyvesant, a section of New York City where drug use and dealing are rampant. He was determined to get an education, and he successfully resisted the temptations to sell or use drugs. In college, he made the acquaintance of a group of mostly White youngsters who were involved with cocaine use. Wanting to fit in, he started to use the drug and eventually became addicted. People who knew him back home were shocked that he had escaped drugs in the so-called ghetto, only to succumb on a peaceful rural campus. His family enrolled him in a drug treatment program, where he received the help he needed. He was able to recover and continue with his education.

Some drug treatment programs specialize in working with young people. If you are looking into such a program, make sure it stresses *rehabilitation,* not *destructive criticism* and *punishment.* Finding a counselor who has had a similar experience to work with the adolescent can help to turn the youngster around.

Another way to help youngsters who are at risk of becoming involved in drugs is to put them in a place that will provide support for them. At times it's almost impossible for adolescents to fight against the pressure to get involved in drugs if that's all that is around them. Consider sending your adolescent to live with a relative in a safer environment if you fear for his or her safety where you live. If your youngster leaves a drug treatment facility rehabilitated, it is particularly important to find him or her a drug-free environment. He or she might not be strong enough initially to reenter the same community with drug contacts and other reminders of addiction.

SEXUALITY AND TEENAGE PREGNANCY

One of the most profound changes that take place in adolescence is the development of sexuality. It's a bittersweet experience characterized by pleasant physical sensations, rewarding personal relationships, and the potential for emotional and interpersonal turmoil, all at the same time.

Because puberty is such a powerful influence, it becomes completely tied up with the adolescent's image of himself or herself. Opposite sex relationships take on great significance, and for Black youngsters it becomes a part of their racial identity.

As we've said before, a Black youngster might feel he or she would never date someone of a different race. He or she might also perceive that another youngster who does so is not sufficiently "Black." When priorities change and dating no longer seems like the most important thing in the world, however, he or she might date across racial lines and not feel as though racial identity is compromised.

Because dating can be an expression of racial identity, we have to make sure our Black adolescents have exposure to Blacks of the opposite sex in ways they find positive and meaningful. If our young people attend predominantly White schools, we have to make sure they have access to other Blacks with whom they can feel comfortable.

Lack of exposure to Black adolescents of the opposite sex can be a problem. Fifteen-year-old Ethan lived with his adoptive

White family but attended a school with a sizable Black student body. He only dated White girls and talked about how comfortable he felt with them and how uncomfortable he felt with Black girls at school. He said the Black girls had "an attitude."

Although it's possible that he'll grow out of it, he is a victim of biased influence and a lack of positive experiences with Black girls. Furthermore, Ethan has probably been rewarded for his negative attitude toward Black girls. It is evident that his growing up in a White family had something to do with his perception. He had little to support his Black identity, and no opportunity to interact in a positive way with Black females in his family. He is now at risk for poor interpersonal contacts in this area of his life as he grows into adulthood. Early negative influences on his development of a positive image of Black females will be at the root of his unsuccessful relationships.

Adolescents often find the sex drive just about impossible to resist. At the same time, peer pressure to engage in sex increases ("Everybody's doing it"). Youngsters have to make serious choices about how to respond. For instance:

- Should they begin to date?
- Should they date different people or be exclusive?
- Should they engage in sex?
- Should they have sex for the experience only?
- Should they have sex with someone they care about?

Even if your youngster has not engaged in sex, these questions are on his or her mind and are discussed with friends.

Our young people need to stay connected to their parents during this critical time. By that we mean they must feel comfortable talking with us about anything that concerns them. Unfortunately, adolescence is a time of conflicting loyalty to parents and peer group. Usually, if the parent does not have influence over the youngster, the peer group will. The result can be premature sexual involvement and sometimes pregnancy.

Why do adolescents let themselves become pregnant? Ignorance is a big factor. Some teenagers believe the most incredible myths about pregnancy. For instance, many assume you can't get pregnant:

- The first time you have sex
- If you don't want to get pregnant
- If you have sex while standing
- If you stand up immediately after sex

Young women often get pregnant just to have someone to love and someone to love them. Some young Black women point to this as a way to establish a more long-term and committed or "serious" relationship with their boyfriends. Fifteen-year-old Cheryl said, "I got pregnant because I thought Kenny would want to get married and take care of us."

As parents, if we work with our youngsters from birth to give them a strong sense of self-worth, they won't need premature sex and pregnancy to make them feel loved and wanted. They need a sympathetic ear and signs that someone understands what they're going through. It might help you to think back to your own adolescence and share the lessons you learned with your youngsters. Remember, they aren't doing anything that our generation didn't do.

Again, the best way to discourage your adolescent from experimenting with sex before he or she is ready is to lay down a positive foundation early. Teach them respect for themselves. Teach them that their bodies are private and that they should share themselves only with someone who is truly worthy of them. Boys should know that although the peer group might stress the value of being sexually active or a "cool lover," they have to respect their bodies. They must understand that sex before they're ready for it could result in degraded feelings in both partners.

From the time Diana was a little girl, her mother taught her the proper name for her genitalia and impressed upon her that those were very private and personal parts of her body. No one had the right to touch them. As Diana got older, her mother talked more openly about sexuality and pregnancy. When Diana expressed a desire to engage in sexual intercourse, her mother asked her about the young man. What was he about? Why did she feel a need to have sex with *this* person? What would happen afterward? What did she expect from him? Her mother also gave Diana some key questions to ask the young man. For instance:

- What do you feel about me?
- What do you like about me?
- Why do you want to have sex with me?
- What kind of birth control do you think we should use?
- How will we prevent a sexually transmitted disease?

The young man said he liked Diana because she was "fine," but he couldn't describe any specific positive character traits he admired in her. Later, Diana told her mother she had decided not to become sexually involved with the young man at that time. She had been disappointed in his answers to her questions. With her mother's help, Diana was able to see that this wasn't the person with whom she wanted to have a sexual experience.

At this point, we have looked at some emotional and the obvious biological risk factors of pregnancy. However, the major physical deterrent to careless sex is the deadly threat of AIDS. The realistic possibility of contracting the AIDS virus must always be of paramount concern. Help your teenager understand that casual sex is not worth his or her life.

RACISM AND THE ADOLESCENT

Like other adult attitudes, racial prejudice begins to crystallize in adolescence. We only have to look at the rash of racial attacks on college campuses across the country to see this. Every Black person will encounter racism. Your adolescent must learn this and be prepared to deal with it.

Black adolescents need to understand that racism is a negative judgment that people have of other people who are different from themselves. These judgments are based on a lack of understanding, stereotyping, and just plain ignorance due to lack of contact.

The racial integration taking place in schools as a result of *Brown* v. *Board of Education of Topeka* and Dr. Kenneth Clark's research has not always had the desired results. Sometimes the consequences of integration have been mistrust, fear, and violence. Long-term cross-racial friendships are rare.

One reason for this is that in most instances integration is not based on *equal-status contact.* In other words, Blacks and Whites of the same socioeconomic classes seldom mix. For instance, busing to achieve school integration exposes disadvantaged Blacks to middle-class or affluent Whites. The perception that Whites are rich and Blacks are poor is perpetuated. Both Blacks and Whites need to know that being poor is not synonymous with crime and drugs. Further, contrary to the portrayal in the news media, crime and drugs are not exclusively a Black problem—Whites also commit crimes and abuse drugs.

A program that brings together people of different races and the same economic background could help youngsters find common ground to relate to one another. Such meetings could be accomplished through church or school exchanges, for instance. This kind of equal-status interaction between the races has been found to be the most effective way to reduce prejudice. At the same time, it's important for people of different racial and economic backgrounds to interact with one another. For instance, it might be helpful for disadvantaged Whites to know that there are affluent Blacks.

Portraying Black people in a positive light has also been effective in changing racial attitudes. White youngsters need to see positive images of Blacks to develop respect for our differences. There are positive models in virtually all professions. Teachers can help by finding ways to implement class discussions of the subject. Topics that can be revealing include:

- Portrayal of Blacks in the media
- Achievements of twentieth-century African-Americans
- Achievements of pre-twentieth-century African-Americans
- Black American accomplishments in science

School psychologists and guidance counselors can help present race-related material to students.

The whole purpose of these kinds of exposure is to break down the barriers of ignorance and the stereotypes that tend to foster conflict between people. If we can accomplish this before adult racial attitudes are formed, adolescents might take a different view of race when they become adults.

BLACKS AND THE JUVENILE JUSTICE SYSTEM

In dealing with the law, Black teenagers perceive that they're thought to be guilty even before they've been openly accused. White society, including law enforcement officials, seems to assume that Blacks, especially adolescents, are inherently criminal.

Jay, one of a group of youths we interviewed, observed that if you go downtown at lunchtime, you will see groups of office workers, mostly White, going to lunch, shopping, or running business errands. No one thinks of them as a White "gang" roaming downtown. Yet when he and his friends go downtown, they attract a lot of attention as a gang. When they enter stores, White women clutch their purses, and store attendants and detectives follow them around and eventually ask them to leave.

Black teenagers who have had to go to court fare no better. They feel that in cases where they are sentenced to jail terms, Whites get probation; when they are put on probation, Whites get their cases dismissed.

The youngsters believe their hairstyles, skin color, and dress all make a difference in how they are treated by police officers. This makes them feel vulnerable and distrustful of the law. In effect, the speech patterns, haircuts, sneakers, pendants, or chains that the youngsters see as expressions of their racial identity put them at odds with the law.

Glen was stopped one night while driving his father's Mercedes. He was casually dressed and was wearing a large African pendant and a cap. The police stopped him and wanted to know who owned the car, and how he came to be driving it. They were convinced he was a drug dealer. Even after he proved who he was, they made a thorough search of the car before letting him go. Glen's father showed him how to assert himself by taking his son to the police station and complaining about the way Glen had been treated.

If your adolescents come home and talk to you about their

experiences with police officers, please take the time to listen to them. Such experiences can be extremely infuriating, humiliating, and sometimes dangerous. Your children need your help in managing their feelings and shaping an appropriate response to such situations. Tell them about similar experiences you had when you were their age. It will help them to realize that dealing with the law is a deep and complex problem that requires a thoughtful response.

HOW SOME TEENAGERS COPE

A group of Black male teenagers explained that they have learned to cope with the difficulties of growing up Black by:

- Thinking things through for themselves and not following others blindly
- Taking pride in themselves
- Resisting negative peer pressure
- Remembering the lessons taught to them by their parents
- Communicating with their parents

Some of the teenagers said they found it easy to communicate with their parents; others said they did not. Many of the latter group said their parents got upset and began to lecture them whenever there was a problem. The youngsters who are able to cope best are those who seem to understand that different environments call for different ways of acting and relating.

When Adolescents Cannot Cope

Sometimes when Black adolescents try to cope with the frustration and humiliation of racism, they are labeled as having certain mental health difficulties. In reality, they are dealing quite rationally with the stresses in their environment.

For example, let's examine the term *paranoia.* A person who is paranoid feels persecuted when there is no basis in reality for those feelings. When Blacks react to racism that others might not be able to understand for lack of experience, it appears that they are reacting to something that doesn't exist.

Lawrence, the boy in chapter 7 who walked out of his classroom in the middle of a film he thought was racist, might have been too angry to articulate his humiliation, but that doesn't mean he had no reason to feel that he was being subtly attacked. In fact, Lawrence said he didn't confront his teacher at the time because "I know they'd all think I was just being paranoid."

Our youngsters must be prepared to see those labels for what they are. Some people deliberately use them to dissuade Blacks from responding to racial attacks. Remind your youngster that if he or she feels that a particular incident is racially motivated, it's best to address the issue assertively, regardless of how someone might choose to label his or her reaction.

Depression is another reaction to stress in the environment. It is an extreme sadness characterized by symptoms such as a change in appetite, change in sleep habits, loss of enjoyment from activity that used to be pleasurable, and difficulty in concentrating. The most extreme symptom is suicide, or placing oneself in potentially destructive situations.

For example, a youngster who lets a conflict grow to a violent stage, knowing that the other party is armed while he is not, is setting himself up to be destroyed. Youngsters who are this desperate may feel that they can't make a difference in society and that they can't achieve and change the quality of their life. They have lost all respect and value for life, including their own. These feelings and behaviors might indicate a wish to die and thereby escape the stress and negativity they are experiencing.

We have worked with gang members recovering from gunshot and stab wounds who have cried about the loneliness and the alienation that led them to join gangs. Black youth clubs or organizations such as those sponsored by local community centers can provide structured activities with a constructive focus. If adolescents don't have support in a positive organization, they will look for it in the negative environments of drugdens and gangs.

A common early warning sign that an adolescent is at risk for this kind of activity is the feeling that he or she doesn't belong. The youngster feels isolated, alienated, angry, and bitter at society. Your best chance for avoiding serious problems is to identify these risk factors early, to establish open discussions, and, if necessary, to seek help for your child. You will only be able to do this if you maintain honest communication with your child.

THE IMPORTANCE OF COMMUNICATION

Communication with adolescents can be difficult. Teenagers experience complex feelings that sometimes they can't even put into words. In their frustration and confusion, they often come into conflict with the people around them, especially those who are closest to them. With an adolescent in the home, tension mounts, conversations become arguments, and nothing seems to get done without a struggle. It's as though battle lines are drawn: parents on one side, adolescents on the other. What should you do when communication gets this tough?

First of all, put yourself in your youngster's shoes. Recall your own youth and how difficult it was for you at times. Try to make your youngsters see that you understand what they are going through. What they need most from you at this time are patience, understanding, and guidance. This is where the techniques of active listening, open responses, and tuning in to nonverbal signals that we talked about in chapter 4 prove their worth.

Craig lived with his mother, Eileen, and his stepfather, William, a prominent attorney. William gave Craig a list of chores: mow the grass, take out the trash, and clean his room. He was also very strict with Craig about schoolwork. Craig resisted. "You are not my father, you can't make me do any of this," he told William. This conflict led to a great deal of hostility between the two. Eileen was caught in the middle, not sure who to support. The family entered therapy to try to find a solution.

Craig told us he felt that William treated him like a slave by having him do chores. He thought William was pressuring him about schoolwork only so he could become an attorney like him. Craig was not interested in law. Later in therapy, Craig admitted that he felt William married his mother but was not interested in him. He interpreted William's strictness as criticism rather than as a desire to see him do well.

There was a clear lack of understanding because the family had never sat down and had an honest, open discussion of their feelings and expectations of one another. When they did this in therapy, their relationship improved considerably.

Alvin was brought up to believe that he should not judge people by the color of their skin. When he started dating a White girl, his mother became extremely angry with him. Her open hostility surprised him: "You don't like yourself. You don't like Black people. Are you crazy? How could you date a White slut?"

Alvin's mother felt she had good reasons for disapproving of interracial dating. She had never communicated them to her son, however. Based on her expressed philosophy, he assumed she would not object. As we've seen before, dating is a very important issue for a teenager. It demands honest, open communication between parent and child.

Later, Alvin's mother admitted she was wrong to say the things she did. She explained to her son that she saw her objection to interracial dating as a matter of Black pride. She also admitted that he had the right to choose his dates himself.

We don't want to trivialize the problems that Black adolescents face. They are formidable. But with the love, understanding, support, and guidance of parents, they can pass through this difficult period with a positive attitude and hopeful about their future.

Don't be deterred by the conflicts and the rebelliousness. It's neither your fault nor theirs. It's all part of growing up. Chances are you went through the same things as a teenager. Try to remember this.

See the disagreements as opportunities to teach your youngsters negotiating and compromising skills. This gives them a certain amount of power, control, and practice in making their own decisions. By learning from their mistakes, they develop as independent adults prepared to function in the community.

Chapter Nine

THE COMMUNITY GARDEN: COMING OF AGE

A GARDEN WITHIN A GARDEN

For Black Americans, coming of age means accepting ourselves as worthwhile individuals who are members of a Black culture that is an integral part of American society. As mature adults, we have a responsibility to support our Black culture but also to interact constructively with White society to promote racial harmony.

In this final chapter, we explore some of the traditions, institutions, and strategies that have helped Black Americans to function in two cultures at the same time. We believe our survival as a culture depends on our ability to preserve those valuable traditions and to pass them on to our children. We also take a look at how, as individuals, we can attempt to break down some of the barriers that prevent us from becoming full participants in American society.

In 1971, researcher William Cross, Jr., outlined a five-stage model of how Black Americans develop Black Consciousness. It's a useful approach in describing how we can evolve a constructive outlook from the negative experience of racism. Briefly, Cross's model looks something like this:

Stage 1: Pre-Encounter. The Black person shares Whites' perception that Black is inferior, and rejects his or her own Blackness. Such a person may engage in self-destructive behavior and act in ways that denigrate Blackness. He or she views Whites as superior and distrusts Blacks.

Stage 2: Encounter. The person adopts a pro-Black and anti-White outlook, usually after some outside event cracks the old accepted perceptions. Driven by a growing sense of Black rage and guilt, he or she begins an intense search for a Black identity.

Stage 3: Immersion-Emersion. The individual feels an overwhelming desire to understand the experience of being Black. He or she studies Black history. "Everything that is Black is good and romantic." Such a person might actively express a distrust of Whites. He or she might even dehumanize Whites as evil or "White devils." In the later part of this stage, the individual brings Black rage together with reason. There is more emphasis on awareness and control of his or her behavior. He or she becomes much more receptive to plans for developing the Black community.

Stage 4: Internalization. Here the individual may take one of four courses:

a. Become disillusioned and return to stage 1
b. Become stuck at the early part of stage 3, overwhelmed with hatred for Whites
c. Become satisfied with Black "things," talk about action but do nothing
d. Make a positive commitment to political action in the Black community

Stage 5: Internalization Commitment. The individual develops a sense of brotherhood with all oppressed people. He or she shows a sincere concern for people who are at lower levels (earlier stages) of consciousness, and begins to take concrete political action.

Stage 5 (Internalization Commitment) represents the developmental point at which a Black American understands and accepts himself or herself as a complete and worthwhile human being. Self-esteem and cultural pride are high. The person no longer lives in reaction to racism. Instead, he or she is concerned with living a full and rewarding life, contributing to society, possibly engaging in political action to advance the cause of the community.

Cross believes, and we agree, that this is a necessary step in Black Americans' individual development. By combining our outrage at racism and our Black pride and self-esteem, we can formulate action that promotes our full participation in American society. Such action can begin when we recognize the Black community for what it is: an effective support system with traditions worth preserving. Indeed, we have no choice but to preserve and support them. Let's look at some of these traditions and how they have served us over the years.

THE BLACK CHURCH

The Black church has been one of the greatest sources of support in Black people's continuing struggle to survive in America. For many who could not afford life's basic necessities, church programs have put food on the table. The church choir was perhaps the first outlet for Black artistic expression. Many of our most respected performers today received informal training, exposure, and support in church. Over the years many social programs took root in basement church halls and blossomed from pulpits into effective political strategy.

Black ministers, in addition to being spiritual leaders, have been our chief intermediaries to the White power structure. They've stood ready to assist where needed. For example, Delois worked for an afterschool program as a teacher's aide. She was the only Black employee in the program. She became aware that the director was having her do all the cleanup work. Her parents advised her to calmly discuss the problem with the director. The director's reaction was to tell Delois to do as she was told if she wanted to keep her job.

In church Delois's minister overheard the family discussing the matter with friends. He offered to accompany Delois to see the director if she thought it might help. Unfortunately, the minister's presence only served to further infuriate the director, who felt that they were challenging her authority. Nothing was accomplished.

On his own initiative, the minister inquired into the director's background. He discovered that she had a history of hiring few Black employees, and of mistreating those she hired. By contacting former Black employees of the program, the minister was able to generate sufficient support to have the director replaced.

In church, Black youths have an opportunity to observe and to participate in cooperative and leadership activities. Many Blacks had their first experience of being important, contributing individuals in church programs, perhaps as Sunday school teachers. Such experiences foster self-confidence and leadership skills in young people.

Conrad recalls that his first "public" duty was to climb into the pulpit every Sunday, read a scripture, and signal the congregation when to stand for each hymn. It was an intimidating experience, he said, and at first he could barely get the words out. But his pastor helped him by showing him how to project his voice even when he was nervous.

The church offers Black children the opportunity to observe ministers, deacons, and other church officials making crucial decisions about the church and about things that affect the lives of people the children know. They learn how responsible people conduct themselves. For instance, when church members visit the sick or care for the indigent, young people learn about *their* responsibility to care for one another.

In school Black children sometimes feel ambivalent about authority. They might feel that the authority figures do not care about them, or their peer group might see it as "cool" to resist authority. In church such youngsters can feel comfortable showing respect for authority because that attitude is promoted there. Young people also know that church authorities care about them. There is less distrust.

In church young Blacks can learn some of the cooperative skills necessary to accomplish a task. Claire, who is active in youth programs in her church, learned a great deal about responsibility. "You can't simply walk away from a task. Each person has a job to perform. If you can't do the job, it's your responsibility to find someone who can help you with it."

Perhaps the most important contribution of the church to the Black community has been to foster a deep spirituality and a firm belief in God. This belief has given us a sense of hope against the relentless challenges of racism. Even in the worst of times we remain optimistic that eventually we *will* triumph. Martin Luther King, Jr., spoke with that optimism when he said, "I've been to the mountain top, and I've seen the promised land. . . . We as a people will get to the promised land."

COMMUNITY-BASED ORGANIZATIONS

Not long ago, young people could count on community-based organizations, such as boys' clubs or community centers, as places where they could go after school to have fun with adult guidance. With the rise in violence and drug use today, such organizations are needed more than ever.

As concerned adults, we have an obligation to advocate for such facilities for young people, whether or not we have children of our own. They can be effective alternatives to the bleak options that many of them face. It might be helpful to recall the kinds of organizations or programs that made a difference to you when you were growing up. Today's Black youngsters need the same kind of support.

Grant recalls that as a young teenager he participated in a youth organization that was sponsored and supervised by a well-respected adult in his community. The organization's goals were as follows:

> To develop leadership and responsibility throughout the community, striving for a common goal of unity which in turn will help us, the youth of tomorrow, to prepare ourselves for the practices of our omnipotent society.

The organization focused on community involvement through educational, social, and recreational activities and political action. They recruited Black leaders in politics, art, music, science, business, and athletics to participate in programs to benefit the community. Members went on field trips and took part in sports competitions, all under the guidance of parents and other adults who supported the group's goals.

We must do whatever we can to promote such ideals and organizations within our communities, even if we have to start the organizations from scratch. The church is still perhaps the best place to find the support to begin such an endeavor.

WORKING IN UNITY

Another tradition that has worked to our advantage has been our ability to stick together and support one another. Blacks who aspire to higher socioeconomic status sometimes think their chances to succeed are better if they limit their association with other Blacks. And to a large degree, American society promotes this belief by perceiving unified Blacks as a threat. But in reality, many of the advances that Blacks have made in America have been the result of our working together as a community for a common cause, whether the March on Washington or a fight to get Black youngsters on a cheerleading squad.

Elaine, a Black student at a predominantly White school, tried out to become the school's first Black cheerleader. She and her friends, Black and White, thought she had performed as well as any of the students who were selected, but she was not chosen. Her mother met with the teacher who had held the tryouts and asked for clarification of what had happened. The teacher became visibly uncomfortable and couldn't give a clear explanation.

Elaine's mother met with a group of Black parents whose daughters were also interested in becoming cheerleaders and planned a strategy. When the girls went to the next tryouts, their parents sat in the school's gym observing the process and making notes. For the first time in the history of the school, they had Black cheerleaders—three in all. Community support made the difference.

INFORMAL COMMUNITY SUPPORT

The Black community supports its members through a variety of informal traditions.

Karyn, Marcia, Laura, and Thalia grew up together. Marcia was interested in fashions. She liked dressing up and would change clothes every hour if she could. She pretended to own a boutique and fitted her friends with "the latest fashions." Karyn wanted to work in an office. She often sat in front of an old typewriter with a pair of eyeglasses at the end of her nose, pretending the other girls worked for her. Laura wanted to be a teacher and social worker. When it was her turn to pretend, they all played school.

At about age ten, the girls formed a "club." Each day when they got together after school, they played out the fantasies of their respective "professions." Laura's mother, aware of the value of this play activity, took the time to encourage the girls to pursue their chosen fields. She went so far as to have them research what they would need to do to achieve their particular goals. Today all but one of the young women are working in the fields they chose as girls. The fourth is successful in another career.

Laura's mother was performing a function demonstrated to be effective in encouraging growth and advancement in the Black community for centuries: Black parents see it as their responsibility to encourage and support other children as if they were their own. Many successful Blacks recall that their community has been a source of direct personal support in their careers. For instance, comedian Eddie Murphy and basketball star Julius Irving come from the same Long Island, New York, community, where they received a great deal of support. Both men have in turn helped others in the community.

This kind of community support begins when individuals see themselves as responsible in some way for the success of others and the community as a whole. It's a realization that you *can* do something to make a difference.

Robin remembers that from time to time her parents took in children who had family problems or who had nowhere to go.

Sometimes an entire family of "strangers" took shelter in their home until they got back on their feet.

This type of informal support is still viable and necessary today as Blacks begin to join the American mainstream. For instance, a group of women frequently meets to discuss ways to help boost one another's careers. One woman is in a Ph.D. program. Another is interested in entering such a program. A third is planning to enter law school. They are all competent, motivated, and capable of doing well in their chosen fields, but they're ambivalent about their ability to complete the necessary training. Their self-esteem wavers now and again. A fourth member of the group, who has already completed a Ph.D. program, helps them by offering advice and encouragement. Each group member contributes to the group from her particular area of strength, and they all support one another.

When it comes to protecting our children from the threat of drugs or gang violence, community-initiated action is critical. Often a youngster who is not interested in gangs will join simply to get protection from other gangs. When Brenda realized her son Wayne was in this predicament, she discussed the matter with the parents of Wayne's friends. They organized car pools to drive the youngsters to and from school while they worked with the police to find a permanent solution to the problem.

Here again, community action helped people to solve their common problem. Many organizations begin with a single concern, but with initiative they can expand to tackle other issues of importance to larger numbers of people.

REINVESTING EXPERIENCE

As we look around for ways we might individually contribute to the strengthening of the Black community, it will be helpful to think of the concept of *reinvesting experience.* It's a simple idea: While none of us can expect to single-handedly save the community, each of us can give back some of the strength that we have drawn from it over the years.

For example, we urge people who were once involved in drugs or gangs, but who managed to put their lives back together, to go back to the community and help youngsters who are threatened by the same dangers. Young people tend to respect counselors who understand what they are going through.

Black law enforcement officers and correction officers who work daily with such problems can sometimes convince youngsters to shun drugs and gangs. Youngsters respond well to authority figures when they are convinced that such people are sincerely concerned about them. The officers can act as positive role models and demonstrate alternative ways of dealing with the "system." For instance, they can help incarcerated youngsters cope with their feelings of being under pressure, and help them find ways to express their anger without violence. Again, the key is convincing them that someone cares about them.

Reinvesting parenthood is another helpful step. It can be the simple act of admonishing two youngsters who are fighting on the way home from school. It can mean taking complete responsibility for a child whose parents do not have the means to support him or her. Informal adoption, in which a family member or friend assumes responsibility for the raising of another person's child, has been one of the strongest features of the Black family and can be effective in the community's fight against drugs and gangs. Many families send their children to live with relatives and friends just to get them out of the reach of drugs.

Formal adoption is another way to help the many Black children who for one reason or another, perhaps just for being Black, are classified as "hard to adopt." Your help might be the only way out of an otherwise hopeless situation.

Whether through formal or informal adoption, or by temporarily helping someone in need, this willingness to care for a child, even a total stranger, is one of the most valuable strengths in Black culture. When we care, we are returning to the community the love, concern, and commitment that helped us survive. We must not lose this sense of responsibility for one another.

Black professionals—doctors, attorneys, scientists, engineers—or anyone who finds his or her work satisfying and fulfilling can help by looking for opportunities to share their work experience with young people. We've talked about role models and how important they are for young people. Being a good role model means more than just being identified as someone who has "made it." You can be a more effective model by meeting young people face-to-face and giving them the opportunity to ask specific questions. Many schools sponsor career speakers and would be happy to hear from someone willing to sit down and talk to young people.

Looking at the Black community today, we can clearly see an erosion of some of the traditions and institutions that have been our strengths. Many Blacks who join the American mainstream abandon their cultural roots. They see Black traditions as incompatible or not necessary to their way of life. The church no longer holds the influence it once had, particularly among young people. The Black minister, once the most respected figure in the community, now competes for the honor with television personalities, star athletes, and drug dealers with their easy money and flashy cars. Concerned individuals in the community must do whatever they can to revive and promote the proven values that are critical to our survival as a culture. We need to teach them to our young people so that they too can guide their behavior from strong inner beliefs. We can do this by adopting these values in our own lives and by teaching them to our children from birth.

FUNCTIONING IN AMERICAN SOCIETY

Once we have learned to hold ourselves in high esteem as Black Americans, and to respect our culture and take steps to preserve it, we must then define our own constructive strategies for functioning in the broader American society. There are simply no realistic alternatives. Besides, we've contributed our blood, our labor, and our creativity to building it. We have every right to help shape its future and to share in its prosperity.

Of course, we cannot deceive ourselves as to the nature of the society around us. Everything that we've looked at so far and our own personal experiences point to an America that's still characterized by racism and bigotry. In just about every important front—education, employment, income, infant mortality, housing, healthcare, etc.—it's clear that racial and ethnic minorities, especially Native Americans, Hispanics, and Black Americans, continue to lag far behind the White majority.

Even economically successful Blacks are not completely accepted. In Hartford, Connecticut, Dr. Geraldine Morris Pinkston hosted a segment of a television program titled "Black Perspective." In this segment, a group of middle-class Blacks discussed how they are perceived in society.

Several women expressed outrage at the continuing opposition to the idea of Black women wearing braids in offices. They felt that corporations' unwillingness to accept Black women with braids reflects the fact that White society continues to see Black cultural expressions as not legitimate.

Another woman complained that Whites frequently ask her, "If you can make it, why can't other Blacks?" She sees this as an unfair question because it's seldom, if ever, asked of any other ethnic group.

"My race still precedes me through the door," was how one successful businessman described the situation. Many people, he said, Black and White, assume that Black-owned businesses aren't run properly. "In our daily bombardment of what's 'good' and what's 'excellent,' we are never told that anything Black is either of those."

These observations suggest that the Black middle class still does not feel welcomed or trusted by the White middle class. At best, they are seen as rare exceptions to widely perceived stereotypes of Blacks. The remarks underscore the need for Black people to support the Black community *economically* as well as culturally. We must patronize and promote Black business enterprises. We must also support individual advancement, such as in employment and promotion, if we are in a position to do so.

America will be able to fully benefit from its racial and cultural diversity only when all its ethnic minorities have equal and complete access to its resources and are respected and acknowledged for their contributions to the society.

With conditions being what they are, how can Blacks function positively in American society? First of all, we must refuse to accept racist or otherwise inhumane treatment by others. Through open, honest, and direct communication, we must address unjust, unfair, and biased behavior as practiced not only by individuals but also by the institutions in society. And in our own struggle for dignity and racial equality we must also be prepared to support other minorities in America and oppressed people in other countries, such as South Africa.

When we understand and accept ourselves as worthwhile and deserving members of a legitimate culture, we find it easier to challenge racial inequality and to stand up for our rights and the rights of others. We are also able to dispense with the petty prejudices and suspicions that limit personal interaction with people of other races and ethnic groups. We become comfortable enough to initiate relationships based on equality and respect for each group's differences.

RELATING TO OTHER RACES AND ETHNIC GROUPS

One way to foster understanding and harmony in our society is to encourage young people from different ethnic backgrounds who are friendly with one another to share their particular cultural experiences. This might mean visiting one another's homes or churches, for example. If we know more about one another, we are less likely to act out of fear and suspicion.

Two freshman became close friends at their predominantly White university. Maureen was White, Denise was Black. On one occasion when the two were shopping, Denise exchanged pleasantries with another Black woman in the store. When the woman left, Maureen asked Denise, "Do you know her?" Denise answered, "No." Maureen couldn't understand how two strangers could be so friendly to each other. Denise explained that it comes from the experience of frequently being one of a few Blacks in a White environment. It was something she experienced constantly at the college. Denise asked Maureen if she would be willing to put herself in a similar situation to see how it felt.

She then took Maureen to a Black church, and to a club in a Black neighborhood at another time. After both experiences Maureen said she was able to feel what it must be like to be a racial minority in a given setting. Obviously, Maureen couldn't fully understand the situation because for her the events were isolated, and she could easily go back to a comfortable White environment at any time. The experience was sufficient to get her to appreciate her friend's outlook, however.

Two of our friends, Betty and Edward, are Jewish. Ed's parents were imprisoned in concentration camps during World War II, and Ed still finds it painful to discuss their experiences. One of the most difficult periods in our friendship was when Jesse Jackson made an anti-Semitic racist remark about Jews. Our friends were understandably disturbed. Though we thought Jackson's remark was insensitive, we continued to support him. We also felt it was necessary to sit down and discuss the matter with Betty and Edward because their friendship was important to us. We were able to talk about it in an atmosphere of love and trust. It took a lot of work and painful discussion, but we came to an understanding about our respective positions.

Our friendship is a source of inspiration to each of us because it reminds us that people of different races and cultures can learn what's important to one another if they take the time to work at it. We can begin on a one-to-one basis and perhaps expand the experience to broader groups. If we are serious about creating change in the racial climate in this country, we have to be willing to sit down and work out our differences.

Because of the resurgence of racism on college campuses, we have had occasion to work with university students to promote racial understanding in college communities. We hired an Asian, a Hispanic, and a Caucasian psychologist to facilitate the workshop with us. We grouped students and administrators by ethnic background. We worked with the Black students and faculty while the other psychologists worked with their respective ethnic groups.

We had them consider such things as what they found to be the most difficult aspects of working with other racial groups, and how they coped with those difficulties. They did experiential exercises, such as thinking back to when and how they first became aware of race. When they all got back together, we had the students talk about common racial stereotypes and the fact that they're just a form of prejudice. They were then encouraged to "brainstorm" about what they could do to promote racial harmony.

At the end of the session, each person was encouraged to approach another person in the group and say something positive about the other person's characteristics or racial group. People who might have focused only on the negative before the discussions were surprised to realize that they had been doing that. They expressed pleasure at the realization that it was up to them to decide how they were going to look at one another.

If you attend college, it's worthwhile to encourage your school to promote such encounters among students. Such exercises tend to promote understanding and provide experience in negotiating differences.

If as a parent you want to promote racial harmony and understanding, request that schools provide forums for students to discuss racial problems with classmates from other racial backgrounds. There is simply no way to break down the barriers aside from facing them squarely.

Even children in elementary school are capable of responding to this kind of support for racial harmony. We've seen encouraging results in one community in which Black and Hispanic youngsters in the eighth through tenth grades were having difficulties with one another. At the junior high school, Black students use one entrance and Hispanics use another. They then "hang out" in their respective halls until classes start. Thirteen-year-old Robbie explained, "If you are Black and you go to the Hispanic door, they give you odd looks and maybe nudge you so you get the message that you're in the wrong place." One group would not sit at a table in the lunchroom if a member of the other group was sitting there.

Suggestions to break the deadlock included having a Black student invite a Hispanic student (or vice versa) to enter the "Black" (or "Hispanic") door with him or her and to offer support. A similar approach might work in the lunchroom.

It's worth noting that it was the director of a social services agency who first identified the problem and encouraged the junior high school students to attend the forum. By the date the meeting was scheduled to be held, two other social services agencies, a group of eighth-grade students and their parents, and students from a nearby college had expressed interest in participating. One individual took the initiative to help create racial harmony.

The situation in the schools in this community are not at all unusual. The same type of friction might exist in your youngster's school. You have the right to advocate for forums in your schools, and you don't need technical expertise. All you need to do is to identify the problem and ask that professionals be brought in by school officials to help solve it.

In relating to other races, we promote *meaningful exchanges* that result in an understanding of other people's differences. The authors are sometimes perceived as militant in our own circles because we assert ourselves and openly take pride in our African heritage. Yet, we have very close friends from other ethnic groups. This is preferable to creating superficial friendships while harboring distrust and suspicion. A key step is to realize that pro-Black does not mean anti-White. One has to be comfortable with his or her own background before he or she can comfortably relate to others from different backgrounds.

Many Blacks who feel comfortable with their own ethnicity still have difficulty relating to other groups, particularly to Whites. Their difficulty stems from the persistence of racism.

Martha is a confident, successful young woman and a corporate officer in a nationally known company. Occasionally, she has what she calls her "I hate White people" days, when she has to deal with obvious racial discrimination that she thought had already disappeared. At those times she feels a need to commiserate with her Black friends, who understand what she is going through. Martha is an outgoing person and has close friends who are White. She clearly does not hate Whites. Her expression is just a way of putting into words the frustration and humiliation of racism.

It's important to remember that when we commit ourselves to work for racial harmony racism doesn't disappear instantly from our lives. We still have to cope with it in our own way while we fight it.

ENCOURAGING SIGNS

In the midst of political setbacks, the resurgence of racial hate groups, the rise in racial attacks on college campuses, and other disappointing signs of racial polarity, there are some encouraging signs.

One indication is the number of Black political candidates being elected to office at all levels of government. While all these officials have their power base in the Black community, they could not be elected without White support. It's an indication that people of different races and ethnic groups can unite behind a common cause regardless of the leader's race.

The images of Blacks on television is changing ever so slightly. This is important because many Americans learn what they know from television. In one episode of the "Cosby Show," Cliff Huxtable's (Cosby's) step-granddaughter, having seen a Black, a White, and a Chinese Santa Claus, asks what color the real Santa was. Huxtable explains that Santa is all different colors. When he comes down the chimney at a Black person's home, he is Black. At a Chinese home, he is Chinese, and so on. We viewed this episode as a thoughtful and sensitive treatment of the issue of ethnic differences in American culture. Too often the issue is ignored. It has been our personal experience that it's almost impossible to find Black Santa Claus dolls or pictures in the shopping malls at Christmastime—even in Black communities.

The success of the "Cosby Show" proves that it is possible to portray Blacks in a respectable manner and still make money. As a result, other television shows occasionally succeed in presenting sensitive, positive portrayals of Black Americans.

The growing appeal of politically conscious Black filmmakers, such as Spike Lee and Robert Townsend, also suggests that perhaps American audiences, not just Blacks, are starting to listen to critical discussions about racism.

More than ever, mental health professionals are addressing the current state of affairs, as it relates to Black children, self-esteem, and racism. In the November 1989 issue of the NAACP's *Crisis* magazine, one of the authors is quoted as saying that Black children need to be taught to be assertive. In the same article, "Educating the Children about Race Relations: The Role of Teachers and Parents," Dr. Alvin Poussaint states, "Parents have to be ready to answer their children's questions intelligently and on a level that they can understand without making them fearful, but giving them a balanced answer. For example, if a Black child hears the news on TV and asks, 'why don't they let Black people vote in South Africa?' Parents may respond by explaining: 'a lot of the Whites in South Africa and the people in power don't want Blacks to vote and they won't allow them and it's wrong.' " Dr. Kenneth B. Clark is quoted as saying, "I think the education decision makers are either skirting the issue of training American children to respect diversity or are accessories in the perpetuation of racism and segregation in the schools . . . they seem to permit our children to remain illiterate socially." We need to teach our children to be assertive. We need to inform them of the conditions of Black people and monitor what they hear in the media. We need to teach our children to respect diversity.

The dilemma remains, however: How do we find ways to raise our children to become self-respecting, productive citizens in a society that has not yet accepted Blacks as legitimate members? We have to find ways to keep our children alive and interested while we fight ignorance, bigotry, and racism. It's a frustrating, humiliating, and exhausting battle that we must win, because the alternative is unthinkable.

RESOURCE GUIDE

This resource guide is a sample of books, educational materials, dolls, and games which can be used to help children develop positive self-esteem and racial identity. Some of the books may be available in bookstores or libraries, however all of them are available through Positive Images Children's Books (593A Macon Street, Brooklyn, New York 11233, 718–453–1111). The owner, Heather Williams, has written summaries which are extremely helpful in deciding which books are most appropriate for children of different ages. Reading the descriptions will help you choose books that your children will be interested in and eager to read. The resource materials are very useful for schools and other educational institutions.

AGES 2 AND UP

Ashanti to Zulu-African Traditions. By Margaret Musgrove. Illustrated by Leo and Diane Dillon. New York: Dial Bks. for Young Readers, 1976.

Caldecott Medal, 1977
The *New York Times* Best Illustrated Books of 1976
The *New York Times* Outstanding Books of 1976
The *Boston Globe*/Horn Book Award Runner-up, 1976
Society of Illustrators Hamilton King Award, 1977

Magnificent illustrations fill this book about some of the customs and traditions of African life, from "talking drums" to women cooking foufou and weaving kente cloth. Ages: 2–10. Price: $4.95.

Baby Animals. By Margaret Wise Brown. Illustrated by Susan Jeffers. New York: Random House, Inc., 1989.

Children will be enticed by the drawings of the animals, the lyrical text, and the tenderness with which the baby animals are cared for by the girl and her family. By the end of the story, all the animals are asleep, the little girl is asleep, and since this is *a bedtime story, hopefully your little one will be asleep as well. Written by the author of the classic bedtime story,* Goodnight Moon. *Ages: 2–7. Price: $10.95 (hardcover).*

Bible Stories for Children. Retold by Geoffrey Horn and Arthur Cavanaugh. Illustrated by Arvis Stewart. New York: Macmillan Publishing Co., Inc., 1980.

Nearly sixty stories from the Bible are retold in a manner designed to be enjoyable for children to listen to and intended to stimulate the child's imagination. A guide is included for parents. Ages: 2–12. Price: $13.95.

Bringing the Rain to Kapiti Plain. By Verna Aardema. Illustrated by Beatriz Vidal. New York: Harper & Row Pbs., Inc., 1979.

A Reading Rainbow Book

This is an outstanding book in every regard. It is based on an old Kenyan folktale of a boy who devised a method for bringing rain to a drought-stricken area. Verna Aardema retells the tale to the rhythm of "The House That Jack Built."

The illustrations are as stunning as the lyrical rhythm of the poem. I attended a performance given by children in an elementary school. They recited the poem while acting out the story. The room was full of excitement generated by the children and their parents in the audience. Ages: 2–10. Price: $3.95.

Colors Around Me. By Vivien Church. Chicago: Afro-Am Publishing Co., Inc., 1971.

This picture book illustrates the many different skin tones of the Black race. It helps young children to develop a positive self-image. Ages: 2–7. Price: $4.95.

Darkness and the Butterfly. Written and illustrated by Ann Grifalconi. Boston: Little, Brown & Co., 1986.

This is a warm and gentle story of a girl named Osa, who finds the confidence within herself to lose her fear of the dark. The book is full of lovely, dramatic illustrations that carry you away just as Osa is carried away in her dream of being free of fear. Ages: 2–7. Price: $14.95 (hardcover).

Grandpa's Face. By Eloise Greenfield. Illustrated by Floyd Cooper. New York: Grosset & Dunlap, Inc., 1988.

Tamika loves her grandfather, especially the warmth expressed in his face. She spends her best times with him, listening to his stories and going on long walks. But one day she sees him rehearsing for a play, and his face frightens her. Tamika is afraid that the frightening face will come back and replace the face she loves. Her grandpa explains to her that his face was only make-believe, and that no matter what he looks like, he will always love her.

This is a story full of love, reassurance, and security. The illustrations are superb. Ages: 2–9. Price: $13.95.

Jambo Means Hello—Swahili Alphabet Book. By Muriel Feelings. Illustrated by Tom Feelings. New York: Dial Bks. for Young Readers, 1974.

A Caldecott Honor Book

Through their art and words, the Feelings provide children with an introduction to some aspects of African culture. Ages: 2–10. Price: $4.95.

Moja Means One—Swahili Counting Book. By Muriel Feelings. Illustrated by Tom Feelings. New York: Dial Bks. for Young Readers, 1971.

A Caldecott Honor Book
American Library Association Notable Children's Book
School Library Journal's Best Book of the Year, 1971
Child Study Association Books of the Year, 1971

In addition to giving the spelling and pronunciation of the Swahili words for the numbers one through ten, this book gives the reader an introduction to East African culture by describing such things as musical instruments, a counting game played by children, and the clothing people wear. Ages: 2–10. Price: $3.95.

Oh Kojo! How Could You. By Verna Aardema. Illustrated by Marc Brown. New York: Dial Bks. for Young Readers, 1984.

Child Study Association Children's Books of the Year
Parents' Choice Award for Literature

Anancy the spider man is actually outwitted in this vividly illustrated Ashanti tale about a lazy young man who constantly allows Anancy to trick him into buying worthless merchandise. Perfect for reading aloud. Ages: 2–8. Price: $3.95.

The Patchwork Quilt. By Valerie Flournoy. Illustrated by Jerry Pinkney. New York: Dial Bks. for Young Readers, 1985.

A Reading Rainbow Book
Coretta Scott King Award for Nonviolent Social Change

This is a story about the extended family and the natural way in which skills and traditions are handed down from one generation to the next. In the story, grandmother, mother, and granddaughter make a quilt together, using fabric from the clothing of each member of the household. Beautiful, vivid illustrations. Ages: 2–8. Price: $11.95 (hardcover).

People. Written and illustrated by Peter Spier. New York: Doubleday & Co., Inc., 1980.

This book is an absolute masterpiece. In a humorous and ingenious way, Peter Spier takes the reader around the world to explore his premise that each of us is a unique human being. Each page has a sentence or two, with the remainder of the page devoted to illustrations of scenes from all over the world, which are sure to evoke curiosity and discussion. One page, for example, is dedicated to illustrations of noses: small noses, large noses, immense noses, flat noses, pointy noses, round noses.

Spier explores skin color, the types of homes people live in, foods, religion, language, class, and much more. The subtitle of the book is "A Picture Book for All Ages," and it is true. We can all learn from this one! Ages: 2–12. Price: $7.95.

Poems for Small Friends. By Bobbi Katz. Illustrated by Gyo Fujikawa. New York: Random House, Inc., 1989.

Four delightful children and a shaggy dog prance across the pages of this book of poems. Children will want to hear these poems over and over *because they are about subjects near and dear to them: leaving home because of a new baby who has to "wear diapers and sleep in some dumb crib," or the Travel Tree with "cozy nooks for dreaming dreams and reading books." Ages: 2–8. Price: $4.95 (hardcover).*

The Quilt Story. By Tony Johnston and Tomie dePaola. New York: The Putnam Publishing Group, 1985.

A colorful patchwork quilt kept a little girl warm, and comforted her when she felt lonely and displaced in her new home. Generations later, after raccoons and mice had found comfort in the quilt, another little girl finds it in the attic. Her mother stitches up the holes, and the quilt again provides comfort and security to a child. This story will hold a special appeal for any child who has been comforted by a "blankie," teddy bear, or other specially loved object. Ages: 2–8. Price: $13.95 (hardcover).

A Story, A Story. An African Tale. Retold and illustrated by Gail E. Haley. New York: Macmillan Publishing Co., Inc., 1988.

This story tells how Spider stories or Anancy stories got their names. Of course, true to form, Anancy the spider outwits those around him. Ages: 2–7. Price: $4.95.

Ten, Nine, Eight. By Molly Bang. New York: Penguin, 1983.

This book doubles as a bedtime story and a counting book. It features drawings of familiar items and a warm family bedtime routine as a father and daughter count down from ten toes to one sleepy little girl all ready for bed. Ages: 2–6. Price: $3.95.

The Village of Round and Square Houses. Written and illustrated by Ann Grifalconi. Boston: Little, Brown & Co., 1987.

A Caldecott Honor Book

This dynamically illustrated book recounts the true story of a village in the Cameroons where the women live in round houses and the men live in square houses. The story is told from the point of view of a little girl who lives in the village, whose grandmother explains that the village is peaceful "because each one has a place to be apart, and a time to be together." Ages: 2–7. Price: $14.95 (hardcover).

What's So Funny, Ketu? By Verna Aardema. Illustrated by Marc Brown. New York: Dial Bks. for Young Readers, 1982.

A hilarious story about a man who was given the "gift" of being able to read animals' minds. Ages: 2–7. Price: $3.95.

Why Mosquitoes Buzz in People's Ears. By Verna Aardema. Illustrated by Leo and Diane Dillon. New York: Dial Bks. for Young Readers, 1975.

Caldecott Award, 1976
The *New York Times* Outstanding Books of the Year, 1975
School Library Journal's Best Book of the Year, 1975
American Library Association Notable Children's Books, 1975

Why mosquitoes buzz in people's ears may never have been a burning issue in your life, but this rhythmic retelling of a West African folktale will enthrall young children, as will the wide-eyed, vibrant drawings of animals. The ending will definitely bring a chuckle. Ages: 2–8. Price: $4.95.

AGES 4 AND UP

Amigo Means Friend. By Louise Everett. Illustrated by Sandy Rabinowitz. Mahwah, N.J.: Troll Assocs., 1988.

This reader uses only fifty-one words, repeating them often to increase the likelihood that the child will remember them. It is the story of a Spanish-speaking boy and an English-speaking boy who become friends and learn to communicate by learning each other's language. Ages: 4–6. Price: $1.95.

Betsy the Babysitter. By William T. Crawford. Illustrated by Judith Fringuello. Mahwah, N.J.: Troll Assocs., 1970.

A little girl describes an evening at home with her favorite babysitter, her big sister Betsy. Ages: 4–6. Price: $1.95.

The Chalk Doll. By Charlotte Pomerantz. Illustrated by Frane Lessac. New York: Lippincott, J. B., Co., 1989.

Rose's mother shares with her memories of growing up in Jamaica, West Indies. She tells of wanting a chalk doll from the store window but not having enough money to buy one. Instead, she made a rag doll from pieces of fabric. This is a very nostalgic story with charming illustrations. Ages: 4–8. Price: $12.95 (hardcover).

Cornrows. By Camille Yarbrough. New York: Putnam Pub. Group, 1979.

This delightful storybook tells how two children learn about the African origins of their hairstyles. Ages: 4–12. Price: $5.95.

Everett Anderson's Goodbye. By Lucille Clifton. Illustrated by Ann Grifalconi. New York: Henry Holt & Co., 1983.

A Reading Rainbow Book
Coretta Scott King Award Winner, 1984
National Council of Teachers of English (NCTE) Choice, 1984

In a very quiet story, Lucille Clifton takes Everett Anderson through the stages of grief after his father's death: denial, anger, bargaining, depression, and acceptance. This book can be of great help to a child trying to cope with the loss of a loved one. Ages: 4–8. Price: $3.95.

Everett Anderson's Nine Month Long. By Lucille Clifton. Illustrated by Ann Grifalconi. New York: Henry Holt & Co., 1978.

Everett Anderson was used to having his mother all to himself. Now she is Mrs. Perry and *she is expecting a baby. Mr. and Mrs. Perry help Everett to come to terms with his new lifestyle, and to realize that his mother will always love him. Ages: 4–8. Price: $3.95.*

Goggles. By Ezra Jack Keats. New York: Macmillan Publishing Co., Inc., 1971.

A Caldecott Honor Book

Peter and Archie are excited about the pair of motorcycle goggles Peter has found near their hideout. When a group of neighborhood "big boys" tries to take the goggles, Peter and Archie must outsmart them to hold on to their find. Peter's dog Willie is instrumental in the escape from the big boys.

Ezra Jack Keats is the author of six books recommended in this section. His excellent books are full of verbal and visual stimulation for a child's imagination and allow your youngster to tell a story based on the pictures. Ages: 4–8. Price: $4.50.

In the Beginning—Creation Stories from Around the World. Retold by Virginia Hamilton. Illustrated by Barry Moser. New York: Harcourt Brace Jovanovich, Inc., 1988.

The creation stories in this book range from Adam and Eve in the Old Testament book of Genesis; to the Eskimo creation story in which the first man comes out of a pea pod; to the Guinea story, in which Death creates the earth, God beautifies it and then marries Death's daughter—as a consequence, all of God's children also belong partly to Death, who can take any of them whenever he chooses.

Each story is only two to three pages long, with illustrations, and therefore can be read to or by young children. At the same time, the subject matter appeals to older children and young adolescents. Ages: 4–13. Price: $18.95.

Jafta's Father. By Hugh Lewin. Illustrated by Lisa Kopper. Minneapolis: Carolrhoda Bks., Inc., 1983.

A Reading Rainbow Book
School Library Journal's Best Books of Spring

Jafta is sometimes sad when he thinks of his father, who is off in the city, working to earn money for the family. Jafta has many good memories, however, of his father's strength and love, and the fun things they have done together. These thoughts will comfort him until his father returns to their South African village in the spring. Ages: 4–8. Price: $3.95.

Jafta's Mother. By Hugh Lewin. Illustrated by Lisa Kopper. Minneapolis: Carolrhoda Bks., Inc., 1983.

A Reading Rainbow Book
School Library Journal's Best Books of Spring

Jafta is a young South African boy, but the feelings of affection and trust he expresses about his mother are universal. He says of her, "My mother is like the earth—full of goodness, warm and brown and strong." Entrancing illustrations. Ages: 4–8. Price: $3.95.

Jamaica's Find. By Juanita Havill. Illustrated by Ann Sibley O'Brien. Boston: Houghton Mifflin Co., 1986.

A Reading Rainbow Book
Winner of the Ezra Jack Keats New Writer Award

Jamaica finds an old stuffed dog in the park and takes it home. After her mother says it probably belongs to another little girl, Jamaica's conscience convinces her to take the dog to the lost-and-found desk in the *park. Jamaica is sad about returning the dog, but then she makes a new friend—the little girl who had lost the dog. Ages: 4–8. Price: $3.95.*

Jamaica Tag Along. By Juanita Havill. Illustrated by Ann Sibley O'Brien. Boston: Houghton Mifflin Co., 1989.

When Jamaica wants to play basketball with her older brother, he brushes her aside, telling her not to tag along. Jamaica decides to build a sand castle but finds that she has her own tag along named Bert, who wants to help her. She pushes Bert aside but soon realizes that she has hurt his feelings just as her brother had hurt hers. She allows Bert to help, and together they build a castle so impressive that even Jamaica's brother wants to tag along and help them. Lovely watercolor illustrations. Ages: 4–8. Price: $13.95 (hardcover).

Josephine's 'Magination. Written and illustrated by Arnold Dobrin. New York: Scholastic, Inc., 1973.

Josephine, a young Haitian girl, follows the advice of an old man and uses her imagination to create a new toy that becomes a big seller for her mother in the village market. Ages: 4–8. Price: $2.25.

Joshua James Likes Trucks. By Catherine Petrie. Illustrated by Jerry Warshaw. Chicago: Children's Pr., 1982.

Joshua James likes all sizes and colors of trucks. In fact, he likes trucks so much that he even dreams about them at night. Ages: 4–7. Price: $2.95.

Just Like Me. By Barbara J. Neasi. Illustrated by Lois Axeman. Chicago: Children's Pr., 1984.

A story of similarities and differences between twin sisters. Ages: 4–7. Price: $2.50.

Just Us Women. By Jeannette Caines. Illustrated by Pat Cummings. New York: Harper & Row Pbs., Inc., 1982.

A Reading Rainbow Book

On Saturday morning, Aunt Martha and her young niece are going to get into the new car and drive at their leisure all the way to North Carolina. They will take their own time and stop and buy peaches, or sightsee, or *pick mushrooms. There will be no one to hurry them along. Warm, expressive illustrations. Ages: 4–8. Price: $3.95.*

A Letter to Amy. By Ezra Jack Keats. New York: Harper & Row Pbs., Inc., 1968.

Peter's trip to the mailbox to send Amy an invitation to his party becomes an adventure of mishaps and confusion, but the party makes it all worthwhile. Ages: 4–8. Price: $4.95.

Messy Mark. By Sharon Peters. Illustrated by Irene Trivas. Mahwah, N.J.: Troll Assocs., 1980.

Mark's room was so messy that he got lost in it. His parents promised to help find him if he would promise to clean his room. But will Mark be able to keep the room clean? This is a great book for helping children to identify common objects. On Mark's floor alone, there are more than twenty-five familiar items. Ages: 4–6. Price: $1.95.

The People Could Fly: American Black Folktales. Retold by Virginia Hamilton. New York: Knopf, Alfred A., Inc., 1985.

This is an entertaining, humorous collection of black folktales divided into four areas: Animal Tales; Tales of the Real, Extravagant, and Fanciful; Tales of the Supernatural; and Slave Tales of Freedom.

The book is complemented by the cassette on which the voices of Virginia Hamilton and James Earl Jones bring the characters to life. I have seen this book and cassette captivate and entertain a five-year-old and a twelve-year-old. Ages: 4 and up. Price: $19.95 (hardcover).

Peter's Chair. By Ezra Jack Keats. New York: Harper & Row Pbs., Inc., 1967.

A Reading Rainbow Book

There is a new baby in the house, and Peter's world has changed. His most prized possessions, his chair and his cradle, now belong to the baby, and to make matters worse, he can no longer make noise in the house. So Peter runs away and hides downstairs until his mother and father ask him to come back and welcome him home with his own grown-up chair. Ages: 4–8. Price: $4.95.

Pet Show. By Ezra Jack Keats. New York: Macmillan Publishing Co., Inc., 1974.

A Reading Rainbow Book

Archie's plans to enter his cat in the pet show go awry when the cat runs away. He cannot find the cat anywhere. Not to be thwarted, Archie comes up with a great idea for a pet, and his surprise entry wins a ribbon in the show. Ages: 4–8. Price: $4.50.

Purple Is Part of a Rainbow. By Carolyn Kowalczyk. Illustrated by Gene Sharp. Chicago: Children's Pr., 1985.

Written in rhyme: "A finger is part of a hand; a drummer is part of a band . . ." This book reinforces reading skills while helping children to make observations about their world. Ages: 4–7. Price: $2.95.

The Snowy Day. By Ezra Jack Keats. New York: Penguin Bks., 1976.

A Caldecott Honor Book

Peter has a wonderful time playing in the snow, looking at his footprints, making angels, and sliding down a snow heap. He is disappointed when the snowball he saved in his pocket disappears, but tomorrow is another day, and the white flakes are still falling. Ages: 4–8. Price: $3.95.

Some of the Days of Everett Anderson. By Lucille Clifton. Illustrated by Evaline Ness. New York: Henry Holt & Co., 1970.

Each day of the week features a poem reflecting the loves, fears, and fantasies of six-year-old Everett Anderson. For example, on Wednesday Everett is lost in a candy shop; on Friday he wishes his mama could stay home and play with him all day. Ages: 4–8. Price: $3.95.

Sometimes Things Change. By Patricia Eastman. Illustrated by Seymour Fleishman. Chicago: Children's Pr., 1983.

This is a soothing book about changes children encounter everyday; for example, "A butterfly was once a caterpillar, a song was once a note, and a friend was once a stranger." Ages: 4–7. Price: $2.95.

Ty's One-Man Band. By Mildred Pitts Walter. Illustrated by Margot Tomes. New York: Scholastic, Inc., 1980.

No one believed Ty when he told them that Andros, the man he met near the pond, was a one-man band. But Ty faithfully collected the "instruments" Andros had requested, and that night Andros had the whole town dancing and singing as he made music with his wooden leg, a washboard, two wooden spoons, a tin pan, and a comb. Before long, the children had also learned to play the "instruments." Ages: 4–8. Price: $3.95.

Whistle for Willie. By Ezra Jack Keats. New York: Penguin Bks., 1977.

Peter decides that he would like to be able to whistle to call his dog Willie. He dresses up like his father, and finds all sorts of other antics to provide him with "inspiration" while teaching himself how to whistle. Ages: 4–8. Price: $3.95.

AGES 5 AND UP

Follow the Drinking Gourd. Written and illustrated by Jeanette Winter. New York: Knopf, Alfred A., Inc., 1988.

Based on a folk song sung by slaves in the American South, this simple book tells the story of how slaves, determined to be free, followed the stars, rivers, and trees to freedom in the North. Jeanette Winter tells the story of how Peg Leg Joe and others on the Underground Railroad helped slaves to move through the night. The story is made even more compelling by the incredible illustrations in which the people's eyes shine as brightly as the very stars they followed to freedom.

These "First Start Easy Readers" can be helpful in teaching reading. There is a list of each word used in the story at the front of the book. Ages: 5–10. Price: $14.95 (hardcover).

Mufaro's Beautiful Daughters—An African Tale. By John Steptoe. New York: Lothrop, Lee & Shepard Bks., 1987.

A Caldecott Honor Book

John Steptoe has written a beautiful fairy tale based on an old Zimbabwean folktale of a proud, selfish girl and her kind, humble sister who would both like to be chosen by the king to become his queen. The illustrations are nothing short of stunning, with lifelike portraits of the two sisters. Ages: 5–10. Price: $15 (hardcover).

Shaka King of the Zulus. By Diane Stanley and Peter Vennema. Illustrated by Diana Stanley. New York: William Morrow and Company, 1988.

This is the story of the young Zulu outcast who through brilliance and determination rose to become a mighty warrior and leader of his people. The authors compassionately tell of Shaka's triumphs as well as his weaknesses. Ages: 5–10. Price: $12.95 (hardcover).

What Mary Jo Shared. By Janice May Udry. Illustrated by Eleanor Mill. New York: Scholastic, Inc., 1966.

Mary Jo was too shy to share in show-and-tell in school. When she finally gathered up enough courage, it seemed that everything she thought of was already being done by the other children. But Mary Jo was determined to be original. Finally, she shared the best thing of all, her father. This lovely family story will be especially appreciated by a shy child who longs to be more outgoing. Ages: 5–8. Price: $2.25.

AGES 6 AND UP

Andrew Young—Freedom Fighter. By Nauris Roberts. Illustrated with photographs. Chicago: Children's Pr., 1983.

Biography of Andrew Young, minister, civil rights organizer, congressman, United States Ambassador to the United Nations, and mayor of Atlanta, Georgia.

Books in the Rookie Readers *series use a limited number of words over and over, with just a few words on each page. The new reader will have a real sense of accomplishment at being able to read a whole book. Ages: 6–10. Price: $2.95.*

Desmond Tutu—Bishop of Peace. By Carol Greene. Illustrated with photographs. Chicago: Children's Pr., 1986.

History of the 1984 Nobel Peace Prize winner's role in the anti-apartheid movement in South Africa. Ages: 6–10. Price: $2.95.

The Hundred Penny Box. By Sharon Bell Mathis. Illustrated by Leo and Diane Dillon. New York: Penguin Bks., 1975.

A Newberry Honor Book

This is a tender story about the relationship between a young boy and his great-great aunt. Michael's favorite pastime is to count the pennies in

Aunt Dew's hundred penny box, one penny for each year of her life. As he counts, Aunt Dew tells him what she remembers about each year. Aunt Dew drifts in and out and sometimes seems to forget everything, but then remembers so much. Michael faces the dual challenge of keeping Aunt Dew's mind on him long enough to tell the stories and saving the hundred penny box from his mother, who plans to burn it and replace it with a new, shiny mahogany box that will have no meaning at all to Aunt Dew. Ages: 6–9. Price: $3.95.

Martin Luther King, Jr.—The Story of a Dream. By June Behrens. Illustrated by Ann Siberell. Chicago: Children's Pr., 1979.

This play doubles as a good storybook, with excellent illustrations. The main characters are Martin Luther King, Jr.; bus driver; Rosa Parks; policeman; Ms. York and her students, Dina, James, Ida, and David. Ages: 6–10. Price: $14.00 (hardcover).

AGES 7 AND UP

Harriet Tubman—The Road to Freedom. 1982.
Jackie Robinson, 1985.
Jesse Owens—Olympic Hero, 1986.
Martin Luther King, 1985.
Young Frederick Douglass—Fight for Freedom, 1983.

These are well researched and well written biographies by Troll Associates, Mahwah, N.J. Martin Luther King *and* Jackie Robinson *are only thirty pages each. The other titles are longer, approximately fifty pages each. Good for book reports. Ages: 7–11. Price: $2.50.*

Julian's Glorious Summer. By Ann Cameron. Illustrated by Dora Leder. New York: Random House, Inc., 1987.

When Julian's best friend, Gloria, gets a bicycle, Julian is too embarrassed to admit that he is terrified of learning how to ride. So, as he often does, he makes up a story to explain his lack of interest, and as usual, the story backfires. Ages: 7–10. Price: $1.95.

Julian, Secret Agent. By Ann Cameron. Illustrated by Diane Allison. New York: Random House, Inc., 1988.

Julian, Gloria, and Julian's little brother, Huey, become crime fighters, handling such diverse cases as rescuing a dog from a locked car and investigating a bank robbery. Ages: 7–10. Price: $1.95.

The Lucky Stone. By Lucille Clifton. Illustrated by Dale Payson. New York: Dell Publishing Co., Inc., 1979.

Tee loves to sit on the porch that wraps around the house and listen to her great-grandmother, Mrs. Elzie F. Pickens (the "F," stands for Free), tell stories of the lucky stone that has been passed down in the family for generations. One day, Tee is lucky enough to have the stone handed down to her. Ages: 7–10. Price: $2.50.

Malcolm X. By Arnold Adoff. Illustrated by John Wilson. New York: Harper & Row Pbs., Inc., 1970.

This book chronicles the life of Malcolm X, stressing his pride in being black and his passionate love for his people. Ages: 7–11. Price: $4.95.

Martin Luther King, Jr.—Free at Last. By David A. Adler. Illustrated by Robert Casilla. New York: Holiday Hse., Inc., 1986.

This story is divided into significant highlights of Dr. King's life. Ages: 7–14. Price: $12.95.

More Stories Julian Tells. By Ann Cameron. Illustrated by Ann Strugnell. New York: Knopf, Alfred A., Inc., 1986.

In this book Julian tells some very funny tall tales, like the story about the day that was so hot even the frogs wore shoes. Ages: 7–10. Price: $2.95.

Mystery at the Zoo. By Robyn Supraner. Illustrated by Bert Dodson. Mahwah, N.J.: Troll Assocs., 1979.

Michael Andrew McCuller searches the zoo, the Museum of Natural History, and the circus, looking for his friend Simba, the homesick African lion. This is a great adventure for the new reader. Ages: 7–9. Price: $2.50.

Plays of Black Americans—Episodes from the Black Experience in America, Dramatized for Young People. Edited by Silvia E. Kamerman. Boston: Plays, Inc., 1987.

The plays and choral readings in this book dramatize the lives and contributions of the following individuals: Crispus Attucks, Sojourner Truth, Harriet Tubman, Frederick Douglass, Jackie Robinson, Wilma Rudolph,

Sugar Ray Leonard, George Washington Carver, John Henry, Mary McLeod Bethune, Daniel Hale Williams, and Martin Luther King, Jr.

This can be a very helpful resource for graduations, Black History Month, Martin Luther King, Jr.'s Birthday, and assemblies. Ages: 7–13. Price: $10.95.

The Stories Julian Tells. By Ann Cameron. Illustrated by Ann Strugnell. New York: Knopf, Alfred A., Inc., 1981.

Hilarious stories about the trouble Julian gets himself into: The time he and his little brother ate all the pudding their father had made for their mother, or the time Julian convinced Huey that cats come from catalogs. These stories will help young readers to realize how much fun reading can be. Ages: 7–10. Price: $2.95.

AGES 8 AND UP

Mummies Made in Egypt. Written and illustrated by Aliki. New York: Harper & Row Junior Bks. Group, 1985.

Many children are intrigued by ancient Egypt with its mummies, sphinxes, and pyramids. This book details the steps the Egyptians took to mummify their dead so that they could "live" forever. Very informative, with excellent illustrations. Ages: 8–12. Price: $3.95.

Sister. By Eloise Greenfield. Illustrated by Moneta Barnett. New York: Harper & Row Pbs., Inc., 1974.

A *New York Times* Outstanding Book of the Year.

At age nine, Doretha began writing about her experiences, thoughts, and dreams in an old notebook her father gave to her. At age thirteen, she rereads her entries, which tell of her crush on the singer from Lonnie and the Liberations; listening to her grandfather tell stories of their ancestors; the sudden death of her father and the turmoil and pain it causes in her sister's life.

By the time she has finished reading her diary, Doretha realizes that all of these experiences, the sad and the happy, the obvious and the bewildering, have contributed to making her a sensitive, perceptive young woman. Ages: 8–12. Price: $2.95.

Song of the Trees. By Mildred D. Taylor. Illustrated by Jerry Pinkney. New York: Bantam Bks., Inc., 1975.

First Prize Winner: Council on Interracial Books Award

Mildred Taylor also wrote Let the Circle Be Unbroken *and* Roll of Thunder Hear My Cry. *This trilogy of stories, told by young Cassie Logan, chronicles the life of a family in Mississippi during the depression. The very moving and inspiring stories tell of prejudice, courage, values, love, and self-respect. Ages: 8–11. Price: $2.50.*

AGES 9 AND UP

Diana Ross: Star Supreme. By James Haskins. Illustrated by Jim Spence. New York: Penguin Bks., 1985.

This biography presents its subject in an objective manner, showing her self-doubt and insecurities as well as her determination to be a star. It lauds her successes and acknowledges her failures. Diana Ross's relationships with the Supremes, Barry Gordy, and Michael Jackson are explored. Ages: 9–12. Price: $3.95.

Iggie's House. By Judy Blume. New York: Dell Publishing Co., Inc., 1970.

This story about the prejudice and animosity experienced by a Black family when they move into a White neighborhood is also a story about courage and growth, and the development of a friendship between the Black children and their White neighbor, Winnie. Ages: 9–12. Price: $2.95.

Mary McLeod Bethune: Voice of Hope. By Milton Meltzer. Illustrated by Stephen Marchesi. New York: Penguin Bks., 1987.

Mary McLeod Bethune began her education by walking five miles each way to a one-room schoolhouse during the four months between the planting and harvesting seasons. She went on to become the founder of Bethune-Cookman College in Daytona, Florida. In addition, she was a community organizer and an advocate for black men exercising the right to vote and later for women's suffrage. She also served in President Roosevelt's administration as the head of the New Deal's National Youth Administration. Ages: 9–12. Price: $3.95.

Women of Our Time Series
Winnie Mandela: The Soul of South Africa. By Milton Meltzer. Illustrated by Stephen Marchesi. New York: Penguin Bks., 1986.

This is a gripping biography of Winnie Mandela and her passionate struggle for freedom in South Africa. Ages: 9–12. Price: $3.95.

AGES 10 AND UP

Black Folktales. Retold by Julius Lester. Illustrated by Tom Feelings. New York: Grove Pr., 1984.

A very humorous, sometimes poignant, modern retelling of black folktales, including How God Made the Butterflies, Why Men Have to Work, Stagolee, and People Who Could Fly. Julius Lester's special down-to-earth writing style makes these stories enjoyable reading for children and adults. They are especially funny when read aloud. Ages: 10 and up. Price: $7.95.

Jesse Jackson. By Patricia McKissack. Illustrated with photographs. New York: Scholastic, Inc., 1989.

The book traces the life of Jesse Jackson from his childhood in Greenville, South Carolina, to his participation in sit-ins organized by the Congress of Racial Equality, to his involvement with the Southern Christian Leadership Conference and Dr. King, to Operation Breadbasket in Chicago, and finally to his historical candidacy for the presidency of the United States. Ages: 10–16. Price: $11.95 (*hardcover*).

Listen Children—An Anthology of Black Literature. Edited by Dorothy Strickland with a foreword by Coretta Scott King. Illustrated by Leo and Diane Dillon. New York: Bantam Bks., Inc., 1982.

This anthology is divided into four themes: Feeling the Joy of Being Me; Feelings About My Roots: Folktales and Folkways; Feeling the Pain and Pride of Struggle; and Feelings About Who I Am and What I Want to Be. It includes the works of Eloise Greenfield, Gwendolyn Brooks, Don L. Lee, Langston Hughes, Martin Luther King, Jr., Nikki Giovanni, Maya Angelou, Lucille Clifton, Wilma Rudolph, and Margaret Walker. Ages: 10 and up. Price: $3.50.

Sounder. By William H. Armstrong. New York: Harper & Row Pbs., Inc., 1969.

Winner of Newberry Medal for the Most Distinguished Contribution to American Literature for Children, 1969

The boy loves his father and the great coon dog Sounder. During a harsh winter, Sounder and the boy's father cannot catch enough food when they go hunting, so the father steals a ham to feed his family. The father is dragged off to jail and Sounder, shot by the sheriff, crawls off into the woods. The boy searches for his father and for Sounder, praying that they will come home again.

This is an extraordinarily moving story about pain, hope, and promise. Ages: 10 and up. Price: $3.95.

AGES 12 AND UP

Long Journey Home. By Julius Lester. New York: Scholastic, Inc., 1972.

Julius Lester brings to life ordinary people engaged in an extraordinary struggle for physical and spiritual freedom. From Rambler, the blues guitar player who is determined never to be a sharecropper and so keeps moving from town to town playing his guitar, to Louis, the young slave who escapes to Ohio and into Canada via the Underground Railroad, the characters are presented as individuals with fears, loves, needs, and weaknesses in a way that we sometimes do not see when we read about well-known heroes. Ages: 12 and up. Price: $2.50.

Roll of Thunder Hear My Cry. By Mildred D. Taylor. New York: Bantam Bks., 1976.

Newberry Medal for the Most Distinguished Contribution to Literature for Children, 1977.

One of a trilogy of stories, told by young Cassie Logan, that chronicle the life of a family in Mississippi during the depression. The very moving and inspiring stories tell of prejudice, courage, values, love, and self-respect. Ages: 12 and up. Price: $2.95.

BLACK HISTORY EDUCATIONAL GAMES

B. T.'s Black Trivia

Trivia game with questions relating to Black history.
The Blakgame Group, P.O. Box 232, Brooklyn, NY 11233. Price: $25.

Inner Vision

Board game with 4,800 questions and answers on black history.
Inner Vision/ Martha Hurse, P.O. Box 554, Mount Prospect, IL 60056. Price: $25.

Martin Luther King, Jr., Game

Educational board game that features highlights in Dr. King's life. The Cadaco Company, 4300 W. 47th St., Chicago, IL 60632. Price: $10.99.

EDUCATIONAL, TEACHING, AND CURRICULUM MATERIALS

These are available through Claudia's Caravan, Multicultural/ Multilingual Materials, P.O. Box 1582, Alameda, CA 94501; (415)521–7871.

Alerta (multicultural approach to teaching young children).

This rich resource manual of learning activities for use with children from different cultural backgrounds includes tips on how to collect cultural information, design a learning environment, and promote a second language. Ages: 3–8. Price: $22.95.

All the Colors of the Race. By Arnold Adoff. Illustrated by John Steptoe. New York: Lothrop, Lee & Shepard Bks., 1982.

Anti-Bias Curriculum (video).

A thirty-minute color video on the new "anti-bias curriculum" by Louise Derman-Sparks and the A.B.C. task force. Produced by Pacific Oaks College. Price: $35.

Black ABC's (poster set).

In this set of twenty-six colorful study prints, each one illustrates an alphabet letter in upper- and lowercase, with a photograph and a sentence featuring the letter. On the back, there are enrichment activities as well as biographies of famous Black Americans. Ages: 2–8. Price: $32.50.

Black History playing cards.

Playing card deck has fifty-two portraits of famous Black Americans. A booklet of biographies is included. Many can also be used as flash cards. Ages: 4 to adult. Price: $5.95.

Black Is Brown Is Tan. Written and illustrated by Arnold Adoff. New York: Harper & Row Pbs., Inc., 1973.

Black Personalities Poster Set.

The set contains fourteen color posters, with biographical notes and a teacher's guide. Poster size: 11½ × 16″. All ages. Price: $8.95.

Diversity in the Classroom.

An easy-to-use resource unit that emphasizes affirming cultural diversity in an early childhood setting. It shows ways to incorporate multicultural activities into all aspects of the classroom environment. Ages: 3–8. Price: $11.95.

Forty Famous Black Americans.

This kit contains pictures, biographies, and quiz cards for forty famous Black Americans. Each card is 5″ × 8″. Includes suggestions for use. Ages: 4 to adult. Price: $8.95.

Free at Last . . . Dr. Martin Luther King, Jr.

Three of the most memorable speeches of Dr. Martin Luther King, Jr., are recorded on this album. Included are "I've Been to the Mountain," "I Have a Dream," and the "Drum Major Instinct." Available in cassette only. All ages. Price: $9.95.

I Know the Colors in the Rainbow.

One of Ella Jenkin's newest releases, this album takes children on a journey through several cultures. Includes many call/response songs with a children's choir. Ages: 2–10. Price: $10.95.

Juneteenth (filmstrip and cassette).

This filmstrip relates the history of Juneteenth, the popular Black American holiday that is celebrated across the United States. Ages: 8–14. Price: $37.

Kwanzaa (filmstrip and cassette).

This filmstrip depicts a family celebrating Kwanzaa. Included is a discussion of the activities and the major symbols and rituals that take place. Ages: 5–12. Price: $35.

Kwanzaa. By Dr. Maulana Karenga.

This resource book on the Black American holiday of Kwanzaa includes sections on origin, symbols, activities, and terminology. All ages. Price: $9.95.

Kwanzaa Coloring Book.

This book illustrates the seven principles of Kwanzaa, with large, simple drawings for coloring. Includes an explanation of each principle. Ages: 3–12. Price: $4.95.

Living in Two Worlds. By Maxine Rosenburg. Photography by George Ancona. New York: Lothrop, Lee & Shepard Bks., 1986.

Martin Luther King, Jr., Free at Last. By David Adler. Illustrated by Robert Casilla. New York: Holiday Hse., Inc., 1986.

Martin Luther King, Jr. . . . A Peaceful Warrior (filmstrip and cassette).

In this filmstrip, students in a classroom discuss and share many interesting highlights in the life of Martin Luther King, Jr. Ages: 5–10. Price: $35.

Martin Luther King, Jr., Story of a Dream. By June Behrens. Illustrated by Ann Siberell. Chicago: Children's Press, 1979.

Multiethnic Studies in the Elementary Classroom.

More than 200 pages of activities are contained in this binder format, including crafts, cooking, music, biographies, holiday information, and an extensive bibliography. Ages: 5–12. Price: $19.95.

My Ancestors Are from Africa.

These activity cards illustrate heritage, including leaders, history, places of interest, language, music, and customs. Price: $7.95.

My First Martin Luther King, Jr., Book. By Dee Lillegard. Illustrated by Helen Endres. Chicago: Children's Press, 1987.

Our Martin Luther King, Jr., Special Day Book. By Patricia McKissack. Illustrated by Helen Endres. Elgin, Ill.: Child's World, Inc., 1986.

Self-Esteem: A Classroom Affair.

More than 100 activities to help children are listed in this book. It's an excellent resource for creating a self-enhancing environment. Ages: 3–12.

This book has a sequel that contains more ideas for enhancing self-esteem. Ages: 7–14. Price: $9.95.

Teaching and Learning in a Diverse World.

Dr. Patricia Ramsey provides a comprehensive look at multicultural education, as well as presenting exciting possibilities for its use in the physical and social settings of the classroom. Ages: 2–9. Price: $15.95.

Tribes (cooperative learning).

This manual explains theory and has detailed instructions for building cooperative learning groups in the classroom. It helps to create a positive learning environment by increasing self-esteem and motivation to learn. Ages: 6 to adult. Price: $19.95.

Wait and See. By Tony Bradman. Illustrated by Eileen Browne. New York: Oxford Univ. Press, Inc., 1987.

BLACK DOLLS

Baby Whitney. Lomel Enterprises, Inc., P.O. Box 2452, Washington, DC 20013.

A 21-inch doll with a face fashioned after an Ashanti fertility doll.

Bronze Bombers. Olmec Corporation, 7 W. 22nd Street, 10th floor, New York, NY 10010.

A collection of black military figures representing all the armed forces.

Brown Sugar. B 7 V Distributors, Inc., P.O. Box 3854, Shawnee Mission, KS 66203.

A 19-inch soft skin doll with big brown eyes and shoulder-length cornrowed hair. A boy doll is also available.

Cherise. Olmec Corporation, 7 W. 22nd Street, 10th floor, New York, NY 10010.

An 18-inch doll with brown hair and eyes wearing a colorful party dress.

Elise. Olmec Corporation, 7 W. 22nd Street, 10th floor, New York, NY 10010.

An African-American version of the standard 9½-inch dolls that little girls love to dress up and play with.

Huggy Bean Dolls. Golden Ribbon Playthings, Inc., 1501 Broadway, #400, New York, NY 10036.

This family collection includes female and male infants, brothers and sisters, cousins and parents. Available in 17- and 12-inch sizes.

Keisha Doll. Keisha Doll Company, 524 W. 174th Street, New York, NY 10033.

More than 40 dolls in a variety of skin tones, some based on historical figures, some in African dress with cornrow or beaded hairstyles.

Shining Star Black Talking Doll. Vous Etes Très Belle, Inc., Doll Department (Shining Star), P.O. Box 44217, Fort Washington, MD 20744.

Doll has records that are inserted into her back and she recites poems promoting positive self-esteem and racial identity. The doll comes with the publication Color Me Beautiful, Color Me Black *which highlights Black leaders of the past, present, and future.*

Sun Man. Olmec Corporation, 7 W. 22nd Street, 10th floor, New York, NY 10010.

Handsome Black action figures with red, yellow, green, and black outfit that has wings on his neck and a shield on his massive chest.

BIBLIOGRAPHY

Akbar, Na'im. *Chains and Images of Psychological Slavery*. Jersey City, N.J.: New Mind Productions, 1984.

Allport, Gordon W. *The Nature of Prejudice.* Reading, Mass.: Addison-Wesley Publishing Co., Inc., 1979.

Billingsley, Andrew. *Black Families in White America.* Englewood Cliffs, N.J.: Prentice-Hall, Inc., 1968.

Cheek, Donald K. *Assertive Black Puzzled White.* San Luis Obispo: Impact Publishers, Inc., 1976.

Clark, Kenneth B. *Prejudice and Your Child.* Boston: Beacon Press, 1963.

Comer, James P., and Alvin F. Poussaint. *Black Child Care.* New York: Simon & Schuster, Inc., 1975.

Corcoran, Chris. "Need for Education of Youngsters in Racial Liberality." *New York City Tribune,* 31 August 1987.

Dewart, Janet. *The State of Black America.* New York: National Urban League, 1988.

Dixon, Vernon J. and Badi Foster. *Beyond Black or White.* Boston: Little, Brown, and Company, Inc., 1971.

Goodstein, Carol. "Educating the Children about Race Relations: The Role of Teachers and Parents." *The Crisis* 96, November 1989.

Hill, Robert. *The Strengths of Black Families.* New York: Emerson-Hall, 1972.

Hopson, Derek S. "Children Learn About Race at an Early Age." *Hartford Courant,* 24 January 1988.

Katz, Judith. *White Awareness: Handbook for Antiracism Training.* Norman, Okla.: University of Oklahoma Press, 1978.

Lee, Spike. *Uplift the Race: The Reconstruction of School Daze.* New York: Simon & Schuster, Inc., 1988.

McGoldrick, Monica, and Randy Gerson. *Genograms in Family Assessment.* New York: W. W. Norton & Co., Inc., 1985.

Michaelson, Judith. "Black Image: We're Not There Yet." *Los Angeles Times,* 9 September 1987.

Painter, Kim. "Black Doll or White? A 1947 Answer." *USA Today,* 31 August 1987.

Powell-Hopson, Darlene. "The Effects of Modeling, Reinforcement, and Color-meaning Word Associations on Doll Color Preferences of Black Preschool Children and White Preschool Children." Ph.D. diss., Hofstra University, New York, 1985.

Powell-Hopson, Darlene, and Derek S. Hopson. "Implications of Doll Color Preferences Among Black Preschool Children and White Preschool Children." *Journal of Black Psychology* 14, 1988.

Press Conference. American Psychological Association Annual Convention, N.Y., August 1987.

Thomas, Alexander, and Samuel Sillen. *Racism and Psychiatry.* New York: Brunner/Mazel, Inc., 1972.

Williams, Juan. "The Color of Their Skin." *Parenting,* March 1988.

INDEX